HIS GRACE IS DISPLEASED

Joan Hutchinson

KSCJ

GW00500033

About the authors

Dr Clara Cullen's most recent publications are *The Building of the State: Science and Engineering with Government on Merrion Street*; co-edited with Orla Feely (2011), and contributions to the *Oxford History of the Irish Book, Vol. 4* (2011) and *Women and Science, 17th Century to the Present* (2011). Her forthcoming publications are *Communities of Knowledge in Nineteenth-Century Ireland: Science, Culture and Society*; edited by Marc Caball and Clara Cullen (2012) and her *The World Upturning: Elsie Henry's Irish Wartime Diaries, 1913–1919* (2013). In recent years she has lectured in UCD on nineteenth and twentieth-century Irish history.

Dr Margaret Ó hÓgartaigh works at Harvard University. She is the author of *Kathleen Lynn: Irishwoman, Patriot, Doctor* (2006, reprinted, 2011), *Edward Hay, Historian of 1798: Catholic Politics in an era of Wolfe Tone and Daniel O'Connell* (2010) and *Quiet Revolutionaries: Irish Women in Education, Medicine and Sport, 1861–1964* (2011). A Fulbright Fellow and Professor in Boston, she won a silver medal for Ireland in the European Masters' Games in Sweden.

HIS GRACE IS DISPLEASED

Selected Correspondence of
John Charles McQuaid

Edited by Clara Cullen and
Margaret Ó hÓgartaigh

MERRION

Dublin • Portland, Oregon

First published in 2013 by Merrion
an imprint of Irish Academic Press

2 Brookside	920 NE 58th Avenue, Suite 300
Dundrum Road	Portland, Oregon,
Dublin 14, Ireland	97213–3786, USA

British Library Cataloguing-in-Publication Data
McQuaid, John Charles.
His Grace is displeased : the selected correspondence of
John Charles McQuaid.
1. McQuaid, John Charles—Correspondence. 2. Catholic
Church—Ireland—Dublin—Bishops—Correspondence.
I. Title II. Cullen, Clara. III. Ó hÓgartaigh, Margaret.
282'.092-dc23

ISBN-13: 9781908928085

978-1-908928-08-5 (cloth)
978-1-908928-09-2 (paper)
978-1-908928-19-1 (Ebook)

Library of Congress Cataloging in Publication Data
An entry can be found on request

Typeset by FiSH Books Ltd, Enfield, London
Printed and bound by SPRINT-Print, Rathcoole, Co. Dublin

Contents

For Archivists and Librarians

Acknowledgements

We are very grateful to the various archivists and librarians at the National Library of Ireland, Royal Irish Academy, Widener Library, Harvard University, UCD Archives and most especially the Dublin Diocesan Archives. Noelle Dowling, archivist of the Dublin Diocesan Archdiocese, was a marvellous co-worker, a worthy successor to David Sheehy, who is still missed. Thanks also to Peter Sobolewski, whose enthusiasm, particularly for Crumlin housewives who were pursuing communists, is a joy. Irish Academic Press and the Merrion imprint, especially Lisa Hyde, our superb editor, and Conor Graham, the Publisher, were marvellous. Colin Eustace, whose work is greatly appreciated, was the perfect marketing man and thanks to Peter O'Connell. Our thanks to the many friends who have listened to our tales from the archives and have given us shrewd advice; Tom Bartlett, Ciara Breathnach, Stephanie Boner, Maeve Convery, Pat Convery, Lindsey Earner-Byrne, Dermot Keogh, Joe Lee, Kevin O'Neill, Margaret Mac Curtain, Deirdre McMahon, Donncha O'Connell, Mairin Cassidy, Anne McLellan, Ciarán Ó hÓgartaigh, Jim Whelan, and to our families for whom, over the last year, His Grace became a very familiar presence in their lives. Our greatest debt is in the dedication.

Clara Cullen, Dublin and Margaret Ó hÓgartaigh, Boston

A View of God and the Devil
By Patrick Kavanagh[1]

I met God the Father in the street
And the adjectives by which I would describe him are these:
Amusing
Experimental
Irresponsible –
About frivolous things.
He was not a man who would be appointed to a Board
Nor impress a bishop
Or gathering of art lovers.
He was not splendid, fearsome or terrible
And yet not insignificant.
This was my God who made the grass
And the sun,
And stones in streams in April;
This was the God I met in Dublin
As I wandered the unconscious streets.

This was the God that brooded over the harrowed field –
Rooneys – beside the main Carrick road
The day my first verses were printed –
I knew him and was never afraid
Of death or damnation;
And I knew that the fear of God was the beginning of folly.

The Devil
I met the Devil too,
And the adjectives by which I would describe him are these:
Solemn,
Boring,
Conservative.
He was a man the world would appoint to a Board,
He would be on the list of invitees for a bishop's garden party,
He would look like an artist.
He was the fellow who wrote in newspapers about music,
Got into a rage when someone laughed;
He was serious about unserious things;
You had to be careful about his inferiority complex
For he was conscious of being uncreative.

Introduction

John Charles McQuaid's private charity and public venom are perfectly encapsulated in his dealings with his contemporary the Monaghan poet Patrick Kavanagh (1904-67). He gave quietly to Kavanagh at Christmas time but would not have countenanced Kavanagh's implicit critique of Irish society in the above poem.

John Charles McQuaid was born in County Cavan, in the north east of Ireland in 1895. All his life he retained the sectarian border antagonisms of his childhood.[2] Located close to the more Protestant counties of Armagh and Down, McQuaid was a 'cold warrior'[3] who resented those, and there were many, that he saw as a threat to his view of the world. Educated at St. Patrick's Diocesan School where he was unhappy and later at Clongowes College, managed by the Jesuits, he entered the French foundation of Holy Ghost Fathers, and studied at University College, Dublin and the Holy Ghost Fathers Pontifical Academy in Rome whilst also attending scripture lectures at the Pontifical Biblical Institute (the Biblicum) in Rome.[4] Revealingly, he had written his first-class honours MA thesis in classics on Seneca, a dark writer whose views chimed with McQuaid's morbid view of the world.[5] However, possibly the most important fact in his middle-class upbringing (his father was a medical doctor) was the death of his biological mother just days after giving birth to him. His father quickly remarried and McQuaid was not told that his actual mother had died until he was a teenager. It is impossible from this distance to calculate the effect of this information on a sensitive son.

The young McQuaid's decision to join a French order did not

surprise as he was a Francophile and was to teach that subject in Blackrock College. Other matters concerned him there besides teaching, as this book makes clear, including a new Irish constitution, mixed athletics and the staffing of a proposed children's hospital. He was appointed president of the college in 1930 and having completed the normal two three-year terms, had his presidency extended for another three years with support from Edward Byrne, the Roman Catholic Archbishop of Dublin (although this was not a diocesan matter). McQuaid's political influence was such that he chose to advise, even if much of this advice was ignored, de Valera on the Irish Constitution of 1937. This again is evident in the letters collected here.

McQuaid's consecration on 27 December 1940 was seen as a significant moment in Irish Catholicism as he was perceived as an efficient administrator, which he was, in an archdiocese which had become somewhat moribund under Byrne (who suffered from Parkinson's disease in the 1930s). The tenure of his archbishopric was one of great change even if he resisted much of it. In many ways it can be divided into three periods. The years from 1940 to 1945 were a time of wartime and post-war shortages. The post-war years saw the massive expansion of services for Dublin Catholics with a huge emphasis on schools. It may be suggested that his apogée was 1961, the Patrician Year, where the fifteenth centenary of the alleged death of St. Patrick, few facts on Ireland's nation saint can be ascertained, was celebrated. Ahead for McQuaid in the 1960s lay the Second Vatican Council; the future was bleak for an autocratic potentate like him.

The experiences gained by McQuaid in chairing the Catholic Headmasters' Association, which also included all convent schools, is evident from the files in the Dublin Diocesan Archives. Significant issues such as the Mother and Child Scheme, which sought to provide free medical care to all mothers and children under 16; plus McQuaid's omnivorous examination of social activities, including the theatre, as well as the horrors he sought to prevent entering the country, such as modern magazines, advertisements for underarm deodorants etc., are all included in the correspondence collected here. Files for University

College Dublin, Trinity College Dublin, the O'Brien Institute and the correspondence with diocesan priests are unavailable to researchers at present. Readers may draw their own conclusions.

When John Charles McQuaid died in April 1973 the tributes and obituaries in the national press reflect the complex character of the late prelate. There was a unanimous acknowledgement of McQuaid's commitment to the care of the poor – publicly in his establishment of the Catholic Social Service Conference and the Catholic Social Welfare Bureau – whilst the correspondence in the Drumcondra Archives contain numerous letters acknowledging his private charity to individuals. His administrative gifts were immense but theology was used to exclude, not include. These administrative talents of the Archbishop were also acknowledged and his correspondence in the Drumcondra archives reflects this talent. For the most part correspondence was answered promptly and McQuaid's attention to detail of all aspects of pastoral and public life in his diocese was all embracing.

Mary E. Daly in assessing one of McQuaid's predecessors, Cardinal Paul Cullen (1803-78), has suggested that the 'episcopacy of John Charles McQuaid (1940-72) can only be understood through the prism of Cullen: their joint determination to construct ostentatious churches and other Catholic institutions and a shared concern that Dublin's educational, medical and professional communities should fully reflect the strong Catholic presence in the city'.[6] In another assessment of Cullen and McQuaid, Gearóid Ó Tuathaigh perceptively suggests that 'reading nineteenth-century Irish Catholic history backwards (and with moral indignation) is a temptation that historians should resist. However, although common personality traits may indeed be striking, we should not read Cullen as a simple prototype or model for Archbishop John Charles McQuaid. Formidable skills in the high politics of church–state relations, utter dedication to the interests of the Catholic Church, an authoritarian and intensely secretive personal style of leadership, impressive organizational skills (in building the physical and pastoral infrastructure of faith-formation, education and care), and a granite-like determination to "Catholicise" the public life of the capital: this agenda constitutes an impressive swathe of common ground between the two prelates'.[7]

Perhaps the last words should be left to His Grace himself:

> Unless you had access to my private archives you could not describe my episcopate. They will remain closed for long after my death. And they will contain many surprises for those who have already attempted to assess my years as Archbishop of Dublin.
>
> You could, of course, state what you have already come to believe is my character ... I could not sanction the praise you might think it necessary to apportion. The blame that you would find in me, I would at once allow to pass without comment. Both you – and your Editor cannot fail to know that I have not yet answered when I was blamed or even reviled. I do not intend to change. All that side of one's life can be very safely left in the hands of God.[8]

Ultimately the correspondence is where readers may find his voice and that of his friends and enemies.

Notes

1   We are grateful to Art Agnew, for a copy of Patrick Kavanagh's poetry. His sister Una Agnew has written perceptively about Kavanagh's spirituality.

2   The best sources for McQuaid are: Deirdre McMahon, 'McQuaid, John Charles' in James McGuire and James Quinn (eds), *Dictionary of Irish biography*, 9 vols (Cambridge, 2009), vi, pp 176–9; Deirdre McMahon, 'John Charles McQuaid, archbishop of Dublin, 1940–72' in James Kelly and Dáire Keogh (eds), *History of the Catholic diocese of Dublin* (Dublin, 2000), pp 349-80; Patrick Murray, 'McQuaid, John Charles Joseph' in *Oxford dictionary of national biography* (http://www.oxforddnb.com) (accessed 16 Aug. 2010); John Cooney, *John Charles McQuaid, ruler of Catholic Ireland* (Dublin, 1999). John Cooney's biography is based on personal interviews and individuals' reminiscences as well as on the archival material.

3   Thomas Bartlett, 'Church and State in Modern Ireland, 1923–1970: An Appraisal Appraised' in Brendan Bradshaw and Dáire Keogh (eds) *Christianity in Ireland. Revisiting the Story* (Dublin, 2003) p.257.

4   Dermot Keogh, *Ireland and the Vatican. The Politics and Diplomacy of the Vatican, Church–State Relations, 1922–1960* (Cork, 1995) p.158.
5   We are grateful to Margaret Mac Curtain for this information.
6   Mary E. Daly, 'Catholic Dublin: the public expression in the age of Paul Cullen' in Dáire Keogh and Albert McDonnell (eds), *Cardinal Paul Cullen and his World* (Dublin, 2011) pp 130–45, p.145.
7   Gearóid Ó Tuathaigh, 'Reassessing Paul Cullen: an afterword' in Dáire Keogh and Albert McDonnell (eds), *Cardinal Paul Cullen and his World* (Dublin, 2011) pp 435–43, p.442.
8   JCM to Louis McRedmond, 2 March 1970.

Chapter one

The 1937 Constitution and J.C. McQuaid

In May 1934 a committee of four senior civil servants[1] was appointed to review the 1922 Constitution and following its recommendations, over the next three years a new constitution was drafted.[2] The role of J.C. McQuaid in the drafting of the 1937 Constitution has frequently been debated by historians but what is certain is that in his papers in the Drumcondra Diocesan Archives there are significant collections of material and correspondence between McQuaid and Éamon de Valera on the subject. Drafts of the proposed new constitution were sent to 'Q', as de Valera termed his former mentor at Blackrock College, and were meticulously annotated and commented on before being returned to the Taoiseach's office. These exchanges continued up to and included 28 April 1937, just before the draft constitution was published. Particular attention was paid by the future archbishop to the articles relating to family, education and the role of the Catholic Church. Some of his drafts are very illuminating.[3]

1. Draft comments on Directive Principles

It has been frequently said that the Directive Principles of Social Policy are but pious aspirations, devoid of effective force. The statement is based on a misunderstand [sic] both of the nature of a Constitution and of the intention of this Constitution.

1. A Constitution purports to lay down the directive lines along
   which the Nation shall strive, in unity of mind and will, to
   attain the common good. A constitution is not a thesis of
   philosophy and theology. It is an enactment guided and
   deliminated by the teachings of Catholic philosophy and
   theology. It enshrines and sets forth the aim of *what ought to be
   our Christian endeavour* in social policy.
2. The intention of *this* Draft Constitution – to one who
   carefully studies it – is clearly set forth: it means seriously *to
   endeavour* to create those circumstances of temporal life which
   shall realize the Christian ideal of Society. We desire – within
   the vast freedom of the Social Encyclicals – to achieve the
   common good of this Nation on Christian lines and by
   Christian methods. If there be one lesson we can learn from
   other countries it is that we must endeavour to avoid in our
   Young Society the evils that have characterised their Social
   organization. "The foremost duty" says Leo XIII in *Rerum
   Novarum*, "of the rulers of the State should be to make sure
   that the laws and institutions, the general character and
   administration of the commonwealth shall be such as of
   themselves to realise public well-being and private prosperity.
   This is the proper scope of wise statesmanship and is the work
   of the heads of state".

That these conditions of Social order and prosperity can be
realized only within a duly ordered Christian social organization is
a truth for which we have the strongest evidence of history and
economics as well as the urgent teaching of the Encyclicals. "The
very times", says the *Sapientiae Christianae*,[4] "in which we live are
warning us to seek remedies where alone they are to be found –
namely, by re-establishing in the family circle and *throughout the
whole range of Society*, the doctrines and practices of the Christian
religion".

2. Draft Preamble to the Constitution

In the name of the most Holy Trinity, from Whom is all authority and to Whom, as our final end, all actions both of men and States must be referred, We, the people of Eire, Motherland of the Irish Race, humbly acknowledging all our obligations to Our Divine Lord Jesus Christ, for Whose true worship we have endured so many centuries of pain, gratefully recalling the heroic and unremitting struggle, especially in these latter times, to regain the Rightful independence of this Nation and seeking to promote the common good by due observance of the Christian principles of Prudence, Justice and Charity, whereby the dignity and freedom of the citizens may be rightfully secured and the true social order adequately established and maintained do now vote and confirm the Constitution.

3. Memo on Constitutional Guarantees

1. The State guarantees to respect and defend the personal rights of each citizen, not only those that are inalienable, indefensible and antecedent to positive law, but also those that have been by law granted and defined.
2. Accordingly, the State shall take all possible measures to prevent abuses, enforce respect for social order and punish offenders against its laws.
3. The State acknowledges that its citizens are, as human persons, equal before the law. It shall, however, in its enactments, have due regard to individual differences of capacity, physical and moral, and of social function. No titles of nobility shall be conferred, but Orders of Merit may be created. Only citizens are eligible for civil or military offices save in special circumstances provided for by law.
4. The State guarantees
   (1) To protect, as best it may, from unjust attack and in the case

of injustice done, to vindicate, the person, life, good name, and property of its citizens.

(2) To permit the exercise of the right
   a) To express freely one's convictions and opinions
   b) To form associations and unions
   c) To assemble peaceably without arms
always provided that the exercise of these rights shall not conflict with religion, right morals or social order.

(3) not to impose disabilities upon or prefer, in the exercise of justice, any citizen, for reasons of his religious convictions

(4) not to deprive a citizen of his personal liberty save for crime, and in accordance with the law

(5) not to enter the dwelling of a citizen, save in accordance with law

(6) to protect, in a special manner, the weak and indigent, and where necessary, to provide by law for just conditions of employment, more especially of women and young persons

5. Upon complaint being made by or on behalf of any person that he is being unlawfully detained, as in Draft, etc.

4. Draft memo on the Family

The State recognises the Family as the primary and fundamental unit of Society, required by human nature, as a moral and juridical institution possessing inalienable and imprescriptable rights, antecedent and superior to all positive law, having for primary purpose the procreation and upbringing of children, in conditions suited to proper human life and development.

The State guarantees to protect the Family in its constitution, authority and government, as being the essential social basis of social life and order and as indispensible to the welfare of the Nation.

The State pledges itself to guard with special care the institution of Marriage, on which the Family is founded, and to protect it against attack; and no law shall be passed which shall impair its essential properties of unity and indissolubility.

5. Draft memo on the rights of women

In what concerns the rights of women.

The natural sphere of women is the family. By her life within the home, she lends to the State a necessary support, without which the common good cannot be achieved.

If beyond the circle of the home, she chooses to enter the wider sphere of economic, social and political life, none the less her task remains that of promoting respect for family life and of protecting public morality.

The State shall see to it that women, especially Mothers and young girls, shall not be obliged to enter avocations, unsuited to their sex and strength.

6. Draft memo on revised draft constitution on Rights of women [Art. 40.1].

By Art. 40.1 women, equally with men are guaranteed equal treatment before the law, that is, equal justice in the Courts – as human persons.

Equally with men they have the same fundamental human nature and human destiny and, therefore, equal rights that flow that nature.

1. It is to misconstrue Art. 40.1 to read into it an attack on women or any special class, or a threat of future attack. It is a graver error, still, to see in it any tincture of modern Fascism. The Article is a mere statement that distributative justice – which has regard to inequalities, natural and acquired, and to diversity of social function – will be observed in the enactments of law. Distributative justice is especially the virtue looked for in rulers. It is an unreality to imagine that the

possession of an electoral vote abolishes either for men or woman or for both diversity of social function. It is but one means of influence upon the State. The electoral vote is not even touched by the Article.

2. Nothing will change the law and fact of nature that woman's natural sphere is the home. She is perfectly free not to marry or to marry; to choose this or that career. No Article in the Draft Constitution even attempts to deny woman's fundamental rights as a human being.

Article 41,2,1, merely acknowledges a fact: the dignity and indispensible role of those women who choose to get married. Article 41,2,2, having acknowledged that fact, guarantees that it will endeavour to see, not that women will be prevented from engaging in this or that career, but that a certain class of women, namely, Mothers, will not be forced, by pressure of need, so to engage in work as to neglect their proper home-duties.

Benedict XV, speaking to the Catholic Union of Italian women put it well:

"The evolution which the actual state of things has brought about, has conferred on women obligations and duties not formerly accorded them. But no change in the opinion of men, no new state of things, nor course of events can ever snatch woman, if she realises her mission, from that sphere which is natural to her – the family."

Again, Cardinal Gasparri has written a striking comment on the new liberty of women:

"If beyond the hearth (which would crumble in ruins, did she cease to be its queen) custom and laws open up more and more to woman the widening sphere of intellectual culture, social action and civic life itself, yet it is incumbent on her, by a special title, to utilize these new means of influence to promote everywhere respect for family life, care for the Christian education of children and the energetic safeguards of public morality" (Letter to M. Duthoit).

3. The complaint that Art.45.4,2 is a restriction on the choice of career is a simple misreading: the Article is only an attempt to safeguard against abuse.

7. *Draft memo on education*

The State acknowledges the Family as the primary and natural educator of the child.

The State guarantees to respect the inalienable right and duty of the parents not only to provide, according to their means, for the religious and moral, intellectual, physical and social education of their children but also to secure the temporal well-being of their family.

Parents shall be free to provide this education in their home or in private schools or in schools established by the State.

The State pledges itself not to oblige parents, in violation of their conscience and lawful preference, to send their children to Schools established by the State.

However, as guardians of the common good, the State:

a) By appropriate means, but always with due respect for the natural and imprescriptable rights of the child, in the exceptional case when the parents, for physical or moral reasons, shall fail in their duty to their children, shall supply the place of the parents.

b) Shall promote the education and instruction of youth by aiding and supplementing with the resources at their disposal, private or corporate initiative.

c) Shall require, in view of actual conditions, a certain minimum education, intellectual and moral, physical and social, and further shall aid and supplement especially by providing free primary education and other facilitates wherever the common good. Further the State shall aid and supplement private and

corporate educational initiative, particularly by providing free
primary (and when the public good require it, other
institutions) with due respect, however, for the rights of the
parents, especially in the matter of religious and other moral
formation.
d) May reserve to itself, in view of national order, the right to
found and direct certain training schools for the public
services, such as the army and its allied services.
e) The State pledges itself not to oblige parents, in violation of
their conscience and lawful preference, by physical or other
means, to send their children to Schools, established by the
State.

8. Draft memo on the media

The education of public opinion is a matter of such grave import
to the common good that they who attempt it ought to observe
prudence, justice and charity.

The State shall therefore see to it that the organs of public
opinion, such as radio, press and cinema, while preserving their
rightful liberty of expression, shall not be used to overthrow social
order or right morality or, especially in times of war, the Authority
of the State.

The publication or utterance of blasphemous, seditious or
indecent matter are offences punishable by law.

It shall not be permitted to keep or conceal the ownership or
directorate of the organs of public opinion.

9. Draft memo on Religion

In respect of the true Church.
1. The State has the duty of professing and protecting not any
sort of religion but only the true religion. Now that religion
alone is the true one, which Jesus Christ, Our Divine Lord,

Himself instituted and gave in charge to his Church to guard and propagate. It follows, then, that the State is bound by the same obligations towards the Church as towards religion itself.

2. Right order demands that Civil Society should assist the Church. Wherever two Societies coexist, embracing the same members, the one pursuing a higher, the other a lower good, the inferior Society is obliged not merely to observe the laws of justice and charity in regard to the higher, but also, in so far as it's proper end will allow, positively to assist it. And this is all the more true when a State is Catholic and therefore a grouping of the members of the Church; nay even itself in a real sense, a member of the Church. The members cannot be indifferent to the end of the whole body, but ought rather to serve the whole body.

3. The Fathers of the Church, Doctors and Sovereign Pontiffs have taught this doctrine in explicit terms ... This they did, either by changing the laws hostile to the Church or by moderating their force at least in interpretation and practice or, while allowing the separation to continue, by striving to bring about a peaceful harmony and mutual collaboration between the State and the Church.

10. Draft memo on the rights of the citizen

The State having due regard to for the natural inequalities of capacity and function that can occur among its citizens.

All citizens shall, as human persons, be held equal before the law. This statement does not mean that the State shall not have regard, in its enactments, to individual differences of capacity.

The State guarantees to respect the personal rights of the citizen.

The Sate guarantees in its laws to respect, and as far as may be practicable, by its laws, to defend and vindicate the personal rights of the citizen.

11. Draft memo on private property (Article 43, 2)

It may be said with truth that a casual reading of the Articles on Rights will not reveal at once that they are not only based on Catholic Social principles, but that they enshrine that teaching, for the most part, in the very words of the papal encyclicals. It is incorrect to state that Art. 43, 2, might find its place quite properly in a Communist Constitution.

1. Art. 43, 2, must be read in conjunction with Art. 43,1, which guarantees the right of private ownership as a natural right, and guarantees to pass no law attempting to abolish that right. That is not a Communist teaching.

2. Art. 43, 2, claims for the State the right to delimit that right of private ownership, but <u>always</u>, with a view to the common good. One must never omit this view-point of the common good. In so claiming, Art. 43, 2 is but quoting *Rerum Novarum*[5]: "The right to possess private property is derived from nature, not from man; and the State has the right to control its use in the interests of the public good alone, but by no means to absorb it altogether".

   And again quoting from *Quadragesimo Anno*[6]: "It follows from the twofold character of ownership which we have termed individual and social, that men must take into account in this matter, not only their own advantage, but also the common good. To define in detail these duties when the need occurs and when the natural law does not do so, is the function of the Government. Provided that the natural and divine law be observed, the public authority, in view of the common good, may specify more accurately what is licit and what is illicit for property owners in the use of their possessions. Moreover Leo XIII had wisely taught that 'the defining of private possession has been left by God to man's own industry and to the laws of individual peoples'".

   And, again, a very cogent proof – if further proof be needed –

quoting from *Quadragesimo Anno*:
"When civil authority adjusts ownership to meet the needs of the public good, it acts not as an enemy, but as the friend of private owners; for it thus effectively prevents the possession of private property, intended by nature's Author in His Wisdom for the sustaining of human life, from creating intolerable burdens and so rushing to its own destruction. It does not therefore abolish, but protects private ownership; and far from weakening the right of private property, it gives it new strength".

3. To read into this Article the meaning that private property might be confiscated without compensation is to forget the emphasis explicitly set in this very Article and constantly reiterated in the Section – on the Common good. The Common good (Social Justice) forbids the refusal to pay compensation.

12. Draft memo on Authority

Too often the word calls up an association of more constraint upon individual freedom. Authority can and does restrict one, but it is a restriction of guidance.

Public authority exists only for the welfare of those who are governed. For man, by his nature, is meant to live in society. Firstly, the social group of his family begets and nurtures and, to a certain extent, educates him. But, it is evident that man, who is by nature a moral being, cannot find within himself or within his family, the means of developing adequately his powers as a person, or indeed nominally, of supporting his physical life. There is needed then a social organization; a durable grouping of others, wherein each collaborates with all his fellows to produce those general conditions wherein it may be possible to live a fully human life. Under such conditions we may be enumerate the reign of peace and order, the sufficient provision of economic or

material goods and the fostering of the higher or cultural goods
by which properly speaking human life is truly human. Society is
a permanent union of men in view of a common purpose: the
general good of those who are thus united.

Over and above the material elements of such society, one must
give primacy to that element which is the sovereign authority, the
band of union without which Society is only an aggregate of
individuals or groups, not a firmly united association pursuing a
common end. In a family there can be neither peace nor progress
nor union, if to the Father and Mother be denied the right to
direct the children to their own and to the family's good. So, the
very notion of a State is futile, if it be not conceded that there exists
within the State one single and sovereign directing power, having
the supreme right effectively to coordinate all wills in the pursuit of
the common good, for which alone the State exists.

Further, the sovereign authority must cease to be effective, if it
have not the inherent right both to determine the laws by which
the common good may be attained and to judge of the
application of such laws in concrete cases. This regulative power
must reach further still: the public authority were useless, if it had
not the moral right to enforce its law and execute its judgments.
Then, by its legislative, judicial and executive powers, the State,
which rests on moral right, which springs from the very nature of
man's social being, and from the Supreme Author of that being,
finds within its own structure all the means that are necessary for
the attainment of its ends: the common good of the governed.

It would help much to intelligent obedience, if we reflected
more often on the helpfulness of the sovereign public authority.
We should see in it a blessing, truly a gift of God, an instrument
of his willing, whereby our lives are protected and developed.
Obedience in this sense would not [seem] a grudging subjection,
but a willing acceptance of the Creator's Sovereignty as it is
exercised by men. There would be less reason for the State to use
the force, which it undoubtedly has the right and duty to use, for

the maintenance of the essential peace and order of the commonwealth.

In the realm of our own national aspirations, it cannot be denied that the ambition to realise the unity of Ireland is lawful. But it depends on the single, sovereign authority of the State to regulate that for this or that mode of action, such unity may be prepared for. It is not the moral right of any individual or group of individuals to choose a means that is contrary to the public good and general justice. The claim to choose such means can never be substantiated by an appeal to the fact or conditions of Easter Week, 1916 nor to the sentiments of the Leaders. We can conceive of these men as wishing only the true good of their country and in the altered conditions of our days it cannot possibly make for the good of Eire to refuse due obedience to the freely elected and Irish Government, which now controls the major portion of our land.

Many times it has been explained to the country that if the policy of the present Rulers seems to be insufficient for the procuring of the common good, there is always at hand the legitimate means of attempting to convince peacefully the electors of a better conceived and more practical plan. What is not lawful however, is to deny obedience to the rightfully constituted Authority, before or during the period that a change of Government is lawfully effected.

It must have become more and more apparent to these people, in these months of war, when small or weaker nations are threatened and consumed, that it behoves us, as a natural and Christian duty, to cooperate with all the goodwill at our disposal, towards the preservation of peace and good order within our realm. To this end, I would earnestly call all our citizens to utilise the means at their disposal to preserve the hard work, to develop the earning capacity of the country, to assist the needs of their fellows and to maintain, with dignity, the Christian traditions of collaboration with the public Authority, in its well meaning efforts for the common Good.

13. Draft memo on the Nation [Draft "X" 2]

Pending the re-integration of the national territory the area of
jurisdiction of the State established by the Constitution shall be
that portion of the national territory recently termed
SAORSTAT EIREANN, without prejudice to the right of that
State to exercise jurisdiction over the whole of the national
territory.

14. Draft memo on [Art. 1] Church and State

1. The State acknowledges the right of Almighty God to public
   worship, in that way which He has shown to be His will.
2. Accordingly, the State shall hold in honour the Name of God
   and shall consider it a duty to favour and protect religion, and
   shall not enact a measure that may impair its credit.
3. The State acknowledges that the true religion is that
   established by Our Divine Lord, Jesus Christ, Himself, which
   He committed to his Church to protect and propagate, as the
   guardian and interpreter of true morality.
4. The State acknowledges that the Church of Christ is the
   Catholic Church.
5. Further the State acknowledges that the Church of Christ is a
   (perfect) society, having within itself full competence and
   sovereign authority, in respect of the spiritual good of men.
6. Whatever may be ranked under the civil and political order is
   rightly subject to the supreme authority of the State, whose
   function it is to procure the temporal well-being, moral and
   material, of Society. In cases where the jurisdiction of Church
   and State requires to be harmoniously coordinated, the State
   may come to a special agreement with the Church and other
   Religious Bodies, upon particular matters, civil, political and
   religious.
7. The State guarantees to its citizens freedom of religious

conviction and liberty to practice their religion, in private and in public, having due regard, however, to social order and right morality.

8. The State pledges itself not to impose any disabilities on the ground of religious conviction, that would be contrary to natural rights and social justice.

9. Every religious association, recognised by the State, shall have the right to manage its own affairs, own, acquire and administer property, moveable and immovable, and maintain institutions for religious and charitable purposes.

10. Legislation providing State aid for schools shall contain no discrimination against schools under the management of a particular religious denomination.

11. The property of a religious denomination shall not be diverted, save for necessary works of public utility and on payment of just compensation.

12. The State pledges itself in virtue of the sovereign authority conferred on it by God within its temporal sphere to enforce respect, by its just laws, for the inalienable rights of its citizens and especially of the human family, and to preserve, as best it can, conditions of right social and moral well-being.

15. Draft of memo on revisions of draft constitution

The recast of Article 43 is a very able piece of work. Evidently the author has a very good background of theory; but I should say that his background is not quite ours.

1. He has retained the substantive parts, with two grave exceptions: viz., the declaration that the exercise of the natural right of private property is not only allowable but, for social needs, absolutely necessary, and the omission of vocational groups.

   a) As to the former: I believe this statement is vital, in view of the trend of modern social organization, if not of legislation, especially in France and England. The tendency is to admit the right of private property, but by methods of cooperative organization and planned economy to deny the private control of property, which is to abolish the right of private property with increasing effectiveness.

b) As to the second point: I believe it is a bad blunder to omit all reference to vocational groups. There are two effective ways of controlling free competition: either by State absolutism, or, by vocational groups. The former is anathema; the latter is called for by Encyclicals and economists. Further, the omission of vocational groups, is, politically, a mistake, for, a heavy attack will be launched on so notable a departure from *Rerum Novarum* and *Quadragesimo*.

2. The drafting is not at all as clear or businesslike as the original, if I may say so. For example:
   No. 3 could well be divided as "In particular ...".
   No. 4 could admit of division at "It shall, however, be the duty ..." and at "It shall in particular so restrain ...".

3. If his No. 1 is to remain, it could run as amended: " ... external goods, and that the exercise of this natural right is not only allowable, but is, for social needs, absolutely necessary. The Oireachtas, therefore, shall make no law ...".

4. I fail to see how in his (3) "reasonable access to the material resources of the nation" is a better formula than "may be so distributed among private individuals <u>and</u> the various classes". Distribution is not only "access to", but also "possession and control of".

5. Similarly I cannot see why 7,1 should be so amended as to omit "the less favoured classes". The infirm etc. are not coextensive with the less favoured. A very valuable idea is thereby forfeited. No reason is assigned for "deleting division of land": a very prominent plank in Leo XIII's programme and Fianna Fail's policy. It does not answer the question to say that,

as the division is being carried out, there is no need to state the principle.

6. The author forgets that he has himself incorporated 9 into his (4). It is not a matter of policy that can change, but a fundamental duty of State policy. Centres of industry, of course, are in quite another category of importance.

7. I consider it is a pity to omit the section on children and women, for the value of the principle stated. The principle is not sufficiently covered in his "protect the public against exploitation".

8. I would fear a contradiction in (4). The State will so restrain free competition that no <u>undue</u> monopoly may pass into the ownership of one or a few, <u>otherwise than may be provided by law</u>. If the monopoly is provided for by law, presumably the law is just and the monopoly ceases to be undue.

16. Letter from John Charles McQuaid to Éamon de Valera, 8 Oct. 1939 –

My dear Taoiseach,

I think the enclosed are quite good as far as they go.

Nowhere is it said, however, that <u>patriotism</u> is a virtue, as part of <u>Justice</u>, and, Therefore, a duty on every man, more especially on a Christian. We read of "natural patriotism" and of "duty of knowing fundamental law", but why there is a duty is not based on:

1) Natural duty of Justice to one's *patria* and
2) Natural congregation in Society
3) Natural need of Authority as central guiding force to the common good, with, in consequence, Government, Laws, police, Social Services.

In National Flag circular, the duty and <u>virtue</u> of patriotism find expression, side by side with "ideals of loyalty and service".

Similarly in An Bunreacht circular.

Page 3 of the latter circular. Shades of Suarez! The author has skipped clean over the "designation" theory, in favour of "delegation" theory of authority. The Constitution text admits either, and so, raises no undue opposition. This statement will cause worry.

Page 11, Section 18 is, I know, a summary but I think it is quite unhappy. It could figure in a Mohommedan State. It is not a question of putting things tactfully, but correctly and thus avoiding the hurt susceptibilities of Christian non-Catholics? The whole ambiguity is found in the word "recognises", by which this author puts all on a dead-level basis. Merely to quote the constitution would be very, very much better.

Page 12. The State limits private property right in view of the common good, according to demands of Social Justice.

The aim of the State is to secure a social order, according to natural law and Christian teaching, wherein Justice and Charity shall inspire and control human activities.

To go back to page 2: would it not be better to say: "It has a purpose – the full temporal welfare of its members, etc."

I think the final paragraph, page 3, of the covering letter is very good.

I hope these jottings may help. I will gladly do anything I can.

With very grateful regards,

Yours respectfully,

J. McQuaid, C.S.Sp.

[Handwritten comment by Éamon de Valera on letter –'I think it better to return this also. You may want it. EdeV.'].

Notes

1. Stephen Roche, Michael McDunphy, John Hearne, Philip O'Donoghue.
2. For more on this see Gerard Hogan, *The drafting of the Irish constitution, 1928–1941* (Dublin, 2012).
3. The correspondence and documents on the drafting of the 1937 Constitution are

held in (DDA, AB/A/ V).

4. *Sapientiae Christianae* (Christians as Citizens) was an encyclical issued by Pope Leo XIII in 1890.

5. *Rerum Novarum* (On the new things) was an encyclical issued by Pope Leo XIII in 1891. With the title 'Rights and duties of capital and labour', it was concerned with the rights and duties of property and the relations between employer and employees.

6. *Quadragesimo Anno* (The fortieth year) was an encyclical issued by Pope Pius XI in 1931. With the sub-title 'The reconstruction of the social order' it addressed the ethical challenges facing workers, employers, the Church and the state and the response to the rise of socialism as an economic system.

Chapter 2

Education

John Charles McQuaid was headmaster of Blackrock College from 1930 to 1939. He also served as a highly energetic chairman of the Catholic Headmasters' Association and the correspondence reflects his interests in educational matters. He had a stern view of mixed athletics, that is male and female athletes competing in the same meetings, as the newspaper reports, including his correspondence, indicate. McQuaid was a strong supporter of archives and the letter from Robert Dudley Edwards, Professor of Modern Irish History at UCD, is indicative of the importance of diocesan archives. As Roman Catholic Archbishop, he did not approve of mixing Catholic and Protestant students. The correspondence regarding the German School, St. Killian's in Dublin makes this all too clear. He also took a keen interest in students with disabilities, in particular those with hearing defects.[1]

MEETING OF CATHOLIC HEADMASTERS'
ASSOCIATION
AT THE GRESHAM HOTEL
On Thursday, October 22nd [1930], at 3 o'clock

AGENDA:

1—Election of Officers.
2—Correspondence.
3—Report on A.S.T.I. Agreement with Major Superiors.
4—Request for Affiliation with C.H.A. of Nine De La Salle Secondary Schools, viz. —Castletown, Bagnelstown, Castlebar,

Roscommon, Kildare, Waterford, Wicklow, Macroom and
Faithlegg (Waterford), also of St. Ita's Male Secondary School
(Lay), Newcastle West, Co. Limerick.

5—Discussion of the recent decision of the National University
not to recognise a Pass in Lower Course Irish in the Leaving
Certificate as equivalent to a Pass in Matriculation.

6—Discussion of the marking of the Certificate Examination
Papers, especially in Irish, and of the steps, if any, to be taken.

7—Proposals to request the Department of Education to increase
the number of Scholarships in the Intermediate Certificate, owing
to the increase in the number of pupils, etc.

8—Proposal to suggest to the Department of Education to
increase the total for Scholarships in Intermediate Certificate with
a view to encouraging wide courses.

9—Positive proposals for minimum course for Intermediate
Certificate.

10—Programme for Matriculation Greek.

11—Conditions for the Award of the Honours Leaving
Certificate.

12—Revision of Religious Knowledge Programme.

13—Income Tax.

14—Insurance of Pupils in Secondary Schools, and of classes in
Science and Manual Instruction.

JAMES STAUNTON, Hon. Sec.[2]
St. Kieran's College, Kilkenny.

The Half-yearly Meeting of the Catholic Headmasters' Association
was held in the Gresham Hotel on March 26th, at 3 o'clock, p.m.
Dr. McQuaid, C.S.Sp., Chairman, presided. Twenty-five members
attended.

1—Votes of aid for educational work were unanimously passed,
viz., £20 to the C.T.S. Conference Education Section, to be held
at Tuam; £20 to the International Catholic Education Congress,

and £10 to Dr. Corcoran, S.J.,³ as a small token of appreciation of
his work as President of the International Catholic Education
Congress, and as organiser of the Irish section and exhibit.
2—The Amendments of the Secondary Schools Programme,
proposed by the Department of Education in a letter of December
3rd, 1935, copies of which were circulated to all the members of
the C.H.A., were fully examined and discussed, point by point, at
the Meeting, and unanimous conclusions were reached on
practically all points. The Standing Committee was authorised to
put the conclusions of the General Meeting in ordered form. This
was done on April 11th, under the Chairmanship of Dr. McQuaid,
whose summary was examined and approved, and was sent by him
to the Department of Education and to the Daily Press. It was as
follows: —

THE FOLLOWING STATEMENT REPRESENTS THE
UNANIMOUS VIEW-POINT OF THE CATHOLIC
HEADMASTERS' ASSOCIATION: —

1—The Catholic Headmasters' Association duly appreciates the
action of the Secondary Department of Education in inviting its
opinion before a decision was taken concerning the proposed
Amendments in the Secondary Programme, and is pleased to see in
these proposed Amendments a sincere desire on the part of the
Secondary Branch to better the existing curriculum and conditions
of examination.
2—The Association is unanimous in its opinion that, for the
future, no change should be made in the existing Programme,
without allowing at least one year for the consideration of the
proposed change.
3—The Association wishes emphatically to record its belief that,
while freedom in the choice of subjects is a distinct advantage to
the Schools, yet that freedom ought not to be allowed to have for
result the reduction of a Secondary School Programme to the

level of a merely higher Primary Education.

4—Therefore, the Catholic Headmasters' Association can view only with grave concern, any measure that would tend either to make more difficult the position of the Classics or to lessen their status as truly cultural subjects of the Secondary Programme.

For the study of the Classics, at least of Latin, is an integral part of traditionally Catholic Secondary Education; and, in addition, has been from very early times, a chief element of Irish culture.

5—Further, the Catholic Headmasters' Association is convinced that the study of the Classics and of modern Continental Languages, is essential to the complete and rightful development of modern Irish literature, if that literature is not almost exclusively to be based, in regard to outlook and form, on merely English culture.

6—Therefore, while reserving its ultimate decision concerning some minor details which seem to be points of legitimate difference of opinion, the Catholic Headmasters' Association regrets that it cannot accept the principal Amendments, by which it is proposed to change the existing Secondary Programme, for the reasons, chiefly, that these changes tend to lower the standard of Secondary Education and to militate against the rightful position of Classical Studies and modern Continental languages.

To take the principal Amendments in detail.

A.—REGULATIONS

1—The Catholic Headmasters' Association is not opposed, in principle, to the separation of History and Geography, but prefers to retain the present arrangement. There would appear to be a certain natural link between these subjects, as may be gathered from their treatment as joint-subjects of the course, for many years.

A change would seem to be even inadvisable: the standard will presumably be raised; and with the pressure of other essential subjects, it will be difficult to find time for further and necessary class-periods; finally the position would be very trying for Schools that wish to retain the Classics.

2—The Association regards the present arrangement as much superior to the Course suggested for recognised Junior Pupils and would not wish to have any change for the moment.

3—It was agreed to postpone, till the October meeting of the Association, the final decision concerning the proposal that no Subject, except Irish, shall be compulsory for the Intermediate Certificate Examination.

4—It is not felt that any comment is required from the Association on a question that does not seem to effect our Schools.

5—It is not desired that any change should be made in the present regulations for the approved course of the Senior Pupils.

6—Similarly, the actual conditions for a Pass in the Leaving Certificate Examination enjoy the preference of the Association.

7—It was agreed to reject (a) and (b); to accept (d) with of course the proviso that Science is excepted; and to regard (c) as requiring no comment from our Association.

The concluding paragraph, referring to the intention of the Department to continue the existing provisions for Lower Course Subjects and 30% Pass Mark in a Full Course Subject—was accepted by the Association.

B. —PROGRAMME

1—The Association is disposed to accept the Amendments of both the Course in Irish History and the periods of Irish and European History in the written examination, the words, however, "down to the present day" being in all three cases omitted.

2—It is considered much more useful to omit the Note on p. 21 of which there is question.

3—Regarding the counter-proposals, Paragraph I. (a) and (b) are to be rejected;

(c) is acceptable, not however in the sense of admitting a Lower Course in Intermediate Mathematics, but in the sense of including on the examination paper a number of easier questions, sufficient to allow of the average pupil obtaining a Pass.

Paragraph II. was not considered worthy of acceptance.

4—(a) The Association is not averse to the principle of an Oral Examination in Irish of all pupils of Secondary Schools, but sees so many practical difficulties in the scheme as to consider it unpractical. Besides, it would seem, that in a course open to annual inspection over a period of six years, there is ample provision, under the existing regulations, for fairly testing all the pupils.

(b) An additional public examination at the end of the second year does not seem advisable, chiefly because of the absence of uniform entrance age.

(Signed)

J. C. McQuaid, C.S.Sp.

Chairman

Catholic Headmasters' Association

———————

The High School,

Dublin, C.19

5th November, 1935.

Headmaster:

JOHN BENNETT, M.A.

Dear Father Staunton,

The following resolution was passed at the Annual General Meeting of the Schoolmasters' Association for transmission to the Department: – "That the 10% Cut in Capitation Grants be restored and that the Ministry be asked to receive a deputation from this Association to discuss the proposal."

The suggestion arose out of a discussion about the fall in the proportion of Registered Teachers employed in the schools which was the subject of our Department's Circular.

My Association has asked me to forward the resolution to the Catholic Headmasters' Association asking for their support.

Yours sincerely,
[Signed] J. Bennett
Hon. Sec. Schoolmasters' Association.

———————

Kilnamona, Shankill
5 Nov. 1936.

Dear Dr. McQuaid,

I hope this rather belated reply to your letter of the 2nd will reach you in time.

It is not very clear to me in what capacity the questions you mention come under my jurisdiction, except perhaps as a newly-elected member of the Board of Studies. If Lower Course Irish is the Leaving Certificate course, I have much sympathy with your side … the position for years back has been that we in the three Colleges have been perfectly willing to have either set books or no set books, but as long as I can help it, I won't be browbeaten by Fr. Corcoran into having both and setting double papers as they very foolishly do in Latin. Personally, I will vote for a return to set books at any time, and if people want no set books, let them sit for the Leaving Cert.

Of course the whole question is a very wide one, and as I say I'm new to it.

With all good wishes
Yours sincerely
Michael

ST KIERAN'S COLLEGE,
KILKENNY.

Resolution 6.

(1) Full confidence in standard until now, confidence shaken by last year's Irish results in Leaving Cert.

(2) Examinations mean so much to students,
   (a) Co Council Scholarships
   (b) in Maynooth and elsewhere
   (c) College Prizes and Bursaries
   the marks should reflect their merit.

(3) If Teachers had not confidence in marking their work would not be wholehearted.

(4) not easy to keep uniformity of standard. Impossible if examiner is not teaching anyone. More difficult if one teacher is teaching University students, another Intermediate only. Hence suggestion, which is only a suggestion, that examiners be engaged in secondary teaching.

1936 – Number of Intermediate Boys examined 3,487
             75.6% passed.

   This is the chief argument, the number of boys examined has gone up from 1834 in 1925, 1751 in 1926, 1899 in 1927, 2504 in 1931 to 3478 in 1936. The number has more than doubled. The standard and keenness of competition has gone up from 10% to 20%. The number of scholarships remain the same.

_____

CUMANN NA MEÁN MHÚINTEÓRÍ.
(*Association of Secondary Teachers, Ireland.*)

Telephone: Ballsbridge 229
General Secretary: T. J. Burke
Head Office: 3 Anglesea Road,
Ballsbridge
Dublin, S.E.1.

21st December 1936
Very Rev. D. Murphy, C.S.Sp., D.D., M.A.,
Provincial,
Kimmage Manor,
Dublin.
Dear Dr. Murphy,

I beg to enclose two copies of a "Proviso" to the "Procedure in Dismissal of Lay Secondary Teacher and Appeal from such Dismissal". The "Proviso" is the outcome of negotiations between the Irish Christian Brothers and the A.S.T.I., and the effect of it is to render the Appeal procedure inapplicable in the case of certain classes of lay Teachers.

A recent meeting of the Central Executive Council of the Association decided to retain uniformity on the Appeal terms for all the Catholic men members of the Association by requesting the Major Superiors of all the Orders who have signed the Appeal Agreement to sign the "Proviso" thereto as well.

Accordingly, I shall thank you to sign the enclosed two copies of the "Proviso", and return both copies to me at your early convenience. We shall then sign both copies and I shall then send one to you to retain.

Wishing you the season's choicest graces and blessings,

Sincerely yous,
[Signed] T.J. Burke.
~~Gen. Secretary~~

———————

[*Irish Times* Wed. 9th Feb. 1934]
WOMEN IN ATHLETICS.
PROTEST FROM BLACKROCK COLLEGE.

The Very Rev. John C. McQuaid, C.S.Sp., President of Blackrock College, Dublin, asks us to publish the following letter of protest which he addressed yesterday to the Honorary Secretary of the National Athletic and Cycling Association :—

"Sir,—I have noted in yesterday's Press a majority decision of the annual Congress of the N.A.C.A.I. in favour of women competing in the same athletic meetings as men.

"I protest against this un-Catholic and un-Irish decision.

"I hereby assure you that no boy from my college will take part in any athletic meeting controlled by your organisation at which women will compete, no matter what attire they may adopt."

12th February 1934.

Dear Father McQuaid,

I sincerely congratulate you on your splendid protest in the recent Athletic proposition. Please God your timely action will prevent the carrying out of the monstrous suggestion.

I thank you for your letter. I was only too glad to add my own little word to the excellent lead from Blackrock.

Kindest regards.
Yours sincerely in Christ,
[signed] John F. Roe Snr

———————

St Mary's Training College
Belfast
8. 2. '34

My Dear Father.

I cannot resist congratulating you on your "Athletic" protest; if there were a few more leaders of the Catholic people to follow your example, we would shortly put an end to the unchristian impositions on a Catholic people. The protest, fearless and uncompromising as it was, will do great good. I hope that you will be able to come up to the C.T. Conference in June – it promises to be really effective.

Hope that you and all in your care are well...

Yours sincerely in Christ
SM Peter

[*Irish Independent* Mon 12-3-34]

N.A.C.A. Change Position
Women's Place in Athletics
Dublin Decision

After discussing the debated question of women competing at the same athletic meetings as men, a conjoint meeting of the General Council and Central Council of the National Athletic and Cycling Association of Ireland, held in Dublin, decided not to implement the decision of Congress that women should be permitted to compete in a limited number of championship events and that an event for ladies be recommended to be inserted in each of the open meetings throughout the country.

Mr. J. Conaghan, of the Council, said that if they implemented the decision of Congress it would be flouting public opinion.

Mr. P.C. Moore, Chairman, said the motion had been

considered by the Standing Committee, but it was felt that it was a matter for the Central Council to decide. The Central Council had all the authority of Congress during the interim.

Mr. M. J. Byrne (Chairman, Co. Dublin Board) said there had been great discussion on the matter at the Dublin Co. Convention, as the motion came from Dublin, and the suggestion eventually passed for Congress was that four events should be included for ladies in the National Championships. Congress was asked to give that a trial.

OUTSIDE OPINION.

Mr. F. de Vere (Mayo) proposed "that having regard to the fact that there has been no representative demand for the holding of women's athletic championships, and that controversy prejudicial to the N.A.C.A. has arisen, the decision of Congress be suspended for one year, and in the meantime the question of holding women's athletic championships be a matter in discretion of various Co. Boards."

"We know," he said, "the difficulty from the point of view of the Pope's Encyclical, and the attitude the clergy are likely to take in consequence. It is for the purpose of getting rid of that difficulty I make the proposition."

The Chairman said part of the original condition was that the women's championships should be held in conjunction with the national athletic championships, but Congress definitely ruled that portion of the motion out, and as the motion then stood it was a recommendation that championships be held in a certain limited number of events, and also a recommendation that one event for ladies be inserted in each of the open meetings throughout the country.

MISUNDERSTANDING.

The Chairman said there had been a great deal of misunderstanding because Congress had definitely decided not to hold women's championships in conjunction with the national championships, and that local sports-promoting associations were not bound to hold such events.

Mr. McManus said the position was that the Co. Dublin Board had only asked for a trial of their recommendation, because pressure had been brought to bear upon officials of the Association that they should support women in athletic affairs.

"I think something should be done to support women in this," he said. "They are taking part in different kinds of sport all over the world."

Mr. M. Byrne said if women wanted an athletic association they should form one for themselves.

After further discussion Mr. de Vere said he did not want to dictate to the Co. Dublin Board, and withdrew his resolution.

The unanimous decision not to implement the decision of the Congress was taken on the motion of Mr. M. Byrne (Dublin), seconded by Mr. de Vere.

Mr. McManus—"no sports programme can have ladies in future?"

Chairman—"The position is the same as last year."

WOMEN ATHLETES BANNED

[*Daily Herald* 11.3.34]

EFFECT IN FREE STATE OF POPE'S MESSAGE

The Pope's Encyclical on the subject of women in athletics has resulted in a ban on women athletes in the Irish Free State.

A proposal that women should be allowed to compete in a limited number of athletic events was rejected by a meeting of the

Councils of the National Athletic and Cycling Association at Dublin, on Saturday.

The recommendation urging the inclusion of women in athletics was passed recently at the annual congress of the association.

Immediately afterwards the president of Blackrock Catholic College, recalling the Pope's Encyclical on the subject, announced that no boy from the college would be permitted to compete at any meeting at which women were to take part.

The council of the association on Saturday unanimously decided that no action be taken to implement the decision of the congress.

WOMEN IN ATHLETICS
[*Irish Independent*, 22.2.34]

Mr James J. McGilton (hon. sec. N.A.C.A.) has sent the following letter to Very Rev. Dr. McQuaid, President, Blackrock College:—

"Your letter of the 8th inst., relative to the proposed participation by women in track and field athletics, was considered at a meeting of the Standing Committee of my Association on Friday, the 16th inst.

I am directed to inform you that Committee was of opinion that the points raised by you appertain to the General Council of our Association and, accordingly, your letter has been referred to the next meeting of that body, which will be held on 10th prox.

I am to add that the Standing Committee appreciate the fact that your protest was made in the best interests of the Association."

[*Sunday Independent* 26-2-34]

WOMEN'S PART IN ATHLETICS
TEACHING OF THE CHURCH
FR. McQUAID'S LETTER TO THE N.A.C.A.

Very Rev. J.C. McQuaid, C.S.Sp., President, Blackrock College, Dublin, has addressed the following letter to the Hon. Secretary, the N.A.C.A.:—

Dear Sir—I thank you for your courteous letter of the 20th inst., in which you inform me that the Standing Committee of the N.A.C.A. has referred my letter of the 8th inst. to the General Council.

I congratulate the Standing Committee on this prompt and sympathetic action; it is, I feel, a presage of the definitive annulment of an unhappy decision.

Much that has been written in the Press on the occasion of my protest has been painfully irrelevant. May I, then, be permitted to focus the attention of your Association on the single point at issue.

NOT FORM OF SPORT.

Firstly, the issue is not: in what forms of athletic sport may women or girls indulge, with safety to their physical well-being. That question should be duly determined by medical science, rightly so called.

Secondly, the issue is not: in what form of athletic sport may women or girls indulge, within the reserved ground of their own Colleges or Associations. That question should be duly solved by the principles both of Christian modesty and of true medical science.

Thirdly, the issue is not: that, as mixed athletics have already made their appearance in our midst, they should be continued. Mixed athletics and all cognate immodesties, are abuses that right-minded people reprobate, wherever and whenever they exist.

Fourthly, the issue is not: that, as mixed athletics have been adopted in other countries, those of us, who are modern, should not lag behind. It is a Christian duty, incumbent on all of us, not to adopt what is morally wrong, God is not modern, nor His Law.

ONLY ISSUE.

Rather, this only is the issue: that women should not compete at the same athletic meetings as men, though the Annual Congress of the N.A.C.A. has decided that they may so compete.

I have called this decision un-Irish and un-Catholic.

It is un-Irish; for, that mixed athletics is a social abuse, outraging our rightful national tradition, is a statement that requires, not proof, but only some reflexion.

It is un-Catholic; for, that mixed athletics are a moral abuse, formally reprobated by the Sovereign Pontiff, Pius XI, is a truth clearly proved by the words of the Encyclical Letter, *Divini Illius Magistri*.

May I quote the actual text from the official source of Papal documents, the *Acta Apostolicae Sedis*, Vol. xxii, num. 2, pages 72-73. It is a passage strongly relevant, for, the Pope is opposing God's plan in respect of the differing sexes to that "deceptive system of modern coeducation, which is the enemy of Christian upbringing," in that its supporters ignore or deny the effects of original sin and, in disarray of mind, regard society "as an unassorted mass of men and woman equal in all respects." The distinction of the sexes, as ordained by God, must, the Pope teaches, "be upheld, nay even cherished."

THE APPLICATION.

Then, at once, Pius XI applies the principles to "all schools and to athletic sports":—

> "Ejus modi vero praecepta, ad christianae prudentiae praescriptum, tempestive atque opportune servanda sunt, non modo in scholis omnibus, praesertim per trepidos adolescentiae annos, unde totius ferme futurae vitae ratio omnino pendet, sed etiam in gymnicis ludis atque exercitationibus, in quibus Christianae peculiari modo modestiae puellarum cavendum,

utpote quas ostentare sese atque ante omnium oculos proponere summopere dedeceat."

You will kindly allow me to translate very literally:—

"Such precepts must be observed, according to the prescriptions of Christian prudence, in due season and opportunely, not only in all schools, particularly throughout the anxious years of adolescence, on which the tenor of well-nigh all the rest of life entirely depends, but also in athletic sports and exercises, wherein the Christian modesty of girls must be, in a special way, safeguarded, for it is supremely unbecoming that they should flaunt themselves and display themselves before the eyes of all."

The issue, I think, is clear.

CAMOGIE SECRETARY'S VIEWS

Speaking at the annual Congress of the Camoguidheacht Association in Dublin yesterday, Mr. Sean O'Duffy, organising secretary, speaking on the controversy regarding the participation of women in athletics, said that the Association would do all in its power to ensure that no girl would appear on any sports ground in a costume to which any exception could be taken.

If they remained Irish in the ordinary acceptation of the word they could not go wrong.

11-2-34

MIXED ATHLETICS

PROPOSAL AROUSES
FIERCE OPPOSITION

"Sunday Chronicle" Correspondent

Dublin, Saturday.

Widespread opposition has been aroused among school authorities and clergy to the decision of the Council of the National Athletic and Cycling Association in favour of women competing at the same athletics meetings as men.

Almost every college authority in Ireland has sent a protest, and I understand that in face of the opposition the council will meet to reconsider their decision.

"The decision, if it stands, will spell the death knell of the N.A. and C.A," said a prominent athlete to me to-day. "We will certainly have nothing to do with any athletic body who intends to follow the lead of Continental bodies in this question. To have women compete with men is all wrong."

[*Irish Press*. Sat. 24th Feb. 1934]

MIXED ATHLETICS

The following letter has been sent to the Hon. Secretary, The N.A.C.A.:—

Dear Sir,—I thank you for your courteous letter of the 20th inst., in which you inform me that the Standing Committee of the N.A.C.A. has referred my letter of the 8th inst. to the General Council.

I congratulate the Standing Committee on this prompt and sympathetic action; it is, I feel, a presage of the definitive annulment of an unhappy decision. Much that has been written in the Press on the occasion of my protest, has been painfully irrelevant. May I, then, be permitted to focus the attention of your Association on the single point at issue.

Firstly, the issue is not: in what forms of athletic sport may women or girls indulge, with safety to their physical well-being. That question should be duly determined by medical science, rightly so called.

Secondly, the issue is not: in what forms of athletic sport may women or girls indulge, within the reserved ground of their own

Colleges or Associations. That question should be duly solved by the principles both of Christian modesty and of true medical science.

Thirdly, the issue is not: that, as mixed athletics have already made their appearance in our midst, they should be continued. Mixed athletics and all cognate immodesties, are abuses that right-minded people reprobate, wherever and whenever they exist.

Fourthly, the issue is not: that, as mixed athletics have been adopted in other countries, those of us, who are modern, should not lag behind. It is a Christian duty, incumbent on all of us, not to adopt what is morally wrong, God is not modern, nor His Law.

Rather, this only is the issue: that women should not compete at the same athletic meetings as men, though the Annual Congress of the N.A.C.A. has decided that they may so compete.

I have called this decision un-Irish and un-Catholic. It is un-Irish; for, that mixed athletics is a social abuse, outraging our rightful national tradition, is a statement that requires, not proof, but only some reflexion. It is un-Catholic; for, that mixed athletics are a moral abuse, formally reprobated by the Sovereign Pontiff, Pius XI, is a truth clearly proved by the words of the Encyclical Letter, *Divini Illius Magistri*.

May I quote the actual text from the official source of Papal documents, the *Acta Apostolicae Sedis*, Vol. xxii, num. 2, pages 72-73. It is a passage strongly relevant, for, the Pope is opposing God's plan in respect of the differing sexes to that "deceptive system of modern coeducation, which is the enemy of Christian upbringing," in that its supporters ignore or deny the effects of original sin and, in disarray of mind, regard society "as an unassorted mass of men and woman equal in all respects." The distinction of the sexes, as ordained by God, must, the Pope teaches, "be upheld, nay even cherished." Then, at once, Pius XI applies the principles to "all schools and to athletic sports":—

"Ejus modi vero praecepta, ad christianae prudentiae praescriptum, tempestive atque opportune servanda sunt, non modo in scholis omnibus,

praesertim per trepidos adolescentiae annos, unde totius ferme futurae vitae
ratio omnino pendet, sed etiam in gymnicis ludis atque exercitationibus, in
quibus christianae peculiari modo modestiae puellarum cavendum, utpote
quas ostentare sese atque ante omnium oculos proponere summopere
dedeceat."

You will kindly allow me to translate very literally:—

"Such precepts must be observed, according to the
prescriptions of Christian prudence, in due season and
opportunely, not only in all schools, particularly throughout the
anxious years of adolescence, on which the tenor of well-nigh all
the rest of life entirely depends, but also in athletic sports and
exercises, wherein the Christian modesty of girls must be, in a
special way, safeguarded, for it is supremely unbecoming that they
should flaunt themselves and display themselves before the eyes of
all." The issue, I think, is clear.—Yours sincerely,

JOHN C. McQUAID, C.S.Sp.
Blackrock College.

Monday, *The Daily Mail* [11.3.34]

IRISH BAN ON MIXED ATHLETICS
A DECISION REVERSED
MEN-ONLY SPORTS EVENTS

Women to Have Their Own Meetings

The Irish National Athletic and Cycling Association at a meeting in
Dublin on Saturday decided not to implement their resolution of
some months ago allowing women to compete with men in athletic
events.

One result of the ban on women from sports meetings may be
the formation of an Irish women athletes' association.

When the National Athletic and Cycling Association adopted
their resolution some months ago allowing women to compete

there was a storm of protest, and a memorable letter was written by the Most Rev. Dr. McQuaid, president of Blackrock College, who said that no boy in his college ever would participate at mixed meetings.

The only protest at Saturday's meeting came from Mr. McManus, of the Dublin County Board, who said that since women were taking part in different kinds of sport all over the world something should be done by the Irish association to organise sports meetings for them.

Mr. Byrne, chairman of the Dublin County Board, disagreed and said he was entirely against women in the association. He thought if women wanted an athletic association for themselves they should form one.

WOMEN'S RETORT

It is understood that steps will......and Cycling Association at a meeting in Dublin on Saturday decided not to implement their resolution of some months ago allowing women to compete with men in athletic events.

One result of the ban on women from sports meetings may be the formation of an Irish women athletes' association.

When the National Athletic and Cycling Association adopted their resolution some months ago allowing women to compete there was a storm of protest, and a memorable letter was written by the Most Rev. Dr. McQuaid, president of Blackrock College, who said that no boy in his college ever would participate at mixed meetings.

The only protest at Saturday's meeting came from Mr. McManus, of the Dublin County Board, who said that since women were taking part in different kinds of sport all over the world something should be done by the Irish association to organise sports meetings for them.

Mr. Byrne, chairman of the Dublin County Board, disagreed and said he was entirely against women in the association. He thought if women wanted an athletic association for themselves they should form one.

WOMEN'S RETORT

It is understood that steps will shortly be taken to form a women's athletic association governing many forms of sport in which women to-day take part.

It has been admitted that there was a demand that women's events should be included, and now Ireland is likely to have meetings for women only and gates at the meetings exclusive to men may suffer.

Miss Dockrell, the 100 yards Irish swimming champion, said yesterday: "The decision of the N.A.C.A. should encourage women to form their own sports association, directed and controlled by women only."

N.A.C.A. VOTE FOR MIXED PROGRAMME

STRONG OPPOSITION TO PROPOSED NEW STEP

AN ULSTER VIEW

Should women compete in athletics at the same meeting as men? This was the question debated at the Annual Congress of the N.A.C.A. of Ireland in Dublin yesterday. A majority decided in favour of their doing so, but strong opposition was also voiced.

The matter was discussed on a motion by the County Dublin Board, recommending the holding of women's events in 100, 220 and 440 yards and one handicap event in each sports meeting.

Mr. O'Keeffe (G.A.A.) in opposing the motion, said it was an important thing for the association to decide, whether women's athletics was a thing to be adopted throughout the country.

It was a very debatable point what the attitude of the Irish people would be to these events. He himself had received very strong complaints regarding ladies participating in athletic events, and had been asked by members of his association and by people of influence in the country, not to allow them into Croke Park.

Dr. Magnier (Cork) supported Mr. O'Keefe, and said that from the moral point it was absolutely wrong to be running young men and women in the same field in the garb now effected for these events.

Mr. O'Brien (Clare) said that the Pope, in a recent encyclical objected to women taking part in tug-o'-war, wrestling and boxing competitions but he did not object to them taking part in the lighter forms of athletics, such as running and jumping.

He himself believed that freer mingling of the sexes on the athletic field would do good.

Mr. O'Reilly (Ulster) said that in the North, women had been competing in the athletic contests for a long time. Public opinion was so much against it, however, that the G.A.A. in Antrim had to prevent women athletes from appearing in Corrigan Park in anything but gym dresses.

Mr. O'Keeffe agreed with Dr. Magnier in that the position was a very delicate one.

WOMEN IN ATHLETICS

Mr. Fleming said that since no applications had been made by local bodies for permission to hold ladies' events, he did not think they were entitled to discuss a purely hypothetical question.

The Chairman said that having regard to the controversy that had arisen and the protest that had come from one of the foremost schools in the country, it would be in the best interest of the Association that no action should be taken to implement the decision of Congress for the time being. That would clear up the position.

ONLY A TRIAL ASKED.

Mr. McManus said the position was that the Co. Dublin Board had only asked for a trial of their recommendation, because pressure had been brought to bear upon officials of the Association that they should support women in athletic affairs.

"I think something should be done to support women in this," declared Mr. McManus. "They are taking part in different kinds of sport all over the world."

He did not see why they should not have sports meetings of their own and associations of their own.

Mr. Byrne said he did not agree with his fellow-member of the County Dublin Board, Mr. McManus. He was entirely against women in the Association. They had enough to do to look after the athletics of the men, and he thought if the women wanted an athletic association they should form one for themselves.

After some further discussion Mr. de Vere said he did not want to dictate to the County Dublin Board, if they were anxious to have women's championships in the County Dublin.

He then withdrew his resolution.

UNANIMOUS DECISION

A resolution was then proposed by Mr. Byrne, and seconded by Mr de Vere, "that the Central Council considers it in the best interests of the Association that no action be taken to implement the decision of Congress as regards the participation of women in athletics."

Mr. P. Larkin—Why not say "because there has been no demand."

The Chairman—"No."

The Chairman having put the motion, declared it "carried unanimously."

Mr. McManus—"No sports programme can have ladies' events in future?"

The Chairman—"The position is the same as last year."

CROSS-COUNTRY EVENTS

It was stated that 10 teams and 7 individuals had entered for the All-Ireland Senior Cross-Country Championship, which is to take place at Thurles next Saturday.

They are: —

O'Callaghan's Mills A and B teams (the holders), Army Metro, Mullingar, Dublin City Harriers, Galteemore, Tipperary, Curragh, Blarney A.C., Cork, Clonliffe, Downhill (Belfast), and Messers. J.J. O'Connor, Limerick City Harriers; W. Walsh, Carrickbyrne A.C., Wexford; H. McFall, Divis View A.C., Belfast; P. Shields, same team; T. Murphy, Donore Harriers; S. Daly, same team; J. Quinn, South Down Harriers.

Mr. T.E. Nolan, Hon. Treasurer, reported on the non-payment of affiliation fees for the year 1933 by several County Boards, and proposed the following resolution, which was seconded by Mr. Palmer, and passed unanimously:—"That the matter of the granting of sports permits to clubs whose County Boards had not affiliated to the Central Board for 1933 be not considered until the outstanding moneys due by such Boards are remitted to the Central Treasurer, and that non-affiliated County Boards be forthwith notified of their position."

It was decided to fix the annual Schools Championships for Whit Monday.

[*Irish Independent* Monday 26-2-34.]

THE CHURCH
AND
MIXED ATHLETICS

POPE'S TEACHING

DR. McQUAID'S LETTER TO THE N.A.C.A.

Very Rev. J.C. McQuaid, C.S.Sp., President, Blackrock College, Dublin, has addressed the following letter to the Hon. Secretary, the N.A.C.A:—

Dear Sir—I thank you for your courteous letter of the 20th inst., in which you inform me that the Standing Committee of the N.A.C.A has referred my letter the 8th inst. to the General Council.

I congratulate the Standing Committee on this prompt and sympathetic action: it is, I feel, a presage of the definitive annulment of an unhappy decision.

Much that has been written in the Press on occasion of my protest had been painfully irrelevant. May I, then, be permitted to focus the attention of your Association on the single point at issue.

NOT THE ISSUE.

Firstly, the issue is not: in what forms of athletic sport may women or girls indulge with safety to their physical well-being? That question should be duly determined by medical science, rightly so called.

Secondly, the issue is not: in what forms of athletic sport may women or girls indulge, within the reserved ground of their own College or Associations? That question should be duly solved by the principles both of Christian modesty and of true medical science.

Thirdly, the issue is not: that, as mixed athletics have already made their appearance in our midst, they should be continued. Mixed athletics and all cognate immodesties are abuses that right-minded people reprobate wherever, and whenever they exist.

Fourthly, the issue is not: that, as mixed athletics have been adopted in other countries, those of us who are modern should not lag behind. It is a Christian duty, incumbent on us all, not to adopt what is morally wrong. God is not modern, nor His law.

UN-IRISH AND UN-CATHOLIC.

Rather, this only is the issue: that women should not compete at the same athletic meetings as men, though the Annual Congress of the N.A.C.A. has decided that they may so compete.

I have called this decision un-Irish and un-Catholic.

It is un-Irish; for, that mixed athletics are a social abuse, outraging our rightful, national tradition, is a statement that requires, not proof but only some reflection.

It is un-Catholic; for, that mixed athletics are a moral abuse, formally reprobated by the Sovereign Pontiff Pius XI, is a truth clearly proved by the words of the Encyclical Letter, *Divini Illius Magistri*.

May I quote the actual text from the official source of Papal documents, the *Acta Apostolicae Sedis*, Vol. xxii., num. 2, pages 72-73. It is a passage strongly relevant, for the Pope is opposing God's plan, in respect of the differing sexes, to the "deceptive system of modern coeducation, which is the enemy of Christian upbringing," in that its supporters ignore or deny the effects of original sin and, in disarray of mind, regard society "as an unassorted mass of men and women, equal in all respects." The distinction of the sexes, as ordained by God, must, the Pope teaches, "be upheld, nay even cherished."

THE POPE'S TEACHING.

Then at once, Pius XI....junction with the national championships, but Congress ruled that portion out, and as the motion then stood, it was a recommendation that championships be held in a certain limited number of events, and also a recommendation that one event for ladies be inserted in each of the open meetings throughout the country.

There had been a great deal of misunderstanding shown in the Press, because Congress had definitely decided not to hold women's championships in conjunction with the national championships, and that local sports-promoting associations were not bound to hold such events.

Controversy in The Press

Having regard to the controversy that had arisen and the protest that had come from one of the foremost schools in the country, it would be in the best interests of the Association that no action should be taken to implement the decision of Congress for the time being. That would clear up the position.

Mr. McManus said the position was that the Co. Dublin Board had only asked for a trial of their recommendation, because pressure had been brought to bear upon officials that they should support women in athletic affairs.

"I think something should be done to support women in this," declared Mr. McManus. "They are taking part in different kinds of sport all over the world. This recommendation was only to help them, with a view to the women organising and forming an Association of their own."

The Chairman—"I don't think that arises. The issue is merely about women competing at the same athletics meetings as men." Mr. Byrne said he did not agree with his fellow-member of the Co. Dublin Board, Mr. McManus. He was entirely against women in the Association.

Mr. J. O. Collins asked how many women were taking part in

running in Ireland? The Chairman—"It only amounts to a dozen or fifteen." Mr. Selby said that as regards cycling, men members of the Association had been disgruntled because women members who had won medals had set themselves up to be as good as the men.

Mr. de Vere said he did not want to dictate to the Co. Dublin Board. If they were anxious to have women's championships in the County Dublin they should do so. The churches had no objection, the schools had no objection, nobody had any objection to that. "It is mixed athletics they are objecting to," he said. He then withdrew his resolution.

The resolution was adopted then, proposed by Mr. Byrne, seconded by Mr. de Vere.

Mr. McManus—No sports programme can have ladies' events in the future? The Chairman—The position is the same as last year. Mr McManus—I think the members ought to consider this seriously. I don't think this is right. The Chairman—The matter is now dealt with. Mr. McManus—I didn't think as much as that was involved. The largest clubs in the city have events for ladies—cycling and all. Mr. Conaghan—We have got to decide against them, or we are going against public opinion. Further discussion will not help the Association.

The following members attended:— Messrs. P. C. Moore, J. J. McGilton (Secretary), T. E. Nolan, Felming, F. V. de Vere, C. Clinch, Conaghan, M. J. Byrne, McManus, Selby, W. Hely, Larkin, J. Sweeney, M. Navin, J. O. Collins and J. J. Connellan.

———————

EAST GALWAY DEMOCRAT
SATURDAY FEBRUARY 10th 1934

Men and Women
In Athletics

Since the Congress of the National and Athletic Association adopted resolutions in favour of having championships for ladies, and also that there be events for them at Sports meetings, much has been said and written against the decision arrived at.

To our minds it is an unwise one.

While we are anxious for the promotion of athletics, we consider that the line must be drawn somewhere, and for that reason we trust the Association will see the wisdom of changing their attitude in the matter.

On the grounds of delicacy and modesty there is grave objection to women taking part in athletics with men, and women should not be blind to this.

The strong protest of the Reverend President of Blackrock College is one that must not go unheeded by those concerned.

Writing to the hon. secretary of the N.A.C.A.I., he says:—

"I have noted in the Press a majority decision of the Annual Congress of the N.A.C.A.I. in favour of women competing in the same athletics meetings as men.

"I protest against the un-Catholic and un-Irish decision.

"I hereby assure you that no boy from my College will take part in any athletic meeting controlled by your organisation at which women will compete, no matter what attire they might adopt."

[*Irish Times*, Monday March 10]

BAN ON WOMEN ATHLETES.
RULING ON N.A.C.A. CHAMPIONSHIPS
NEW ASSOCIATION MAY BE FORMED

Women are now forbidden to take part in athletics events at meetings conducted by the National Athletic and Cycling Association or Ireland, and a new and separate women's sports association may be formed. A joint meeting of the General and Joint Councils of the Association refused to carry into effect a recommendation of the Association's recent congress "that championships for women be held in a limited number of events, and that one event for women be inserted in each of the open meetings throughout the country."

The congress decision had evoked much protest, the foremost expression of disagreement being that of Dr. McQuaid, President of Blackrock College, who declared that no boy of his college would compete at any N.A.C.A. sports meeting in which women took part.

Mr. McManus, of the Dublin Board, protested that women are taking part in different kinds of sport all over the world. "I don't see why we should hinder them here," he said, "or allow anyone to stop us from helping them. It is very unfair if the ladies are to be driven out of sport."

A retort to Mr. McManus was: "We cannot flout public opinion."

DECISION SUSPENDED.

Mr. F. V. de Vere, of Mayo, proposed a resolution "that, having regard to the fact that there has been no representative demand for the holding of women's athletic championships, and that controversy prejudicial to the N.A.C.A. has arisen, the decision of

congress be suspended for one year, and in the meantime the
question of holding women's athletic championships be a matter
in the discretion of the various county boards."

"We know," said Mr. de Vere, "the difficulty from the point of
view of the Pope's Encyclical, and the attitude the clergy are likely
to take in consequence. It is for the purpose of getting rid of that
difficulty I make the proposition."

The Chairman said there had been a great deal of
misunderstanding shown in the Press, because congress had
definitely decided not to hold women's championships in
conjunction with the national championships, and that local
sports-promoting associations were not bound to hold such
events. It would be in the best interests of athletes that no action
should be taken to implement the decision of congress for the
time being. That would clear up the position.

Mr McManus said that the County Dublin Board had only
asked for a trial of their recommendation.

FORM THEIR OWN.

Mr. Byrne said that he was entirely against women in the
Association. If the women wanted an athletic association, they
should form it themselves.

Mr. de Vere said that if they were anxious to have women's
championships in the County Dublin, they should do so since the
Church had no objections.

When the resolution banning women was adopted, Mr.
McManus said that the largest clubs in the city have events for
ladies—cycling and all.

Mr. Conaghan—"We have got to decide against them or we
are going against public opinion."

PROVIDING GROUNDS.

An *Irish Times* reporter who yesterday interviewed women prominent in Irish sport found the general opinion on the N.A.C.A. decision was that expressed by Miss Dockrell, Irish women's 100 yards swimming champion. "The women must go ahead and form an association of their own for athletics, since the N.A.C.A. has banned them," she said, and added: "It is hard to understand that ban, since there was no question of 'mixed athletics.'"

Miss Dockrell said that since the N.A.C.A.'s assistance was not available in this respect, the women would be faced with the difficult problem of providing their own grounds and organisation. In England and France, however, women's athletics had been strongly established, and she did not think Irish women athletes, who were enthusiastic if not numerous, would be cut off from the sport by the N.A.C.A. action.

Blackrock College
Dublin
6th February 1934

Sir,

I have noted in yesterday's Press a majority decision of the General Congress of the N.A.C.A.I., in favour of women competing in the same athletic meetings as men.

I protest against this un-Catholic and un-Irish decision... I hereby assure you, that no boy from my College will take part in any athletic meeting controlled by your Organization, at which women will compete, no matter what attire they may adopt.

I am, Sir,
Yours sincerely,
John C McQuaid CSSR
President

The Hon. Secretary,
The N.A.C.A.I.,
Shamrock Chambers.,
Dame Street, Dublin.

NATIONAL ATHLETIC AND CYCLING ASSOCIATION OF
IRELAND

9th February 1934

Dr. J. C. McQuaid, C.S. Sp.
President,
Blackrock College,
Dublin

Dear Dr. McQuaid,
 I have the honour to acknowledge receipt of your letter of the
6th. instant and while I appreciate the motive which prompted
you to forward your protest on the question of athletics for
women, I cannot give you any definite reply until the question
has been considered by the Council of my Association.
Very truly yours,
[signed] James P. McGillan
Honorary Secretary.

Blackrock College,
Dublin,
Feb. 23rd 1933

Dear Sir,
 I thank you for your courteous letter of the 20th inst., in which
you inform me that the Standing Committee of the N.A.C.A. has
referred my letter of the 8th inst. to the General Council.
 I congratulate the Standing Committee on this prompt and

sympathetic motion; it is, I feel, a presage of the definitive annulment of an unhappy decision.

Much that has been written in the Press on the occasion of my protest, has been painfully irrelevant. May I, then, be permitted to focus the attention of your Association on the single point at issue.

Firstly, the issue is not: in what forms of athletic sport may women or girls indulge, with safety to their physical well-being. That question should be duly determined by medical science, rightly so called.

Secondly, the issue is not: in what form of athletic sport may women or girls indulge, within the reserved ground of their own Colleges or Associations. That question should be duly solved by the principles both of Christian modesty and of true medical science.

Thirdly, the issue is not: that, as mixed athletics have already made their appearance in our midst, they should be continued. Mixed athletics and all cognate immodesty, [such as mixed swimming and mixed sun-bathing] are abuses that right-minded people reprobate, wherever and whenever they exist.

Fourthly, the issue is not: that, as mixed athletics have been adopted in other countries, those of us, who are modern, should not lag behind. It is a Christian duty, incumbent on all of us, not to adopt what is morally wrong. God is not modern; nor His law.

Rather, this only is the issue: that women should not compete at the same athletic meetings as men, though the Annual Congress of the N.A.C.A. has decided that they may so compete.

I have called this decision un-Irish and un-Catholic.

It is un-Irish; for, that mixed athletics is a social abuse outraging our rightful national tradition is a statement that requires not proof, but only some reflexion.

It is un-Catholic; for, that mixed athletics are a moral abuse, formally reprobated by the Sovereign Pontiff, Pius XI, is a truth clearly proved by the words of the Encyclical Letter, *Divini Illius Magistri*.

May I quote the actual text from the official source of Papal documents, the *Acta Apostolicae Sedis*, Vol. xxii, num. 2, pages 72-73. It is a passage strongly relevant, for, the Pope is opposing God's plan in respect of the differing sexes to that "deceptive system of modern coeducation which is the enemy of Christian upbringing", in that its supporters ignore or deny the effects of original sin and, in disarray of mind, regard society "as an unassorted mass of men and women equal in all respects." The distinction of the sexes, as ordained by God, must, the Pope teaches, "be upheld, nay even cherished".

Then at once, Pius XI applies the principles to all schools and to athletic sports.

"Ejus modi vero praecepta, ad christianae prudentiae praescriptum, tempestive atque opportune servanda sunt, non modo in scholis omnibus, praesertim per trepidos adolescentiae annos, unde totius ferme futurae vite ratio omnino pendet, sed etiam in gymnicis ludis atque exercitationibus, in quibus christianae peculiari modo modestiae puellarum cavendum, utpote quas ostentare sese atque ante omnium oculos proponere summopere dedeceat".

You will kindly allow me to translate very literally:-

"Such precepts must be observed, according to the prescriptions of Christian prudence, in due season and opportunely, not only in all schools, particularly throughout the anxious years of adolescence, on which the tenor of well-nigh all the rest of life entirely depends, but also in athletic sports and exercises wherein the Christian modesty of girls must be, in a special way, safeguarded, for it is supremely unbecoming that they should flaunt themselves and display themselves before the eyes of all".

The issue, I think, is clear.

I am, dear Sir,
> Yours sincerely,

_____

> Blackrock College
> Date: 25 March 1934

Dear Mr McGillan

I am grateful for your letter of 21st inst. In which you kindly assure me that the General and Central Council at meeting... "unanimously agreed that it was in the best interests of the association that no action be taken to implement the recommendations of Congress as regards the proposed participation of women in athletics."

May I be allowed to congratulate Your Council on this... courageous decision.

I am, Dear Mr McGillan,
Yours sincerely in Christ,
J McQuaid C.S.Sp.

_____

> Blackrock College
> Dublin
> 6th February 1934

Sir,
Would you kindly do me the favour of publishing the enclosed letter of protest sent by me today to the Hon. Secretary of the N.A.C.A.I.

Sir,
I have noted in yesterday's Press a majority decision of the Annual Congress of the N.A.C.A.I., in favour of women competing in the same athletics meetings as men.

I protest against this un-Catholic and un-Irish decision. I

hereby assure you, that no boy from my College will take part in any athletic meeting controlled by your Organization, at which women will compete, no matter what attire they may adopt.

I am, Sir,

Yours sincerely,

———————

20th February 1934

Rev. Dr. McQuaid, C.S.Sp.,
President,
Blackrock College,
Blackrock,
Co. Dublin.

Very Reverend and dear Father,

Your letter of the 8th instant, relative to the proposed participation by Women in Track and Field Athletics, was considered at a meeting of the Standing Committee of my Association on Friday, the 16th instant.

I am directed to inform you that Committee was of opinion that the points raised by you appertain to the General Council of our Association and, accordingly, your letter has been referred to the next meeting of that Body, which will be held on 10th proximo.

I am to add that the Standing Committee appreciate the fact that your protest was made in the best interests of the Association.

I have the honour to remain,
Very reverend Father,
Yours faithfully,

James J. McGilton
Honorary Secretary

———————

Editorial Department
Burgh Quay
Dublin
8 – 2 – 36

Dear Dr McQuaid
Many thanks for your kind letter, and for your thoughtfulness
and courtesy in sending it. I am also grateful to you.

Sincerely
Frank Gallagher[4]

Blackrock College
Dublin
6th February 1934

Sir,
Would you kindly do me the favour of publishing the enclosed
letter of protest sent by me to the Hon. Secretary of the
N.A.C.A.I.

Sir,
I have noted in yesterday's Press a majority decision of the
Annual Congress of the N.A.C.A.I., in favour of women
competing in the same athletics meetings as men.
I protest against this un-Catholic and un-Irish decision. I
hereby assure you, that no boy from my College will take part in
any athletic meeting controlled by your Organization, at which
women will compete, no matter what attire they may adopt.
I am, Sir,
Yours Sincerely,

Coláiste Iarfhlatha Naomhtha,
Tuaim,

ST. JARLATH'S COLLEGE,
TUAM.

12 Feby. 1934.

My Dear Dr McQuaid.

I should have written to you some days ago, but I am fighting a cold so you will understand I cannot do all I would like to do.

I want to congratulate you very heartily and very sincerely on the stand you have taken against the action of the N.A.C.A. Your intervention was both timely and dignified, and you must have the satisfaction of feeling that you have led the way to victory in a really important fight. I certainly have no doubt about the victory of our cause; I thank you for your magnificent lead and I hope you will be long spared to lead the way whenever similar perils threaten our country.

Again thanking you and with kind regards,

I remain,
Sincerely Yours,

S. Walsh

NATIONAL ATHLETIC AND CYCLING ASSOCIATION OF IRELAND

SECRETARY'S OFFICE
SHAMROCK CHAMBERS
59 DAME STREET
DUBLIN C.1.

Hon. President: P.C. Moore
Hon. Treasurer: T.E. Nolan
Hon. Secretary: J.J. McGilton

21st. March 1934.

Very Rev. Dr. McQuaid,
President,
Blackrock College,
Blackrock,
Co. Dublin.

Very Reverend and dear Father,

I am directed to inform you that at a meeting of the General and Central Council held on the 10th. inst. the question of the proposed participation of Women in Track and Field Athletics in Ireland was fully considered. The proposal of Mr. W. Byrne, Chairman County Dublin Board seconded by Mr. F. De Vere, Chairman Mayo County Council Board that "The Central Council considers it is in the best interests of the Association that no motion be taken to implement the recommendation of Congress as regards the proposed participation of Women in Athletics" was carried unanimously.

I must apologise for the delay in advising you of this decision which, owing to pressure of work in connection with the National and International Cross-Country Contests, was inadvertently overlooked.

I have the honour to remain,

Very Reverend Father,
Yours faithfully,

[signed] James J. McGilton
Honorary Secretary

IRISH COMMITTEE OF HISTORICAL SCIENCES

Rev. R.J. Glennon,
Secretary to His Grace the Archbishop of Dublin.   27 vi 1941

Dear Fr Glennon,

Many thanks for your letter of June 24.

This organization has undertaken a campaign for the preservation of historical records from destruction to which they are particularly exposed at this time since the acute shortage of pulpable material has intensified the activities of the waste paper merchants. It has been decided to make representations to institutions to induce them to take steps to preserve their records. Already government departments, local councils and professional associations have been approached, and indirect appeals have been made to various religious bodies and institutions.

The dangers to which records are exposed by modern warfare can only be overcome by making photographic copies, duplicates or abstracts. Many institutions have been established to carry on such work. Prominent American bodies have for years been working in Europe and through the utilization of an adapted film camera have been able to make vast collections which can be accommodated in relatively small space. The Catholic Record Society of England in the half century of its existence has been able to publish a number of substantial volumes which will thus restrict the loss to Catholic history should even the whole mass of English Catholic records be destroyed. The foundation of the Catholic Record Society of Ireland in 1911 aimed at the carrying out of a similar programme of work. Since 1922, however nothing has been added to the eight volumes published under its auspices. Recently an effort was made to revive the society and a further volume is now going through the press but the lack of support makes it unlikely that more than one publication will appear in every five years. There are very few persons interested in Irish ecclesiastical history. At the first annual general meeting of the Catholic Record Society, on 17 November 1913, it was pointed out that "Catholics looking for information about births, marriages and deaths were handicapped by the fact that they did not know in what churches old registers had been preserved, and at what date these registers began". An appeal was accordingly issued on 25 April 1914 by the secretary, Dr James MacCaffrey, asking for some brief particulars as to existing parochial records. The failure of his effort is clearly exemplified in the lists subsequently published in Archivium Hibernium which show that less than 600 parish priests supplied the required particulars. In 1934 the Protestant Episcopal Church in Ireland took steps to secure similar information about parish records and have since obtained them from every church in the country; the data is available to anyone who wishes to consult them at the library of the Church Representative Body in St Stephen's Green. It is felt that only by the concerted action of the Catholic Hierarchy will it be possible to take such a preliminary step towards the preservation of Catholic records. My object in seeking an interview with His Grace the Archbishop of Dublin was to obtain his advice on the best method of taking action to secure

a) the listing and if possible the duplicating of diocesan and parochial records and
b) the intervention of parochial clergy to prevent the destruction of records of local schools, houses etc.

I had hoped also to discuss with him the possibility of securing the appointment of trained archivists and research workers with a view to the ultimate publication of a competent history of the Irish dioceses.

I enclose copies of several documents of interest, including a suggested questionnaire for the clergy.

Yours faithfully,
R. Dudley Edwards.

Archbishop's House,
Dublin 9.

8th April 1961.

H.M. O'Farrell, Esp.,
15 Stillorgan Road, Donnybrook,
Dublin.

Dear Sir,

His Grace the Archbishop directs me to acknowledge the receipt of your letter of 6th inst., proposing that St Kilian's School should develop ultimately from the present pre-preparatory stage to a full secondary school.

The matter is one which should properly be referred to the Vicar General in charge of pre-secondary school affairs, Right Reverend Monsignor W. Fitzpatrick.

His Grace the Archbishop is surprised to learn that 18 non-Catholics are in attendance.

His Grace tolerated the attendance of a few non-Catholics on the strict understanding that the school in management, teachers and curriculum, be completely Catholic, and, in particular, that no distinction be made in favour of any interdenominational approach.

If there are present in our City so many non-Catholic Germans, the obvious solution is for the German authorities to arrange for properly non-Catholic schools, primary and secondary, in accordance with the conscience of non-Catholic parents, and with the established principles of separate denominational schools, recognised by our Constitution.

I am,
Yours very faithfully

Secretary.
[L. Martin.]

25th April 1961
For His Grace the Archbishop
Re:
Attached report of Father Condon, on St Kilian's School.

Father Condon, inter alia, makes reference to mixed classes – in respect of the sexes – . I had not known that this was the practice. See the second last page where he sums up.

10th May 1961

Rt. Rev. Msgr W. Fitzpatrick P.P., V.G.,
390 Howth Road Raheny

Right Reverend Monsignor,

I thank you for your kind letter of yesterday's date and will telephone you as arranged about the matter discussed in the letter.

I am taking it for granted that the two objections you spoke of are (a) mixed classes of boys and girls and (b) mixed religion amongst the pupils.

Once I have cleared the matter with you on Friday I will bring the letter of Mr Farrell to His Grace's attention.

I am, Right Reverend Monsignor,
Yours very sincerely,
    Secr.

10th May 1961

My dear Monsignor,

I wish to thank you for your kind letter with enclosed letter from Deutscher Schulverein.

As no doubt he expressed himself to you, His Grace has informed me that he will not consent to the form of school proposed. He will write, directly or indirectly tomorrow.

I hope to telephone tomorrow at a time convenient about the agenda for the next meeting.

I am,

Yours very respectfully,

Secretary.

Rt. Rev. Msgr W. Fitzpatrick P.P., V.G.,
390 Howth Road Raheny

———————

10th May 1961

Rt. Rev. Msgr W. Fitzpatrick P.P., V.G.,
390 Howth Road, Raheny.

Right Reverend Monsignor,
I thank you for your kind letter of yesterday's date and will telephone you as arranged about the matter discussed in the letter.
I am taking it for granted that the two objections you spoke of are (a) mixed classes of boys and girls and (b) mixed religion amongst the pupils.
Once I have cleared the matter with you on Friday I will bring the letter of Mr Farrell to His Grace's attention.

I am, Right Reverend Monsignor,
Yours very sincerely,
Secr.

My dear Monsignor,
I should be grateful if you told the St Kilian's School Committee that I do not, and will not, sanction a co-education school or a mixed religion school, either primary or secondary.
The obvious plan is to build a school for non-Catholics.
You can emphasise to this group that they are the first to violate the order accepted in our country and guaranteed by our Constitution.
They will not receive a priest director, nor will I sanction a German priest as headmaster.

I remain,

Yours very sincerely,

[signed] + John C. McQuaid.

Archbishop of Dublin,

      etc.

The Right Reverend Msgr W. Fitzpatrick V.G.
Raheny

                      Dublin, 26th May, 1961.

THE AMBASSADOR
THE FEDERAL REPUBLIC OF GERMANY

His Grace
The Most Reverend Dr. John C. McQuaid
Archbishop of Dublin and Primate of Ireland
Archbishop's House
Dublin

Your Grace,

I have the honour to apply to your kind understanding and assistance in the following matter.

The Council of St. Kilian's School has informed me that Your Grace has expressed in a letter written to Monsignor Fitzpatrick objections to the sanction of this school. I hope I am right in assuming that the letter is based on a misunderstanding.

I have before me the text of a note my predecessor Dr. Prill laid down after having had the honour of being received by Your Grace in August 1959. At that time Your Grace declared – knowing the spirit in which the St. Kilian's School is run and being informed about all details of the school's management – your entire satisfaction concerning this spirit and the management.

As nothing has been changed at the school since the time you had this conversation with my predecessor you will forgive me if I am taking the liberty to ask you if there are any reasons unknown to me that may have changed your mind.

Your Grace will be aware that this school is furthered by my Government with a view to strengthen the friendly relations between our two peoples.

Your Grace will understand that at the present moment where Irish-German cultural relations are visibly improving I am particularly sensitive about anything which could do harm to these relations.

May I add that a member of the Council of the school or I myself are prepared to explain to Your Grace at an audience granted by you, if you should deem it necessary, the special situation of the school.

Please accept, Your Grace, the assurance of my highest consideration.

[signed]
[Dr. Adolph Reifferscheidt]

ST. KILIAN'S SCHOOL
KINDERGARTEN, PREPARATORY & SECONDARY
SCHOOL
FOR BOYS & GIRLS
15 STILLORGAN ROAD, DONNYBROOK
DUBLIN
17th August, 1961

His Grace John Charles,
Archbishop of Dublin,
Primate of Ireland,
Archbishop's House,
Dublin

Your Grace,

We are pleased to be informed by the German Ambassador that the recent misunderstandings regarding the policy of St. Kilian's School have been resolved to your satisfaction and I am instructed by the Council to write to you and reassure you for our part that the policy of St. Kilian's School has not changed from the original agreements made with you, nor is it the intention to change them. The proposal to form a secondary dept. has been deferred indefinitely. But you may rest assured that any future development of the school will be in accordance with your wishes. It has always been and will continue to be our desire, to have a German and Catholic school.

I remain,

Your obedient servant,
[signed]
N. Stephenson
Hon. Secretary

Provincial Mother House
Telephone: Castletown 8

26th, July, 1961

Deaf children

My Lord Archbishop,

In recent years it has become evident that there are some children attending Primary Schools who because of defective hearing are unable to keep up with the other children in the class. In some cases, these children have been classed as mentally defective whereas in fact they have normal intelligence.

Last year, therefore, the Department of Education with the assistance of the Department of Health inaugurated a scheme whereby these children might receive special instruction from teachers specially qualified to teach deaf children. Permission was given to three Sisters in Primary Schools – one Irish Sister of

Charity and two Dominican Sisters – to attend the Course for Teachers of the Deaf at University College, Dublin. These Sisters have now received their Diplomas and it is proposed that a special class for hard of hearing children be set up in the Primary Schools for Girls at Cabra, Ballyfermot and Cork.

Among the children in the Cabra and Ballyfermot areas who are in need of special instruction are some boys between the ages of eight and fourteen years. Would Your Grace approve of the suggestion that these special classes should cater for both boys and girls? The maximum number in each class will be twelve. Should permission be given to have boys and girls in the same class there will be six boys in the class in Cabra and three boys in the class in Ballyfermot.

In time it should be possible for some of the teachers in the Boys' Primary Schools, either Brothers of lay men, to qualify as teachers of the deaf, but at the moment there are none ready to take these special classes.

> Begging Your Grace's blessing,
> I remain, my Lord Archbishop,
> Your obedient servant and grateful child in Christ,

[signed] Sister M. Catherine O.P.
Vicaress General

16.10.61

My dear Brother Walsh,

Now that you are Superior, may I ask you to take up the question of lip reading.

For years I have been vainly hoping that the Brothers would modernise their methods, somewhat after the energetic and far-seeing policy of the [Dominican] Sisters.

In the meantime, I am being written to by parents and having difficulty in keeping boys out of Protestant institutions

I feel sure that if you look into the matter, a change will very

soon be made.
    With kind wishes,
        I remain,
                Yours very sincerely
                [signed] + John C. McQuaid

Very Reverend Brother P.J. Walsh,
Superior,
St Joseph's, Christian Brothers, Cabra.

10th March, 1969

Rev. Mother M. Jordana, O.P.,
Secretary,
Catholic Education Secretariat,
Mater Dei Institute,
Clonliffe Road,
Dublin 3.

School Medical Inspection Reports on Booterstown School, Cross Avenue and on The School for Deaf Boys, Beech Park, Stillorgan.

My dear Mother Jordana,
    On behalf of His Grace the Archbishop I wish to thank you for your kind letter and advices on the above.
    Your information on the School has been noted and it is presumed that the General Purposes Room question will have been solved at this stage.
    With regard to the School for Deaf Boys at Beech Park, Stillorgan, I thank you for the suggestion that you have made of having the matter brought to the notice of the Superior at Beech Park. I think it will be enough, as you say, to bring it to their notice.
    With many thanks for your helpfulness.

Yours very sincerely in Christ,
Secretary.

Notes

1 For further details, see Margaret Ó hÓgartaigh, *Quiet Revolutionaries, Irish Women in Education, Medicine and Sport, 1861–1964* (Dublin, 2011). The sources for this section are in the Dublin Diocesan Archives, ABBB/A/SE(C), AB8/A/II and AB8/B/XXIV.
2 James Staunton would become the Roman Catholic Bishop of Ferns in 1938, he also features in the Mother and Child debate, as he was secretary to the hierarchy.
3 Timothy Corcoran was Professor of Education at University College, Dublin.
4 Editor of the *Irish Press*.

Chapter three

Medicine

McQuaid took a very close interest in medicine, particularly medical politics. Even while Headmaster in Blackrock, he was a central figure in the moves to establish a large children's hospital in Dublin. He corresponded with his predecessor, Edward Byrne, on these matters in order to prevent St. Ultan's Infants' Hospital becoming a large children's hospital. However he was also active in saving lives. His work in establishing the Catholic Social Welfare Bureau which fed thousands of families has been comprehensively examined by Lindsey Earner-Byrne.[1] Refugee children were also on the agenda, with Catholic connections being used to facilitate children fleeing war-torn continental Europe. More spectacularly, between 1948 and 1951, when there were attempts by the Minister for Health, Noel Browne, to introduce a scheme to provide free health care for all mothers and children under 16, McQuaid monitored the doomed progress of this innovation. In the words of Dermot Keogh, 'what the crisis does reveal was the growing integralist impulse of the leadership of the Catholic hierarchy – a desire to secure Catholic principles as the underpinning for social legislation.'[2]

Blackrock College,
Dublin.

Most Reverend Edward J. Byrne. D.D.
Archbishop of Dublin

That your Grace may direct.

I am further perplexed by an acute situation that has just been reported to me. Mr Doran has been anxious to amalgamate in fact, if not in name, St Ultan's and Harcourt Street [Hospital]. But what is worse; it appears that a new hospital is to be built in Crumlin at the insistence of Dr Collis[3] for chronic rheumatic children. Such an institution in non-Catholic hands is the very negation of all that Your Grace has worked for, because in such a Hospital, the children and the adults or adolescents would remain for over/even three years.

When I receive any further information, I shall ask Your Grace to be good enough to see me that I may report fully and in person.

Asking a blessing on myself and my work,
I remain, my Lord Archbishop,
Your Grace's humble and devoted servant,
John McQuaid.

By hand.
Secret.

Blackrock College
Dublin
11th Dec 1936

Dear Doctor,

I have just learned some items, which I think His Grace ought to be told at once.[4]

Dr Trevor-Smith called Dr Lea-Wilson aside to discuss her name being put up for the vacancy on the Council. Dr L-W was admirable. She protested against the way the Staff had treated her. T-S agreed. Mrs Walsh — he said — was a deluded person but good and devoted. Dr L-W should not go forward for a little while.

Asked the reason, T-S gave it "in great confidence". Moorehead, at the 2nd last Council meeting, Mrs Walsh being absent, assured the Council "in great secrecy" that in <u>six</u> weeks he would have a clear answer from the Hospital Sweeps concerning their amalgamation; he was very friendly with this Commission; that he was doing his utmost to bring about amalgamation of Harcourt St and St Ultan's, to prevent the Archbishop building his new Children's Hospital; that failing amalgamation, he was working hard for the very large extension of St Ultan's, with the same purpose of blocking His Grace's scheme.

Dr L-W asked where "in the world was this new Hospital of His...

...to be built? It must be the new Municipal hospital" !!!

"Nonsense" said T.S. "I don't know where exactly. Somewhere on ...south side. The Archbishop would not have a Municipal hospital, ...to be a big new Children's Hospital".

Isn't St Luke's inimitable?

It is clear then, that:

a) The Hospital Sweeps knows His Grace's wishes.

b) ...has been dined and wined successively by Moorehead, Rowlette and Abrahamson.

c) Moorehead is and remains the (venomous) spearhead of the Masonic opposition. I know he was not idle, but he took a long time to declare his plans. If both plans fail, he will make Harcourt St buy the adjacent Hotel. If Dr L...is not put on the council (or as I suggested Mr B...), then T.S. says Collis will go on and he (T.S.) will resign in protest.

d) Only two weeks remain of the six weeks Moorehead mentioned.

I will do what I can at my end.

Please see me on your return.

With Kind regards,

Yours sincerely,

J. McQuaid C.S.Sp.

Telegraphic Address:
"CROSDEARG, DUBLIN."

Cumann Croise Deirge na hÉireann
THE IRISH RED CROSS SOCIETY

Uachtarán an Chumann   21 ST. STEPHEN'S GREEN.
President of the Society   DUBLIN
THE PRESIDENT OF IRELAND 6th July, 1944
DR. DOUGLAS HYDE

Ref: 18/4

My Lord Archbishop,
   We of the Red Cross Society, with the approval of the
Government, have promised to care for 500 children from France
if and when it is possible to send them here. The question of
when we may be called on to receive them is dependent on many
and incalculable factors. We must, however, now make preparations
for the housing and maintenance of the children if and when they
arrive. The subsequent disposal of them can later be considered. As
you may possibly know the A.R.P. authorities in Dublin had made
provisional arrangements for the accommodation in case of danger
to evacuees from the City. They have informed us that we may
have the use of a number of large houses to which it was
proposed to send children. The list includes one house in your
diocese: – Marine Hotel, Wicklow.
   We are having them inspected so as to inform ourselves of their
suitability for housing the refugee children. As we believe that
most of the refugees will be Catholics we consider it most
desirable that religious orders should provide the controlling staff
in the various houses. It is expected that the numbers in each
house will approximately number 100. We presume that half will
be girls.

May we ask your help in securing the co-operation of one or more religious orders to provide the necessary staff? It would be very helpful if we could have some French speakers amongst them. I may add that we have inquired from the Principal of the College of Domestic Science, Cathal Brugha Street, whether we can obtain the services of a girl trained in domestic economy to look after the catering, and she has assured us that she has some very competent girls.

You will realise that although the arrangements now to be made are tentative and provisional, it is necessary to have our plans in such shape that the machinery can be put into operation at very short notice. Accordingly, we would be glad to learn from Your Grace if it is possible to arrange for priests and nuns to take charge of the children in the house I have mentioned.

In view of the nature of the problem you will probably find it necessary to reveal its main outlines to a number of persons. You are free to discuss it with anybody you wish. The number consulted, however, should be kept as small as possible and all should be asked to treat the matter for the present as confidential.

I have the honour to be,
Your Grace's obedient servant,
[signed]
(Conor A. Maguire)
CHAIRMAN

His Grace, The Most Rev. John C. McQuaid, D.D.,
Archbishop of Dublin and Primate of Ireland,
Archbishop's House,
DUBLIN

ARCHBISHOP'S HOUSE
DUBLIN, N.E.3.
14th July, 1944

CONFIDENTIAL

Dear Mother Paul,

A scheme for receiving the French refugee children is being considered. A centre in the country is proposed, say a Preparatory College.

I suggested to the Government that your Sisters are best able to handle a house of refugees, because of your training in France and elsewhere.

Might I ask you to ring up Mr. Boland of External Affairs (who will expect a ring) and arrange to see him as soon as you can.

I should be very happy to see you, not strangers if it be possible, tackling this very grave problem of Catholic children.

With grateful regards,
Yours very sincerely,
+ John C. McQuaid.

————————

COPY

ARCHBISHOP'S HOUSE,
DUBLIN, N.E.3.
14th July, 1944

Dear Mr. Justice Maguire,

I have considered carefully your letter requesting my help in the provision of accommodation for French refugee children.

I shall be glad to assist to the best of my ability.

In the present stage, I can but suggest that you approach the Provincials of the Orders or Congregations actually in the

Diocese, stating that I have proposed to you this measure.

I can recommend one Congregation of women (St. Joseph de Cluny) Mount Sackville, Chapelizod, which, from its training in France and experience, would seem to me very well suited for so hard a task.

May I point out that no scheme will succeed which does not segregate boys and girls, which does not provide education, and which does not take into consideration the grave problem among French people of class-distinctions.

I have spoken at length to Mr. Boland, of the Department of External Affairs, who, if I may say it, has a singularly clear understanding of your problem in all its aspects.

I remain, dear Mr. Justice Maguire,

Yours sincerely,

+ John C. McQuaid,

Archbishop of Dublin.

Mr. Justice Conor A. Maguire,
Chairman,
Irish Red Cross Society,
21 St Stephen's Green, Dublin.

Personal   23/11/49.

Dear Minister,

I have read with great interest your statement in Galway at University College, wherein you spoke of the need of a new approach in education, and of the necessity of allowing the Church freedom in moral and spiritual spheres.

It is very disappointing that only a tiny excerpt should have appeared in the Press, for one misses the context and the sequence of development.

I would be grateful if you could favour me with a copy of your text, at least of the parts referring to education.

The statement interests me, particularly in view of the very grave and radical disability under which we Catholics are obliged to live: I refer to the less than pagan Charter of the National University.

Until that Charter is changed, the Church cannot possibly have the liberty that you have courageously and rightly advocated.

> With kind wishes,
> I remain, dear Minister,
> Yours sincerely,
> John C. McQuaid

Sean McBride, Esq., The Minister for External Affairs.

———————

10th October 1950

Dear Taoiseach,

The Archbishops and Bishops of Ireland at their meeting on October 10th had under consideration the proposals for Mother and Child health service and other kindred medical services. They recognise that these proposals are motivated by a sincere desire to improve public health but they feel bound by their office to consider whether the proposals are in accordance with Catholic moral teaching.

In their opinion the powers taken by the State in the proposed Mother and Child health service are in direct opposition to the rights of the family and of the individual and are liable to very great abuse. Their character is such that no assurance that they would be used in moderation could justify their enactment. If adopted in law they would constitute a ready-made instrument for future totalitarian aggression.

The right to provide for the health of children belongs to parents, not to the State. The State has the right to intervene only in a subsidiary capacity, to supplement not to supplant.

It may help indigent or neglectful parents: it may not deprive 90% of parents of their rights because of 10% necessitous or negligent parents.

It is not sound social policy to impose a state medical service on the whole community on the pretext of relieving the necessitous 10% from the so-called indignity of the means test.

The right to provide for the physical education of children belongs to the family and not to the State. Experience has shown that physical or health education is closely interwoven with important moral questions on which the Catholic Church has definite teaching.

Education in regard to motherhood includes instruction in regard to sex relations, chastity and marriage. The State has not competence to give instruction on such matters. We regard with the greatest apprehension the proposal to give to local medical officers the right to tell Catholic girls and women how they should behave in regard to this sphere of conduct at once so delicate and sacred.

Gynaecological care may be, and in some other countries is, interpreted to include provision for birth limitation and abortion. We have no guarantee that State officials will respect Catholic principles in regard to these matters. Doctors trained in institutions in which we have no confidence may be appointed as medical officers under the proposed services, and may give gynaecological care not in accordance with Catholic principles.

The proposed service also destroys the confidential relation between doctor and patient and regards all cases of illnesses as matter for public records and research without regard to the individual's right to privacy.

The elimination of private medial practitioners by a state-paid service has not been shown to be necessary or even advantageous to the patient, the public in general or the medical profession.

The Bishops are most favourable to measures which would benefit public health, but they consider that instead of imposing a costly bureaucratic scheme of nationalised medical service the State might well consider the advisability of providing the maternity hospitals and other institutional facilities which are at present lacking and should give adequate maternity benefits and taxation relief for large families.

The Bishops desire that your Government should give careful consideration to the dangers inherent in the present proposals before they are adopted by the Government for legislative enactment and therefore they feel it their duty to submit their views on this subject to you privately and at the earliest opportunity, since they regard the issues involved as of the gravest moral and religious importance.

I remain, dear Taoiseach,
Yours very sincerely,
JAMES STAUNTON,
Bishop of Ferns, Secretary to the Hierarchy

His Lordship, Bishop of Galway

9th Dec. 1950.

My Lord Bishop,

In answer to Your Lordship's query, I wish to say that I saw the Taoiseach immediately after our interview with the Minister, again on Tuesday, 7th November, three days after my return from Rome, and again on Saturday, 25th November. The Taoiseach has had our pronouncement in hand for these three interviews.

I have also seen the Tanaiste on two occasions, the Minister for Justice on one occasion and the Attorney-General on one occasion.

The possibility of the Mother and Child proposals being accepted by the Cabinet and implemented, as they exist in the Draft, is not even to be considered.

Negotiations are being conducted since the result of the Doctors' Referendum was made known, between the Doctors and the Taoiseach and the Tanaiste. These are confidential talks. Time and silence are proving very helpful!

I prefer not to write what I know, but my information is most reassuring from the very commencement of my own negotiations.

I shall report at our Standing Committee meeting.

With kind wishes for Christmas,

I remain, My Lord Bishop,

Yours sincerely,

JOHN C. MCQUAID.

Archbishop's House,
Dublin, N.E.3.

8th March, 1951.

Dear Minister,

I beg to thank you for your letter of the 6th instant received by me today, enclosing a pamphlet which purports to explain the Proposed Mother and Child Health Service.

I welcome any legitimate improvement of medical services for those whose basic family wage or income does not readily assure the necessary facilities.

And, if proof be needed of my attitude, I may be permitted to point to many actions of my Episcopate, in particular to the work of the Catholic Social Service Conference founded by me, more especially to its Maternity Welfare Centres.

I regret, however, as I stated on the occasion when, on behalf of the Hierarchy, I asked you to meet me with Their Lordships of Ferns and Galway, I may not approve of this Mother and Child Health Service, as it is proposed by you to implement the Scheme.

Now, as Archbishop of Dublin, I regret that I must reiterate each and every objection made by me on that occasion and unresolved, either then or later, by the Minister for Health.

Inasmuch as I was authorised to deal with the Taoiseach, on behalf of the Hierarchy, I have felt it my duty to send to the Taoiseach today, for his information, a copy of this letter.

I shall report to the Hierarchy, at its General Meeting, the receipt today of your letter, with enclosed pamphlet.

I am,

Yours sincerely,

(Sd) John C. McQuaid

Archbishop of Dublin,

Primate of Ireland.

Noel C. Browne, Esq., T.D., M.B.,

The Minister for Health,

Custom House, DUBLIN.

————————

22nd March, 1951

Dear Dr. Browne,

I have your reply of the 21st March, 1951, to my letter of the same date. I did not in that letter address myself to the reasons which you had advanced in support of your suggestion that the Hierarchy are not opposed to the Mother and Child Scheme as outlined by you. I did not do so because it is for the Hierarchy alone to say whether or no the Scheme contained anything contrary to Catholic moral teaching. It is clear from the letter which His Grace the Archbishop of Dublin addressed to you on the 8th March 1951, that the objections put forward on the occasion of your interview with him and with Their Lordships of Ferns and Galway on the 11th October last were "unresolved either then or later". It is clear from the same letter that His Grace sent me a copy of it in as much as he was authorised to deal with me "on behalf of the Hierarchy."

My actions in regard to this matter since I received the letter from His Lordship the Bishop of Ferns on the 10th October last have been entirely actuated by what I conceived to be a friendly desire to help a colleague and I take it somewhat amiss to find misconstrued my endeavours to have the objections to the Scheme which had been advanced on behalf of the Hierarchy satisfactorily resolved.

In the hope that these objections could be satisfactorily disposed of I refrained from replying to the letter from His Lordship the Bishop of Ferns of the 10th October. I explained to His Grace the Archbishop of Dublin my reasons for so refraining and he communicated these to the Hierarchy. I need hardly say that I accept unreservedly your statement that you would abide by any pronouncement from the Hierarchy as to what is Catholic moral teaching in reference to this matter.

> Yours Sincerely,
> Sgn. John A. Costello

Dr. Noel Browne, T.D.,
Minister for Health.

DEPARTMENT of TAOISEACH
Dublin.
30th March, 1951

A Chara,

You wrote to me on the 15th February, 1951, protesting against the proposed Social Security Scheme on the grounds that it was being proceeded with in spite of criticisms which you said have been levelled at it by "eminent Catholic sociologists". I must in the first instance, apologise for the delay in replying to your letter. Pressure of work prevented my doing so earlier. In regard to the social security proposals I can assure you that neither I nor any of my colleagues in the Government would be party to proposals which would in any way contravene the teachings of the Catholic Church. Since the White Paper on Social Security was published

by the Government there have been two meetings of the
Hierarchy and one meeting of the Standing Committee of the
Hierarchy. From none of these meetings has there emerged any
unfavourable comment of any kind on the Government's
proposals for social security. This is unquestionable evidence that
there is nothing in the proposals which contravenes Catholic
teaching because the Hierarchy is the only authority competent to
speak on matters affecting faith and morals.

Mise, le meas,

(Sgd.) JOHN A. COSTELLO.

———————

COPY

Archbishop's House
Dublin.
6th April, 1951.

My Lord Archbishop,

I am glad to be able to report that yesterday afternoon at 5
o'clock, I called, by arrangement, at Government buildings and
handed our letter to the Taoiseach.

I spent one hour and twenty minutes pointing out the meaning
of the document, in its various sections, according to the sense of
our two meetings.

The Taoiseach at once and fully accepted our decision – as one
would expect.

The same night he gave a copy to the Minister in question,
who, the Taoiseach has told me this morning – read it through
and then announced to the Tanaiste that "it was quite all right.
The Bishops had not condemned the Scheme on the ground of
Faith and Morals."

A Parliamentary Secretary, who was present, remarked: "If I had
not heard the remark, I could not believe it possible". The
comment of the Minister confirms my report to the Standing
Committee.

It is not known what the Minister will do next.

I took occasion at once to explain to the Taoiseach that the phrase "Catholic Social teaching" used by the Bishops meant "Catholic moral teaching in regard to all things social" and that our document was a clear-cut, forth-right condemnation of the Scheme on moral grounds.

I am keeping in close touch with the Taoiseach and, though I may not write in a letter all that I know, I shall keep Your Grace well informed, until we can meet at a later date.

With kind wishes,

I remain, my dear Lord Archbishop,

Yours sincerely,

+ JOHN C. MCQUAID

[His] Grace of Armagh

ARCHBISHOP'S HOUSE
DUBLIN N.E. 3
10th April, 1951

[Copy]

Dear Taoiseach,

I have the honour to acknowledge the receipt to-day of your letter giving the answer of the Government to the letter which, on behalf of the Hierarchy, I handed to you on the 5th instant, when you were good enough to receive me at Government Buildings.

It will be my duty to convey the decision of the Government to the Standing Committee of the Bishops without delay, and to the General Meeting of the Hierarchy in mid-June.

I may, however, be permitted to anticipate the formal reply of the Hierarchy by expressing to you as Head of the Government my deep appreciation of the generous loyalty shown by you and by your colleagues in graciously deferring to the judgement of the

Hierarchy concerning the moral aspects of the particular Health Scheme advocated by the Minister for Health.

In view of the clear attitude of the Hierarchy I may too be allowed to express my conviction that the decision of the Government to proceed to formulate another Scheme consonant with Catholic principles, will receive the very welcome support of the Bishops. It is our urgent desire, evidenced in our communications with the Government, that due provision should be made by the Government for the health of those mothers and children, whose insufficient means would not allow them to avail themselves of the best modern facilities.

The present intention of the Government to prepare such a Scheme is at once a guarantee of the blessing of God on your deliberations and a presage of practical and peaceful achievement.

I have the honour to remain,

My dear Taoiseach,

Yours respectfully and sincerely,

[signed] + John C. McQuaid

Archbishop of Dublin,

Primate of Ireland

John A. Costello, Esq., T.D., S.C.

Office of the Minister for Health

Dublin.

21 March, 1951

Dear Taoiseach,

I should have thought it unnecessary to point out that from the beginning it has been my concern to see that the Mother and Child Scheme contained nothing contrary to Catholic moral teaching. I hope I need not assure you that as a Catholic I will unhesitatingly and immediately accept any pronouncement from the Hierarchy as to what is Catholic moral teaching in reference to this matter.

I see no reason, however, in your letter of the 21st instant to change the opinion I expressed in mine of the 19th instant. For the reasons set out in that letter I am not satisfied that the Hierarchy are opposed to the Scheme on grounds of Faith and Morals. I note that you have not addressed yourself to any of those reasons except that you do not admit that following upon your interview with His Grace the Archbishop of Dublin on October 12th, 1950, and assured me that His Grace and Their Lordships of Ferns and Galway were satisfied. My recollection of that is fortified by the note which I made of your statement to me on that occasion and the recollection of other persions [sic] to whom I then conveyed your statement.

Have you overlooked the fact that the letter from His Lordship the Bishop of Ferns is dated October 10th, that is to say, the day before my interview with His Grace and Their Lordships? I assumed that this is the letter which His Grace the Archbishop of Dublin referred to when he spoke to me on my way into the conference to meet Their Lordships of Ferns and Galway and which he said it was proposed to hand to you on the following day. In fact the first mention you made to me of the receipt of the letter was on November 9th, 1950, and which in your letter of the 21st instant you stated you received "only some time after your interview".

I took the view that this letter which had already been discussed, and in my view satisfactorily discussed, was given to you merely as a matter of record. I intended the reply which I gave to you and which substantially represented the case I made to His Grace and Their Lordships to be likewise for record. I was under the impression that you had sent it as a reply to the letter of His Lordship the Bishop of Ferns and I was horrified to learn for the first time only a few days ago that you had in fact never sent it.

If, however, as you now say in your letter of 21st instant, you understood that His Grace and Their Lordships were not satisfied after the interview of 11th October, that belief on your part is quite inconsistent with your subsequent conduct in the matter. In particular you allowed the Scheme to develop without ever suggesting that the objections of His Grace the Archbishop of Dublin and Their Lordships of Ferns and Galway were still unresolved, and you never discussed that aspect of the matter with me or questioned me about it until 14th Inst. You are quoted by a circular issued by the Irish Medical Association on December 12th as asserting:

"It was his considered opinion that neither the Dail nor noSenate [*sic*] would approve any amendment of the Act of Regulations which would envisage the omission of a free service for all in connection with the Scheme"

Furthermore, in your interview with the Irish Medical Association on December 12th, 1950, there was no suggestion of any difficulty in the way of the implementation of the Scheme other than those raised by the Irish Medical Association. It seems strange that at this late hour when the discussions with the Irish Medical Association have reached a crucial point that you advance, as the only remaining objection to the Scheme, the one which of all possible objections, namely, the supposed opposition of the Hierarchy, should have first been satisfactorily disposed of before any steps were taken in furtherance of the Mother and Child Scheme and which I, naturally, would have been most anxious to dispose of if I did not believe, as I did and still believe, that matters were satisfactorily arranged at the interview which I had with His Grace the Archbishop of Dublin and Their Lordships of Ferns and Galway on October 11th last,

Yours sincerely,
Noel C. Browne

From the *Irish Times*, 16/2/1952.

Dr Noel Browne speaking at Trinity College:

> Ireland had become noted as a nation of deeply religious and
> Christian people, which would be encouraged to take its place
> by the side of those others with ostensibly similar beliefs in a
> Holy War to fight for Christendom. That was again a trick and
> a well used lie.....

The next day Dr Browne was invited to address Catholic students
in University College Dublin and delivered an attack on the
Voluntary Hospitals and the Medical profession (vide "Sunday
Press" 17/2/1952 which as usual gave him wide publicity).

These statements taken in conjunction with his earlier
references to "Clerical dialetics", "unctious hypocrites" and "tongue
twisting arguments and banquets of dialectical poppycock" form
part of a systematic and insidious attack on the Church.

Capt Cowan's attacks on the "secretive, occult and
objectionable prctice" [*sic*] of the Hierarchy may be more direct
but they are less harmful and less clever than Browne's or
Hartnett's. They are both good speakers and can easily sway an
audience of impressionable young students.

Could nothing be done to ensure that these people are not
provided with platforms from which they can pursue their
campaign against the Church? Can nothing be done to counteract
their campaign?

COPY.

ARCHBISHOP'S HOUSE
DUBLIN N.E. 3.
7th November, 1952.

Excellency,

I beg to enclose a memorandum on the White Paper on new
and extended Health Services, which we discussed some days ago.

The memorandum takes the form of my report to the Hierarchy, as Chairman of the special Episcopal Committee formed to deal with the situation.

To this report I have added some notes on the position as it actually exists, with documents to illustrate the attitude of the Irish Medical Association.

It may be helpful at this stage to point out that the whole situation, in its origin and development, very usefully illustrates the profound difference that the Hierarchy must expect to find between the Government of Mr. de Valera and that of Mr. Costello.

To deal with Mr. Costello's Cabinet was, with the exception of Mr. Browne, Minister for Health, and Mr. McBride, Minister for External Affairs, a very pleasant experience; for one met with a Premier who was not only an excellent Catholic, but also an educated Catholic, in immediate sympathy with the Church and the teaching of the Church. Nor was Mr. Costello unduly worried about placating the Liberals and Freemasons of North or South. Neither was he anxious to remain in the position of being the political leader. Had he been a man of less integrity, he could have avoided many difficulties. When the crisis came in The Mother-and-Child Scheme of Dr. Browne, Mr. Costello immediately and, when the need for declaration arose, publicly, made his own the decision of the Hierarchy.

To deal with Mr. de Valera and his Ministers is indeed a different matter.

From Mr. de Valera's re-assumption of political leadership, the chief element of note, as far as the Church is concerned, is a policy of distance. That policy is seen in the failure to consult any Bishop on the provisions of a Health Scheme. All the present difficulty results from that failure.

It will be remembered that Mr. de Valera had promised to give a Health Scheme based on 'the Constitution and Social Directive thereof'. It would not be in character for him to make any reference to the Hierarchy; such a reference would be felt to be inappropriate in view of the Protestant support and the voting-power of the Liberal Independents on whom he has been obliged to lean for a continuance in office. Further, any consultation of the Hierarchy would, if later discovered, bitterly antagonise the North of Ireland Protestants, whom Mr. de Valera always considers, in the hope to remove Partition.

Besides, in assessing the attitude of Fianna Fail Government, one may never forget the revolutionary past of the Party. On so many occasions, the Party was on the side opposed to Episcopal directions. While, then, the outward courtesies will be accorded, the inner spirit of sympathetic and open collaboration with the Hierarchy will be missing from a Fianna Fail Government. Not that anti-Catholic measures may be expected from men who faithfully practice now the faith, but, as I have said in my present *Quinquennial Relatio*, a definite Liberalism is always present.

In my opinion, that Liberalism must be incessantly watched. And what I particularly fear is the effect on the rising generation of an attitude which would successfully oppose the Hierarchy on the present Mother and Infant Scheme.

That there are definite signs of the younger people wishing to know and to assimilate a Catholic philosophy in things social and political, is one of the most encouraging features of the present Irish Scene. But the presence of a Protestant minority, with its focus of operations in Trinity College, powerful in finance and the professions and very firmly organised on a Masonic basis with strong affiliations in London and Belfast, will always demand an unrelaxed vigilance on the part of the Church, particularly in education.

Such are the features of the present situation which I think ought to be presented to Your Excellency and the Holy See.

Your Excellency may rest assured that I will continue to do all in my power to obtain from the Government the most favourable solution that is possible in the present situation.

With sentiments of deep esteem, I beg to remain, Excellency, Yours very devotedly in Christ,

+ John C. McQuaid,

Archbishop of Dublin,

etc.

His Excellency,
The Most Reverend Gerald P. O'Hara, D.D.,
Apostolic Nuncio,
Dublin.

I telephoned, as directed by His Grace.

Mr. Forde agreed and asked that the Minister be informed as soon as convenient.

M.P.O'C.

Mr. Forde, Secretary, to Dr. Ryan, Minister for Health, telephoned at 4.40 to say:

"Dr. Ryan asked me to telephone His Grace to say that he is now ready to meet His Grace and the members of the Committee and suggests any time suitable to His Grace on Wednesday morning, 10th December. Dr. Ryan will be accompanied by the Tanaiste".

42961 Ext. 21.

[Handwritten at bottom]

Kindly telephone:

HGaB will be pleased to meet the Minister for Health [and Tanaiste – inserted] and will at once endeavour to have Committee present by 11 o'c 10th inst.[5]

Mount St Mary's
Galway
4 Dec. 1952

Your Grace

It is hard weather for travel but I hope to attend on Wednesday next at 11. The Minister has been getting some broadsides from Galway!

Yours sincerely,

+ Michael, Galway[6]

Archbishop's House

Dublin
18th July 1953

Copy

Dear Minister,

I wish to thank you for the courtesy of sending me the draft of the section which with His Grace of Cashel I had discussed with you.

I am, dear minister,

+ John C. McQuaid.

Archbishop of Dublin.

Etc.

Seamas O Riain. Esq.. T.D. M.B.
The Minister for Health.
The Custom House.
Dublin.

Today wrote Dr Tierney[7] to inquire if he thought the draft sufficiently safe.

University College, Dublin
President's Office,
Earlsfort Terrace
Dublin, C.19 . . . 21 July 1953

His Grace The Most Reverend John C. McQuaid,
Archbishop of Dublin,
Archbishop's House,
DRUMCONDRA,
Dublin

Your Grace,

The Minister's proposed new section of the Health Bill seems to me to represent fairly our own proposals to him as re-worded by the parliamentary draftsman. In one respect it improves on our proposals. This is the provision for half and half representation on Selection Boards.

On the face of it the reference in the Minister's sub-section 2 to "one or more such Colleges" and the phrase "or Colleges" in the last line might seem to suggest that University College, Dublin, for example, would only be given equal representation on such Boards at some future date with other medical schools. I think however that this is merely a notional contingency which need never be allowed to arise. The Minister would always have the power to confine representation to one College, and there is little likelihood that we in Dublin will ever find ourselves in the situation which at present faces Cork and Galway.

The new section seems to be entirely satisfactory from the Cork and Galway point of view, and I think we should be prepared to accept it without any further discussion.

With kindest regards,
Very sincerely yours,
[signed] Michael Tierney

[Handwritten, above the letter's text]
I am grateful for your note, which informs my opinion. The draft
is substantially that on which we had agreed and as good a
measure as we could obtain.
    +J.C. 22.7.53]

——————————

ARCHBISHOP'S HOUSE
DUBLIN N.E.3.

On Sunday, 15th February, having heard that the Health Bill
would be taken on the coming Thursday, I wrote to Dr. Ryan
asking him to see me.

Dr. Ryan called on Tuesday, 17th February at 3.30 p.m. and stayed
for an hour and a half. The interview was very cordial.

1. I pointed out that the new Draft was a distinct improvement on
the 1947 Act, and that I was grateful for the acceptance of our
suggestions.

2. Dr. Ryan remarked that he had been asked whether the Bill
had the approval of the Bishops. I answered that the question was
surprising and said it was such as a Captain Cowan would ask. The
Minister then revealed that his answer had been: "The Bill has
neither the approval nor the disapproval of the Bishops" – which
is a fair summary of the position to date.

3. I pointed out that Sect.18 (1), day-pupils of Secondary Schools,
came as a distinct surprise: it was never mentioned in the White
Paper or in our discussions and in very many cases was altogether
unnecessary. In fact, the provision gave one to think that parents
could not or would not mind their own children.
    The Minister saw the point and agreed to amend the Section
and let me have the amendments. He stated that in some

Secondary Schools very poor or poor pupils would be found and that it would probably be necessary to exempt a whole School, rather than individual pupils within a School.

4. I drew attention to the provision for child-welfare services for all children up to 6 years, as being surely unnecessary in very many families. The Minister explained that this provision exists since 1919, that he did not like it and would amend it.

I pointed out what seems to be a difference of principle in Sects. 15, 16 and 19 (b).

5. I then emphasised the most disconcerting feature: the absence of reference to freedom of choice of Doctor, such as was found in Par. 27 and in Par. 40 A (c), B (b) and C (b), in the case of the three income groups. The Minister said that the absence of reference was solely due to the fact that reference was unnecessary, that freedom of choice of Doctor was inherent in the provisions of the Bill.

I pointed out the further absence of reference to choice of Hospital of Institution and asked if perhaps choice was to be covered by "regulations" to be made by a health authority in Sections 13 to 20, or if in Sect. 21 the power of the Minister to regulate the working of Sections 13 to 20 covered this essential question of choice.

I urged that reference ought to be explicitly made to freedom of choice of Doctor as in our view crucial. The Minister agreed to embody the principle. He explained, however, the legal difficulty of drafting. For instance, if choice had to be a legal right, must a Health Authority keep two Doctors on an outlying island?

6. I then discussed the £1 contribution and requested an explanation. Was it an actuarial computation? The feeling was that £1 was a token payment, not a genuine contribution; that it might be hard to collect and so would be dropped.

The Minister explained that the average is one child in 3 years and thus £1 per year would be about half the figure £5 to £7 which it was proposed to pay a Doctor for each confinement. A woman would have thus, on an average, contributed about half the cost of each confinement.

7. I had intended pointing out an apparent contradiction in the tenor of Sect. 4 and Sec. 30, but had not the opportunity as the Minister had to leave.

In my opinion, a Manager should first obtain the consent of the parents, in the spirit of Sect. 4. The fine will have been noticed.

I shall take up the point again.

Further, I intend to refer to the provision for post-graduate training. It has reference, in my opinion, only to St. Kevin's Hospital (the former Workhouse)[8], Dublin, which has been the subject of negotiation between Dr. Noel Browne and University College, Dublin. Actually, a Committee recommended a post-graduate school in St. Kevin's.

> For interview with Dr Ryan
> at 3.30 p.m. on Thursday 17th February 1953.

1./ Bill is much improved on 1947 Act.

2./ Grateful for that and for acceptance of our suggestions.

3./ Suggestion about day pupils of secondary Schools – 18 (1)

  a./ a great surprise, as was never mentioned.

  b./ is surely unnecessary in very many cases.

  c./ reads like attitude that parents cannot mind their own children.

4./ Similarly, child welfare services up to 6 years, is surely unnecessary in very many cases.

  Difference of principle in Sect. 15 and 16. and 19 (b)

5./ Most surprising is all omission of reference in Bill for exploratory memo. to freedom of choice of Doctor, as formula in Par. 27 of White Paper.

In summary of White Paper, Par. 40A(c), B(b) and C(b) medical and nursing care for mothers and infants (with choice of doctor) is referred to for each of 3 income groups. Nothing in White Paper or Bill as to choice of Hospital or of any "Institution".

If choice is meant it is perhaps to be covered by "regulations" which are to be made in Sect. 13 to 20 by a health authority. And Sect 21 gives minister free hand to make regulations for working of Sects. 13 – 20.

7./ The provision of £1 per year seems to us merely a means of saving principle.

Is it a token payment? or genuine contribution? If latter will it suffice?

Will it be too hard to collect this sum? Will not few contribute?

8./ Tenor of Sect. 30 seems to contradict section 4.

Could not manager require consent of parents to be first obtained as Sect. 4 seems to require?

Concerning Left-wing Labour: When I broadcast on the issue of the Italian Elections, I took occasion to give the warning that the attack on the Church would come in Ireland under the guises of patriotism and social reform. The present issue is a perfect example of the technique used in our country.

The Leftists are urging that the Church has blocked social progress, has failed to help the poor, has wished to impose a means-test.

But much more subtle is the other approach of the Leftists. They say: The Bishops have pronounced on morals and that is indeed their function, and a good Catholic will accept; but, unfortunately, the decision of the Bishops is damaging to the cause of national unity; it will now be impossible to remove Partition.

The conclusion is left to be drawn; get rid of the influence of the Bishops, if we are ever to succeed in bringing in the Northern Protestants.

I know for certain that the present judgement given by the Bishops on a moral issue is regarded by the Leftists as the most important event of the last twenty-five years.

That opinion is very shrewdly correct; but the event is much more important.

A Catholic member of the Judiciary, very highly placed, of the highest integrity and gifted with a vision that has often amazed me, has assured me that the action of the Bishops in condemning Dr. Browne's Scheme and of the Government in accepting the Bishop's judgement is the most important event since Catholic Emancipation.

In his view, a clash was bound to come on some issue between Church and State.

That the clash should have come in this particular form and under this Government, with Mr. Costello at its head, is a very happy success for the Church. The decision of the Government has thrown back Socialism and Communism for a very long time. No Government, for years to come, unless it is frankly Communist, can afford to disregard the moral teaching of the Bishops.

How necessary may be the direction of the Bishops may be judged from the suggestions that to bring in the Protestant North, we in the Republic ought to permit to Protestants divorce, birth-prevention and removal of censorship of publications.

The outcry in the Protestant North, following the unjust presentation of the Bishop's judgement by the Irish Times, is indeed typical. But what many fail to see is that the Protestants now see clearly under what conditions of Catholic morality they would have to be governed in the Republic. The political enticements held out to them are now judged by them to be only snared to trap them in a Republic dominated by the Catholic Church. Thus, the arguments of the liberal Catholics, who seem to put national unity before the interests of the Faith, have been discredited in the eyes of Northern Protestants…

Such in summary, Excellency, is the crucial situation, through which we have lived since last October.

I have been at great pains to assess the position correctly. Other aspects I can more easily discuss when next I have the pleasure of calling.

With kind personal regards and sentiments of deep esteem,

I have the honour to remain, Excellency,

Yours devotedly in Christ,

John C. McQuaid.

His Excellency, the Most Rev. Ettore Felici.

———————

DEPUTY COWAN ON FATHER GEMELLI.

Deputy Cowan speaking in the Dail on the Mother and Child Scheme of Dr. Browne, on Tuesday, 17th April, 1951, stated that "an eminent authority takes a line entirely opposed to the line taken by the Hierarchy of Ireland." This authority is Father Gemelli of Milan.

Father Gemelli delivered a lecture on Health Services during a Congress on Social Security held at Bologna, 24th-29th September, 1949.

Dr. Browne's Ministry for Health circulated to the Press its translation of this lecture, but it added a preface of its own making.

It is interesting to note that Deputy Cowan uses the exact words of his preface in the Dail.

Examining the translation of Dr. Browne's Ministry and the original Italian text of Father Gemelli's lecture, "La Difesa della Salute in un Sistema di Sicurezza Sociale" (The Defence of Health in a System of Social Security) published in the official Bulletin of the Congress, "La Sicurezza Sociale" (Istituto Cattolico du Attivita Sociale, Edizioni dell'Ateneo), we find the following facts:—

I. The Ministry's translation omits all that Father Gemelli says about social <u>insurance</u>, as the basis of medical reforms; e.g.
   a) Lines 8 to 24 of page 199 of the Italian version are cut out;
   b) Pages 218 to 222 of the Italian version are cut out. These pages limit the function and scope of the State in medical services;
   c) Point 3 on pages 227-220 of the Italian version is cut out. Point 3 deals especially with social <u>insurance</u>.

Nowhere in his lecture did Gemelli contradict a single point taught by the Irish Bishops,
Deputy Cowan has been grievously misled.
Someone in the Ministry from Health issued a translation of Gemelli's lecture mutilated to suit the purposes of the Ministry for Health.

———

CATHOLIC EDUCATION
1. <u>MODERN EDUCATION AND THE SECULARISATION OF MODERN CULTURE.</u>

1. A most serious obligation, pars. 1–3.
2. Based on the fact of the Incarnation, pars. 4–6.
3. The child, a wounded creature in need of support, par. 7.
4. Forming the true and perfect Christian, pars. 8–9.
5. God, the highest reality, pars. 10–11.
6. Faith, the unifying force in the life of scholarship, pars. 12–13.
7. Faith, applied to the student's own field, pars. 14–16.
8. The (doctrine of the) Mystical Body and the principles of social philosophy, pars. 17–18.

Par. 1   The history of western civilisation is the history of our educational traditions. It began and was formed in the Paideia Hellenica, as a conscious social discipline.

Par. 2   This tradition was taken over by Roman society and passed over to form the new monastic education which was the basis of mediaeval culture.

Par. 3.   Every cycle of European history has implied a new form of education that has moulded the epoch in question. This Scholastic philosophy in the 13th. century, Humanism in the 15th and 16th centuries, and Rationalism in the 18th. In modern times it is more difficult to define the change. There would seem to be two different and seemingly contradictory tendencies. On the one hand the specialisation of the sciences prodiced [sic] the development of technical research and technical progress.

Par. 4   On the other hand, from the 18th. century the movement spread for the so called basic education of all in literacy.

But this universal education became impoverished, just as the specialisation of the sciences caused culture of lose its unifying elements.

Par. 5   In the past, education never lost sight of its function of unification in culture. Thus the study of the classics constituted a common intellectual tradition in the independent national literatures of Europe. And this was not the only common element in the educational tradition of the West. Besides this there wwas [sic] the elementary religious education common to all the people, and the higher theological culture of the clergy who formed the majority among teachers in these two other levels of education. The education of the common people formed the most important of the three, in that it determined the common religious beliefs and moral convictions governing mens [sic] lives. Nowadays thethe [sic] Church is only one among many educative institutions. (eg, radio, press, films etc)

In the past the Church penetrated the entire body of culture, so that in the Church men found instruction and inspiration, alone. Without doubt, it was not education in the modern sense of the word. It was oral and visual, founded on the liturgy which was a visual dramatised version of Christian doctrine, enriched by all the artistic values that society possessed. And it was thus that the masses acquired a religious education and culture superior to the economic level at which they lived. So much so that we wonder at the architectural and artistic wonders produced by a society so poor in material resources.

The Reformation dispersed all the accumulation of the art and symbolism of the Middle Ages, insofar as it touched on religion, depriving the masses, in the North European countries, of their traditional means of education. This does not mean that it killed

all education, of the people. Because of the importance attached
to the individual's study of the text of the Bible, letters in the
vulgar tongue were taught so that everyone would be able to read
the Scriptures.

The Reformation thus effected, wherever it prevailed, especially in
its Calvinist form, a notable increase in literacy for the common
people and inaugurated a a [sic] new form of general education.
But it emphasised the literary at the expense of the aesthetic, and
underlined the role of the individual in the community. These two
changes, in their turn, impoverished the life of the community
and hastened the secularisation of culture. This effect was
completely alien from the ideals of Protestantism, its views being
limited to the reading of the Bible and the teaching of
Cathechism [sic]. But precisely because of this limitation, it led to
the impoverishment of culture.

Under the culture of the baroque, the mediaeval Catholic
tradition lived on, to the 17th century, producing its final
expression in the 18th century. At first sight, the tradition of
education in the baroque and Protestant culture seems the same.
Both had the same humanistic trends, the same methods, the same
models, and even the same texts. But the spirit of the two cultures
was quite different. The sphere of influence of the baroque was
much greater, as it did not limit itself to polite letters taught to the
educated classes, but extended, through music and the arts, to all
the people. The strength of this culture, and the education it
implied, did not consist in scientific progress or in the extension
of literacy among the masses. It consisted in the spiritual unity
which brought the expression of the greatest geniuses into contact
with the common people. The degree of literary culture was not
elevated in these countries, and education did not do as much as
that in Protestant countries to apply scientific knowledge to social
or economic ends. But music and the arts were used as
instruments of universal instruction, and not as in Protestant
countries as mere amusement or distraction of the leisured classes.

This loss of the universal education implicit in the culture of the baroque marks the turning point in the history of modern Europe. And this fact has been ignored by the majority of historians who undervalue baroque culture, the cause of its decay, and the consequences of its disappearance.

The decay and the disappearance of the culture of the baroque was not due to the culture of the Protestant countries. It was caused by the internal conflicts in the culture of the Catholic countires [sic], conflicts that arose between the classicism of the age of Louis XIV and the old baroque culture. This classical French culture acted as a vehicle for Rationalism, making this the exclusive canon of culture. And these in turn led to the revolutionary criticism of of [sic] the Catholic Faith ... It was a second Reformation in the culture of Catholic Europe. What Rationalism destroyed was the community and universality of instruction which was the heart of the culture of the baroque. This community of instruction was founded on religion, and on an elite, rather than on scientific and technical discovery, and from that time on, culture and education was uprooted from the life of the common people. On the other hand, the educated class, in the narrowest sense of the word, immensely increased, but the culture given it was very limited and superficial, compared to the old humanistic culture, and much more than the old religious culture.

Par. 10   Thus the progress of modern education implies the progressive secularisation of modern culture. And 19th. cent. Liberalism not only considered this as inevitable, but also a good thing in itself.

Today this ingenuous Liberalism has been abandoned almost by all, but the secularist ideal has not disappeared. The successor to the Liberal is the Communist, preaching a creed as authoritarian as any of the old religions.

On the other hand, there is an increasing consciousness of the inadequacy of rationalism either as a philosophy of life or as a method of education. Modern psychology has shown that human actions are not always completely determined by rational motives, in the attainment of either individual or social ends. An education limited to the cultivation of the intelligence, and ignoring the existence of the unconscious forces of psychical life cannot give satisfaction nowadays. Such an education leads to a split in the human personality and in human culture. Sooner or later the unconscious forces thus ignored irrupt [sic] into the sphere of the conscious and lead to the destruction of the human personality and of the unity of culture. It is true that modern psychologists give their rationalist and materialist explanation of the play of these forces. But this explanation had led them to reduce all to one single aspect- that of the repression of the sexual impulse- and originated in clinical observation of the individual. It is not possible to explain social problems in the terms of the Freudian dualism of the conscious and the unconscious. Human life and culture has tthree [sic] levels.

There is, in the first place, the subrational life of instinct and impulse, playing a great part especially in the life of the masses. Then there is a second level where conscious effort comes into play, the level, par excellence, of the culture of human society. And there is a third level of the suprarational and the spiritual, which is the level, not only of religion, but also of philosophy, literature, and art, where intuition seems to transcend the calculation of reason.

In the past, all the great civilisations of the ancient and the modern world have recognised the supreme importance of the third and higher kind of knowledge for human culture and for education in particular. And only in the last two centuries has

Western man tried to deny the existence of this knowledge, and to create a completely rationalist and secularist culture.

Barely was this new kind of culture opened to the masses than it showed itself quite incapable of of [sic] controlling the subrational forces always beneath the surface of any culture. And in the present century these forces released themselves in a series of wars and revolutions that threatened to destroy civilisation. The real cause of this phenomenon is not economic or religious, but psychological, resulting directly from the frustration and starvation of the spiritual nature of man caused by the secularisation of education. And this conflict between a society based on this education and the spiritual nature of man cannot be resolved on the third and highest psychological level mentioned above. The real centre of unity is to be found at this level of religious faith, spiritual experience, and artistic and scientific intuition. And here culture finds its material resources, in the last analysis, but on the spiritual conception of its greatest minds, and on the way these are transmitted to the mass of the people by education.

When education no longer transmits this unifying experience to the people, a culture dies. And this is what has happened to modern secularised culture.

Western civilisation can only be saved from self destruction by rediscovering this last dimension of culture. And this is the true task of education today.

As was pointed out in the beginning, every change in European culture is accompanied by a change in European education. Today we are at a turning point in our culture, and consequently the time is ripe for a new orientation in education. It is true that the change would be difficult, because the great advances in technical science have led our culture from its spiritual centre. But this state of things is neither inevitable or hopeless. The changes of the last 150 years have not destroyed all the strata of European culture. These strata have only been buried, or ignored. The time has come to restablish [sic] equilibrium between the external world of mechanised activity, and the internal world of spiritual experience, through the medium of education. This renewal can be conceived in two ways. It can be seen as the return to Christian education, or as a movement to bring modern education into strict relation to the psychological bases of society, this restablishing [sic] the internal equilibrium of our culture.

These two alternatives are not in opposition to one another. They are two aspects of the same problem. Through education the Christian tradition should be understood as the moral and spiritual basis of our culture. This should be relatively easy in those countries where the process of secularisation has not wholly touched all the aspects of life. But such countries are rapidly becoming the exception. In the greater part of Europe, and especially in the USA secularisation has gone so far as to be accepted as inevitable, even by Catholics. So that a return to the Christian tradition in culture by means of education will not be accomplished without great sacrifices.

Notes

1 See Lindsey Earner-Byrne, *Mother and Child: Maternity and Child Welfare in Dublin, 1922–60* (Manchester, 2007)
2 Dermot Keogh in *Building Trust in Ireland: Studies Commissioned by the Forum for Peace and Reconciliation* (Belfast, 1996) p.131. The sources for this section are in the Dublin Diocesan Archives, AB8/A/IV and AB8/A/XVIII.
3 Doran was an administrator and Collis a doctor at Harcourt Street Children's Hospital, see Margaret Ó hÓgartaigh, *Kathleen Lynn, Irishwoman, Patriot Doctor* (Dublin, 2006), chapter four for more details.
4 Various doctors are mentioned here, Marie Lea-Wilson worked in Harcourt Street with Robert (Bob) Collis, while Trevor Smith was based in Donnybrook at the Royal Hospital, Thomas Gilman Moorehead was the Regius Professor of Medicine in Trinity College, Dublin and both Rowlette and Leonard Abrahamson had extensive private practices, for more details, see *Medical Registers*.
5 This is His Grace, the Archbishop. McQuaid frequently signed his annotations with this. The Tanaiste was the deputy Taoiseach.
6 Michael Brown was Roman Catholic Bishop of Galway, he signed his letters with a Cross, hence the nick name, Cross Michael.
7 Michael Tierney was President of UCD.
8 This is now St. James's Hospital, a teaching hospital for Trinity College, Dublin.

Chapter four

Republicans

Given the belief of John Charles McQuaid that it was not the moral right of any individual or group of individuals to choose a means that is contrary to the public good and general justice or to the established government of Ireland to achieve their own ends it is not surprising that there are substantial files on subversive organisations among the Archbishop's papers in the Diocesan Archives in Drumcondra. This chapter will focus on one of these organisations, the IRA. These files also contain a number of pamphlets – one sent to John Charles McQuaid (JCM) by J. McGarrity, 31 Jan. 1961 (AB 8/B/XXIV/ 1/40/3-4), one *The Separatist* purchased by JCM (AB 8/B/XXIV/ 1/44) July 1966[1].

Also among the McQuaid papers, there is one rare personal document, that relating to the death of his half-brother Eugene, in an IRA ambush in Mayo during the Civil War. This has been included in this chapter as it may throw some light on the attitude of J.C. McQuaid to republicanism.

> 1. *Copy of the letter sent on the 10th March 1923 by Capt. J.*
> *[Joseph] Togher to Dr.McQuaide [sic] relating the circumstances*
> *under which poor Dene met his death.*[2]

Dear Dr McQuaide [sic],
Received your letter yesterday. I expect to the quite C.E. in a couple of weeks, D.V. I saw by the paper, the respect in which

your family is held, and the last tribute to a brave man is indeed
fitting. You ask me to give a full account of the affair of 22nd ult.
Well, it is in a way, hard to give an account of the death of one
whom I had grown to hold in the highest esteem and confidence,
but I shall endeavour to give a correct account of everything. To
commence: at 11 p.m. 21.3.23 I drew up two Operation Orders,
one covered an operation in Srahmore and the other one in Achill
Island. The Srahmore party left per cars at 3.30 a.m. 22.2.23 and
the Achill Party at 7 p.m. per boat across Clew bay. Mac
[McQuaid] asked me which one was most likely to be "hit up"
and I told him that my party (Srahmore) would probably have a
scrap. "Right" said he "I'm going with you". It was only possible
to bring the cars 2 miles to North of Newport owing to broken
bridges. I gave instructions to Transport to come to the first
broken bridge at 2 p.m. for the column on their return trip. The
Drivers of the lorries heard the firing when they reached the
bridges that evening. They returned to Newport and reported it.
They went on to Westport for reinforcements as there were none
in Newport. I expected that there would be no men to spare in
Westport owing to the Achill operation, but fortunately, on the
arrival of the boat at Mallaranny it was too rough to land and they
had to return. As the evening drew to a close I had issued Orders
for a General retirement of all men fit to move. They were to
break the Irregular Line at the head of the road and fight a
rearguard action into Newport when Dusk fell. The wounded
including Mac & Myself were to be left behind to the tender
mercy of the enemy, but it was the only way. Our Slogan was
always "The 1st Western never surrender" and it was instilled into
every Officer and man of our Unit, that while one man could pull
a trigger it was a disgrace to surrender, and I believe that every
man of that Unit, would prefer to die fighting than come back
disarmed, and disgraced as soldiers. As to the scrap itself. We ran
into the Ambush at 12.30 p.m. returning from Srahmore to
Newport at Furnace schoolhouse. I enclose a little Sketch

showing the position more or less. We were surrounded on three sides by mountains and the Lake cut us off on the fourth side. The road was bleak and gave very little cover. There were no walls or ditches. The Mountains began to rise in a sharpe [sic] slope about 100 yards from the road and they overlooked the school-house, which was on a little eminence on the side of the road. There were walls around the school, but it was in a frightfully exposed position. I was leading the first party of 20 with Mac beside me. The second party of 25 came a mile behind. I considered it would be possible to flank the enemy in case of an attack with such an extension. That was an error on my part arising from my ignorance of the topography of the country. I had never been there before. When I reached the School-house the 2nd party had come within the other Sector of the horse-shoe bend in the Mountains. The Irregulars held both hills at the end of the horse shoe, and had trenches & cover constructed on the Mountain side. Both parties were then inside the irregular line and could not get out. The enemy then opened fire on both parties with Tomson [sic] Guns, Rifles and Mausers. I ordered the whole party to take cover and settled them in what I considered safe position. Just as I had finished and was advancing to the head of column at the school house to use the rifle grenade, I was hit in the leg. I shouted to Mac that I was hit. He pointed to the School House. I hopped in and Mac followed me. He dressed my wound very carefully and told me I would be quite O.K. as the bone wasn't hit. There was a perfect hail of lead outside and inside 5 minutes there was a call for the Red Cross. Mac. went out quite coolly. I fully expected that he would be hit as a sniper had the door of the School house covered and his shooting was remarkably accurate. However, Mac came back alright and settled me up again. He told me the boys were getting on O.K. and not to worry that we would win through alright. He cheered me considerably as the more I saw of the position, the more I realized what a veritable death-trap we were in. Never before had I led my detachment

into a fight in which we did not assume superiority after the first
15 minutes. In all my engagements in Kerry or elsewhere my total
casualties was one man wounded, but here I was placed very
awkwardly with the probability of the whole detachment being
wiped out. The Sergt. Major came in then and told me that the
Irregulars were trying to get across the lake a point [sic] just
beyond the hill to our right. I immediately had a party told off to
advance on that flank and prevent their crossing. That particular
point came under heavy fire to cover the Irregulars flanking
movement. One man was killed there and two wounded. Again
the call came for the Red Cross and again Mac. went out to
attend the wounded. The teacher and the children were in the
School all this time. We moved them into one corner and made
them lie down. They were comparatively safe. Two hours passed
and Mac. didn't return. I was under the impression that the fire
was so intense he couldn't get back. The Sergt. Major who was
watching came from door [sic] now and again to report progress
and get instructions. He told me that the "Doc" had a very
narrow shave the bullet striking the wall beside him. He told me
that he was on the other side of the road, and was down near the
lake. A few mins. after that Capt. Colleran of the Newport
Garrison came in carrying Mac. Mac. looked very pale and was as
cold as ice. He had been lying on the ground outside for over an
hour badly wounded. The Officer who brought him in, did so at
the risk of his own life. He was a brave chap. We got the childrens
coats, capes and cloaks and made a temporary bed for him on the
floor. We then got the fire going with pieces of wood and turf,
and covered him with our own great coates [sic], etc. I lay beside
him and rubbed his hands whilst the Sergt. Major rubbed his feet,
but it was impossible to keep him warm. He lost a fearful amount
of blood and his clothing was saturated. I could hear him
breathing through the hole in his lung, and I was in positive
agony, not knowing what to do for him. We bound him up and
plugged the wound with dressing. I said an Act of Contrition and

he repeated it after me, although at the time I considered it
unnecessary, knowing Mac. as I did, and that he had been to
Confession the previous Saturday. He was in great pain. At last, in
despair I sent one of the children with a white apron to a house
to ask for blankets, clean sheets and some water and milk mixed.
The Irregulars collared the kiddy and didn't let him get what he
was sent for. They gave him a note for me instead. A copy of the
note with my reply is enclosed. There were further notes but the
answer was always the same, "No surrender". I asked for a loan of
their Doctor but I could only get him on one condition
"Surrender". I told my second in command that I would never
take that course and he agreed. I would not have asked the
Irregulars Doctor if anyone but Mac. had been hit. You can realize
how small I felt asking a favour of our enemies in a fight, but it
was the only way. All this time Mac. was lying quiet and then he
started trying to clear his throat. He asked me to lift him up. I lay
down and shoved his shoulders up to enable him to spit out. He
did so. It was a clot of blood. "That's a piece of my lung, Joe" he
said. To cheer him up I said not at all that would happen to
anybody, I often spit blood. But Mac. knew and said nothing.
Later he wanted to spit again but he either [sic] too weak or the
pain too great. He couldn't. I never spent such a time. Trying to
watch the fight, our fellows and Mac. The teacher although an
Irregular sympathizer, did everything he could for Mac. He got
the children to say the Rosary in which we all joined. He was
very careful to specify the Rosary as being for "the poor Doctor"
not for our success, or for our rescue. Even under the cirs [sic]. I
had to smile when I thought of it all. It was best so and we all said
it for Mac. After the second note all troops & Irregulars ceased fire
to let the children and teacher home. One Irregular sniper kept
firing the whole time. At about 7.30 p.m. reinforcements arrived
with the Doctor & stretchers and Mac. was moved to Westport,
thence to Claremorris. We had eight prisoners. They were only
arrested on suspicion, but officers and men went so mad when

they saw Mac. and they wanted to shoot the lot. I explained we weren't sure about them, and I think that's all that saved them. I never saw men so mad. The "Doc" was a Universal favourite, and I think he had more influence with the fellows than I had myself, even though I had scrapped all through the South with them. It was impossible not to love him, he was such a gentlemanly chap, so cheerful and unassuming, and with all that refinement which comes from a perfect home life, and liberal education. From Mac's ways, I could nearly tell what "Pals" you and he must have been. He was always ready, and if I wanted advice on anything or any particular thing done, I could rely implicity [sic] on Mac. I take great pride in our army and am consequently hard to satisfy but nothing would please me more than having Officers of Mac's type. They are not found every day.

If there is anything else on which you would like to be informed, I will answer your query by return post. Even after being wounded I believe Mac did settle the man he had been dressing. Can't say for certain as I did not see many of the boys after the fight as I was sent to Claremorris.

Kindest regards and sympathy to you all,
Yours very sincerely,
J. Togher

2. Eithne McSuibhne to JCM [John Charles McQuaid], [from 4 Plas Belgrave, Cork] 4, 17 March 1941

'Your Grace, I beg you will read, with consideration, the enclosed communication sent to the Cork Corporation, and other public bodies, by the Cork Sinn Fein Executive.

Your Grace's knowledge of Irish History will make clear the futility of Mr. de Valera's attempt to brand as convicts, those who stand for the Republic of Ireland.

As I pointed out in the enclosure, Irishmen arrested in similar circumstances have always refused to submit to convict treatment.

Such deplorable incidents are the direct result of injustice inflicted on those who stand for the rights of their land. In 1931 a police Inspector was shot in Tipperary, and Mr. de Valera was called to account for it by Mr. Cosgrave, who then occupied the position that Mr. de Valera holds now.

Mr. de Valera did not think the matter called for any condemnation at that time. What must be said of him, when, on succeeding Mr. Cosgrave at head of the FreeState [sic], he wants to hang a young Republican because, in a scuffle with policemen, he drew a revolver in self-defence, and is alleged to have shot one of his attackers. It is admitted that he was held by his captors when the shot was fired. Could not that bullet have been very easily deflected?

I appeal to Your Grace in interests of Justice. I appeal to you to use your influence in securing that this attempt to clothe [sic] Thomas MacCurtain[3] in convict garb should cease, and that his clothes be immediately returned to him,

I wonder might I ask your Grace to represent to Mr. de Valera that he would be somewhat less unworthy to stand before the G.P.O. on Easter Sunday, to celebrate the Silver Jubilee of the 1916 Rising, if he opens his goal gates and internment camps, and sets free every soldier and citizen of the Irish Republic that he holds imprisoned for fidelity to the Republic. Mr. de Valera will not, of course, admit he holds them prisoners for fidelity to Ireland. He calls it treason. So did England.

Our Holy Father's motto is ours: Peace based on Justice.

Begging a prayer from Your Grace, I am, very respectfully your, Eithne Mac Suibhne'.[4]

3. Una C.A. de Staic to JCM, from Mansion House Dublin Reprieve Committee, 1 Aug. 1942[5]

My Lord Archbishop,

I have been directed by the reprieve committee to respectfully ask

you if you would be so kind as to make arrangement in the event
of Thomas Williams,[6] the condemned man in Belfast, [to] have
prayers requested for the repose of his soul in the city churches
where 11 o'clock Mass is usually said.

The corporation have recommended a cessation of work from 11
A.M. till noon.

We think the workers would like to attend Mass during that
period and give him the benefit of their prayers.

We would like to thank Your Grace to let us know this evening if
you can accede to our request.

I remain,

yours respectfully,

Una C.A. de Staic.[7]

4.   JCM to Mrs Stack [sic], 1 Sept. 1943[8]

Dear Mrs Stack,

I have received your note sent to me on behalf of the Reprieve
Committee asking if I would arrange to have prayers offered in
City Churches, in the event of the execution of Thomas Williams,
for the happy repose of his soul.

Whilst I thank you for the courtesy of your request, may I point
out that it is open to any of the faithful to approach the City
clergy to have prayers requested for the purpose. The intervention
of the Archbishop at this hour is not at all required.

I am,

Yours sincerely,

John C. McQuaid, Abp. Of Dublin'.

5. Una C.A. de Staic, with address, Mansion House, Dublin, Reprieve Committee to JCM, 3 Sept. 1942 -

My Lord Archbishop,

Permit me to thank you for replying so promptly to my letter about the prayers for the poor executed boy.

I am sure you have been told how immense were the numbers of people who attended Mass for the repose of his soul, many of them remained the entire hour in the church.

Again thanking Your Grace,

I remain, etc.

6. *Séan MacBride, Mansion House Dublin to JCM, 27 Aug. 1942.*

[Letter headed Six County Prisoners Reprieve Committee.]

My lord Archbishop, The Reprieve Committee, which is working to secure the reprieve of the six young Irishmen at present awaiting execution in Belfast Jail, has arranged for a public meeting in support of the reprieve movement to be held on Monday the 31st August at 8 p.m. in the Mansion House, Dublin.

The Committee would be greatly honoured if your Grace could see fit to attend this meeting, whose object has already the support of Irishmen of all denominations.

Knowing of your Grace's numerous duties, however, the Committee fully appreciate that it may not be possible for your Grace to attend. In this event the Committee would be greatly honoured to receive any message of support which your Grace may deem fit to send.

I remain, my Lord Archbishop,

with the utmost reverence and respect,

Séan MacBride,[9] Chairman.

7. *JCM to Seán MacBride, 31 Aug. 1942*

Confidential and Personal

Dear Mr MacBride,

Your letter has reached me down the country and I hasten to

thank you for the courtesy of your invitation.

May I assure you that I have done everything possible for the reprieve of all the condemned men. I am continuing to work for that end in every conceivable manner. My name has never yet appeared but you will trust me when I say that I have been able to work much more powerfully in that manner. For that reason, I have asked you to treat this letter with fullest confidence.

With kind wishes,

I remain, dear Mr MacBride,

John C. McQuaid, Acp. Of Dublin.

8. *Telegram from Cahirciveen Reprieve Committee to JCM, 7 Nov. 1942*

'Request your influence reprieve O'Neill'.

9. *J.J. O'Kelly of 173, Botanic Rd, Glasnevin to JCM, 8 Sept. 1942*

Request for JCM to intervene in the case of the young man, Maurice O'Neill, condemned to face the firing squad at a date to be fixed. Maurice O'Neill, I happen to know from generations of association and kinship, belongs to the most widely connected family in Iveragh. His aunt is a teacher at Roundwood, while her daughter teaches at Crumlin. His brother, who taught in Dorset-Street, is interned in the Curragh, and his uncle, a retired Kerry teacher lives in Cork whilst his other immediate relations are, in the main, of industrious farming stock, not unworthily represented in the Church. His evidence before the Tribunal, so far as its publication has been permitted, speaks for his motive and for itself, and shows clearly that it was not he fired the fatal shot. When the leaders of the present Administration decided to abandon the Republic to which they had sworn allegiance and seek to capture the Free State administration against which, until

then, they had been actively in arms, the Ministers who remained
faithful to the republic delegated [to] the Army of the republic the
authority vested in them. As required by decrees of the First Dail
... Count Plunkett,[10] the late Miss [McSwiney],[11] Prof. Stockley,[12]
Brian O'Higgins[13] and the others ... had the voluntary assurance
from the heads of the Republican Army that not a shot would be
fired in Ireland, certainly not in Southern Ireland, while they
exercised the authority thus declared to them. If there have been
regrettable shootings since, it is mainly because over-zealous, over-
ambitious and not unprejudiced plain-clothes police have
provoked men to self-defence, whose constant thought was and is
to avoid conflict with them. The Republicans, who for more than
a generation have been making the supreme sacrifice for Irish
liberty, desired a Government whose ministers by unselfish and
efficient service would win the confidence and the love of all our
people, instead of earning such widespread odium by their
incompetence and arrogance that they will venture to appear in
public only under heavy armed guard. Men who thus manifestly
fail in the first Essentials of Government should have the grace to
resign and seek such avocations as they may be competent to
undertake. One must add that, in a time of peace, the signing of
death warrants against men by no means second to himself in
Christian loyalty and idealism should not be one of the major
functions of the President who, in the Phoenix Park enjoys
princely emoluments at the public expense while Christian
citizens feel the pain of hunger and enforced exile.
The barbaric censorship which now muzzles men of patriotic
instincts while the Senate can be openly used as a privileged
platform to England's interest, will pass. So too, the man-hunt now
masquerading as law will end, as the Elizabethan and Cromwellian
tyrannies ended. But the authors will be remembered for their
public conduct and their wanton flouting of Ireland's sacred
tradition of Sanctuary, while the victims, in my judgment, will live
in public veneration beside the martyr priests and people who

won loyalty for the Church by their shining sacrifice during the Penal days.

I am far from wishing your Grace to do anything unbecoming your sacred office, but I would like to take the liberty to suggest that you may find an opportunity to urge that the spirited young man whose life hangs in the balance be not executed for adhering to the principles which openly [activated] every member of the present Administration until they attained to power.

I am,

Yours very respectfully,

J.J. O'Kelly'.[14]

10. Copy of statement, headed Dail Eireann, 8 Dec. 1938 and signed by Sean Ua Ceallaigh, Ceann Comhairle, Brian O hUiginn, Cathal O Murchada, Maire Nic Shuibhne, Uilliam F.P. Stoclaigh, Tomas MacGuidhir

11. JCM to O'Kelly, 9 Nov. 1942

Dear Mr O'Kelly,

I have received your note and I wish to thank you for the courtesy of your request.

I very much regret that I cannot see my way to intervene to obtain a stay of justice, in the case of persons duly convicted of offenses against the legitimate Government of Eire.

With your own expression of regret for the shootings that have occurred, I take this occasion to unite my reprobation of the shootings which have caused death to the Officers of the lawful Authority, and I would ask you to use your influence to secure that the possibility of such crimes should at once be removed.

I return herewith the Document of December 8th 1938, which you were good enough to allow me to read.

I remain, dear Mr O'Kelly,

Yours faithfully,
John C. McQuaid, Archbishop of Dublin, etc.

12.1942? No sender name, incomplete

1. 'Mr Diarmuid Fitzpatrick is in Jail (The Curragh) since the end
of last June. He was arrested on suspicion of being a member of
the I.R.A. and of allowing his shop to be used as a depot for
I.R.A. correspondence. His house (Hollybank Road,
Drumcondra) and shop (Cathedral St.) were searched while he
was being conducted to the Bridewell. Nothing of an
incriminating nature was found in his house or shop. Immediately
after his arrest his brother Louis Fitzpatrick (Executive Officer,
Ministry of Supplies, Ballsbridge, Knight of Columbanus) got
influence at work. The family solicitor, Mr. John Shiels (a member
of some "Board" associated with Mountjoy Prison) with Louis
Fitzpatrick visited the prisoner. During the interview Diarmuid
said he was not a member of the I.R.A. and that his shop had not
been used by the organisation.
After a few days Diarmuid was asked to sign a document
disassociating himself from the I.R.A. His brother was told this
signature would secure Diarmuid's release. But Diarmuid refused
to sign saying it was against his principles. Thereupon he was sent
to be interned at the Curragh for the duration of the war.
2. He has a wife and 4 children – aged 7, 6 (twins) and 3 yrs. His
wife tries to carry on the business. The twins live with their uncle
and the girls (aged 7 & 3) live with their mother. The business is
heavily in debt, the house in Hollybank Road was mortgaged –
Diarmuid's mother has now paid off the mortgage and put the
house in the name of Diarmuid's wife. His wife dispensed with
the services of the shop assistant. She goes every day to the shop
leaving home with the two children (as she cannot have a maid)
at 8.30 a.m. The two children are left with their grandmother for
the day and are left back in the shop at 7 p.m. when their mother

closes the shop and takes them home.

Diarmuid's wife is a very good practical Catholic. Diarmuid used to make a visit to the Blessed Sacrament in Gardiner St. every day at lunch time. This has been his custom all his life. One of the charges against him was that he used to go to the Church for the purpose of collecting political notes left under a Statue in Gardiner St. by members of the I.R.A. This Diarmuid denied. His wife states that he is not a member of the I.R.A. Members of the Dependence Fund Committee of that organisation called to her (though she had made no application for help) to state that Diarmuid was not a member of their organisation.

13. Caitlín Brugha, Temple Gardens, [Dublin], to JCM 23 Feb. 1943

[The letter headed – Irish National Aid Society. (Republican Prisoners Dependents' Fund)]

My Lord Archbishop,

It is barely nine months since we were placed under an obligation of deep gratitude to your Grace for your generous contribution to our funds – an interval so short, that in normal circumstances, we would not dream of approaching you again. At present, however, we find ourselves with such inadequate resources that our position is not merely precarious but desperate.

As your Grace is aware we try to help both by gifts of money and of clothes, the necessitous relatives of breadwinning political prisoners. With the huge increase in the number of these latter in recent times, demands of quite unprecedented proportions have been made on us. Poverty and misery are so widespread among these dependents, that every appeal for help has its own imperative and impelling claim. A letter received only three days ago, for example, stated that a family of seven children had to go without a fire for two weeks, as all the money sent by us had to be spent on food. Many weeks find us unable to give our small ambitioned

average of 4/= or 5/= per person. That is, surely, a meagre
allowance, and when one remembers that the charity of these
unfortunate people urges them to put a little of it towards
cigarettes for the prisoners – the only thing allowed by prison
regulations we can imagine their sorry plight [sic]. The
committee's effort to collect has become increasingly difficult
owing to the high price of clothing.

Forced as we are to face these sad facts, we instinctively turn to
your Grace, of whose hidden princely generosity we are
conscious. It is with well-founded confidence we approach you
once more, and we are fully aware that the only gratitude we can
promise you is the prayer of many a grateful heart for an
unknown benefactor – and that is perhaps, as your Grace would
have it.

I beg to remain, my lord Archbishop,

Yours most respectfully,

Caitlín Bean C. Brugha'.

[Hand-written note on letter by JCM, dated 25 Feb. 1943 'Will
send through Dr. [Cooney] as I began with him. +J.C.'].

14. *Copies of letters, dated 22 May 1943, to the Governor of the
Internment Camp on the Curragh*

The letters inform the governor that the undersigned prisoners, Sean
MacCumhaill (Donegal), Sean S. Saxwell [sic] (Leitrim), Peadar Houston
(Dublin City), J.G. O'Doherty (Derry City), Seamus Gerard Bohan (Co.
Dublin), John Curran (Kerry), Christopher O'Callaghan (Kerry) and
Terence McLoughlin (Roscommon), were going on hunger strike on
24 May. File contains copies to Cardinal MacRory, the Papal Nuncio
Pascal Robinson and Eamon de Valera- none to JCM.

15. Letter from Brian Doyle, Cumann Cabhruighthe na hÉireann
(Irish National Aid Society Auxiliary Committee), 9 North
Frederick Street, Dublin, to JCM, dated 15 Sept. 1944

Your Grace,

My Committee has asked me to make our annual appeal on
behalf of the dependent mothers, wives and children of the
internees in Irish jails and internment camps. Some of these
bread-winners are now entering on their fifth year of isolation
from their families.

Your Grace will remember having helped us on previous occasions through Dr. A.F. Cooney — one of our Committee
members —, and I am to sincerely thank Your Grace for the
munificent benevolence towards these helpless ones whose suffer-
ings we are endeavouring to alleviate.

I remain,

Your Grace's most obedient servant,

Brian Doyle, Hon. Sec.

[There is a handwritten note [not by JCM] to check with Brian
O'Higgins]

16. Draft of letter from JCM to Mr O'Higgins, 3 Oct. 1944
[having checked that request for funds was genuine]

I am asked by HGaB [His Grace the Archbishop] to send you a
cheque for £50, with the request that you would be good enough
to give the sum in cash, at your discretion, to the Irish National Aid
Society Auxiliary Committee. The Secretary of the latter
Committee has written asking for a subscription.

HG [His Grace]. wishes to have an assurance that this contribution will not be published, for the reason that it is given on the
strict understanding that it has no political meaning whatever, but
is meant to be purely a charitable gift towards distressed mothers
and children. The AB [Archbishop] wishes further that this aspect

be firmly stressed with the Auxiliary Committee.

I am, dear Mr O'Higgins,
Yours faithfully,
Secretary.

17. *Roger McHugh,[15] Hon. Sec. Charles Kerin's [sic] Reprieve Committee, Mansion House Dublin to JCM, 24 Nov. 1944 –*

A chara,
We enclose a form and shall be grateful if you will sign and collect other influential signatures to the petition for the reprieve of Charles Kerins.[16]
The Lord Mayor[17] is presiding at a Public Meeting called by the Kerry County Council, to be held in the Mansion House on Monday evening, 27th inst. at 7.30 p.m. We hope that you will associate yourself with this meeting.
Unfortunately we have great difficulty in getting publicity, as press notices have been refused, telegrams held up, and many workers for the Reprieve Committee have been arrested.
Hoping that you will co-operate with us in this very critical and urgent matter. Is mise do chara, etc.

[Handwritten note on letter by JCM, 'No answer'].

18. *Printed letter from Una Bean A. Staic (Mrs Austin Stack) to JCM, 28 Nov. 1944 –*

A Chara,
I would like to ask the people of Ireland, through your columns, to join with me in a Triduum of Masses and Holy Communions beginning Wednesday, November 29th, and ending on 1st December (First Friday) for a very special intention.
Is mise,
Una Bean A. Staic (Mrs Austin Stack).

The above letter has been sent to all Dublin papers and has not appeared.

Is it possible that Mr. de Valera, through his censor, is prohibiting the saying of prayers for Charlie Kerins, who is to be hanged in Mountjoy Jail on Friday.

May I appeal for a general Communion on Friday morning for Charles Kerins, not that this young man needs our prayers, but rather that the tragedy and splendour of his noble death should turn the eyes of people towards God again, and should revive in our hearts that Christian sense of duty towards our country, which has of late years deserted our people.

The sacrifice of Kerins will not be in vain if it brings back the memory of Rory, Liam, Dick and Joe, and all the dead who died for Ireland.

[No comment or response from JCM in the file].

19. Telegram, dated 9 May 1946 from George Griffin, Mogeely, Cork, to JCM –

Your Grace,

at this the eleventh hour I most earnestly request you to intervene on behalf of Messrs Fleming and McGaughey [sic] hunger strikers and obtain their release as his Eminence the late Cardinal McRory obtained the reprieve of Thomas McCurtain for me. I feel confident that Mr Boland or the Taoiseach will not refuse you a general amnesty might expedite this end of partition [sic].

20. Letter from Seán Fitzpatrick, Hon. Sec., National Graves Association, 74 Dame Street, Dublin to JCM, 21 Aug. 1948 –

Your Grace,

The Relatives of the Six I.R.A. men who were executed by the late Government have written to my Committee asking them to

apply for the Remains to enable them to have a Christian Burial.
We understand there is a Canon law governing these matters. I
had a letter from The Most Rev. Dr. Keogh of the Diocese of
Carlow granting us permission in the case of Richard Goss and
George Plant[18] (the latter is not of our persuasion) and who were
executed at Portlaoighise [Portlaoise].
I would be very grateful if you would do likewise in the cases of
– Patrick MacGrath, Thomas Harte, Maurice O'Neill and Charles
Kerins, whose executions took place at Mountjoy prison, Dublin.
Thanking you for an early reply,
Is mise, etc.

21. JCM draft to Seán Fitzpatrick, 24 Aug. 1948 –

I am directed by HGaB. to acknowledge the receipt this morning
of your letter dated 21st inst., in which you state that Relatives of
six I.R.A. men executed by the former government have written
to your Committee asking you to apply for the remains to enable
them to have a Christian burial, and accordingly, as you understand Canon law to be involved in such a request, to desire the
AB. to grant permission.
HGaB. requires me to be point out that each of the five persons
mentioned in your letter, who were executed in his Diocese, were
buried as Catholics, with the assistance of a priest, in a blessed
grave.
When therefore you request that these men should receive a
Christian burial, your words are open to the implication that the
AB. refused in his competence as AB. some rites which were due
to these men who died in the Catholic Faith.
HG. deeply regrets the implication which your words contain and
would prefer to believe that the implication cannot have been
meant by you as a reflection on the actions of the AB. in such
cases.
The Canon Law to which you make allusion has reference only

to the exhumation of a corpse which has received permanent Christian burial.

Accordingly, if it was meant that these men had not already received Christian burial, there is no occasion to cite the Canon Law or to refer to the Archbishop.

I am, etc.

Maurice P. O'Connell,

Secretary.

22. Seán Fitzpatrick, Hon. Sec., National Graves Association, to JCM, 28 Aug. 1948 –

Your Grace,

At a Special Meeting called for the purpose of considering your letter received on the 26th inst. I was instructed to hurriedly reply stating that it was not the Committee's intention to imply that these executed men did not receive the Rites of the Church, or to cast any reflection on your Grace, and earnestly beg you to accept their apologies.

Is mise, etc'.

23. Seán Fitzpatrick, of National Graves Association to JCM, 2 Sept. 1948 –

Your Grace,

My Committee respectfully beg to refer to recent correspondence with your Grace on the question if [sic] the dis-internment [sic] of the executed men.

Subject to your Grace's permission it is proposed that the remains of the men referred to be removed from the prison at Mountjoy and brought to the Church of the Franciscan Fathers at Merchants' Quay – being allowed to remain there overnight for subsequent re-burial with their friends.

My Committee has been informed by the Rev. Father in charge

at Franciscan Church, Merchants' Quay, that written permission
from Your Grace is necessary before he can allow the remains to
be placed within the Church.
My Committee will therefore feel obliged if you will let them
have such written permission.
The favour of an early reply, will oblige, etc.'.

[Handwritten note on letter 'Sept 17 – one night'].

24. Handwritten draft by JCM to Seán Fitzpatrick, 3 Sept. 1948 and copy of typed letter signed by the Secretary, L. Martin –

Dear Sir,
I am asked by His Grace the Archbishop to acknowledge the
receipt of your letter of the 28th ult. and to thank you for your
avowal that in your previous letter it was not intended to suggest
that the four executed men had not received the Rites of the
Church or any reflection upon the action of the Archbishop.
In view of your further letter, His Grace desires me to state that,
in so far as Canon 1214 of the Code of Canon Law is involved,
the Archbishop will not have any objection to the petition that
the remains of the four executed men should be exhumed.
I am, etc.

25. Sean Dowling, President, Fourth Battalion, Dublin Brigade, Association of Old I.R.A., 12, Thomas St., Dublin to JCM, 30 Oct. 1948 –

My Lord Archbishop,
The Commemoration of 1798 which will take place in
November begins on Sunday 14th with an elaborate procession
which is being organised by Major-General Hugo O'Neill. It will
start at College Green and, passing through what has become
known as the '98 way, and end at the Croppies Hole at Arbour
Hill.

The Corporation have appealed to citizens to decorate their homes and have undertaken the suitable making of historical sites etc. They have informed us however that the official decoration of the streets will end at City hall, leaving the rest of the route – and that the most important part – to private enterprise.

From the City Hall, through High Street, Thomas St., Francis St., James's St., Stephen's Lane, the route lies in the old Fourth Battalion area. We are deeply concerned that it should be decorated in a worthy manner and we propose to appeal to the inhabitants to exert themselves.

It was felt that if we could count on the co-operation of the Catholic Clergy in High St., Meath St., Francis St., and James's St., in the matter, success would be certain and when we made an approach in this direction help was promptly and warmly offered. On pursuing the matter further however we found ourselves faced with some difficulty which appears to arise either from a reluctance on the part of the Clergy to recommend to their flocks what may seem to be a purely secular activity, or, from an uncertainty as to whether the Commemoration has the approval of the Church.

We know that Your Grace is celebrating High Mass in the Pro-Cathedral as part of the ceremonies but this has not yet been officially announced and will not be generally known until the programme which is in the hands of the printers is published. This will be too late for the end we have in view.

If we had Your Grace's permission to inform the Parish Priests in the area that you are favourably disposed to the Commemoration or if, alternatively, that it could be conveyed to them by Your Grace we feel that both they and we would be helped over a difficulty.

May we respectfully ask Your Grace to consider how far you can assist us in this matter which is one of extreme urgency as only just a fortnight remains to organise the whole business,

I am, etc.

26. Handwritten draft reply by JCM to Sean Dowling, 1 Nov. 1948 –

Dear Mr Dowling,
I am asked by HGaB. to acknowledge the courtesy of your letter concerning the Army's celebration of the 1798 Anniversary.
HG. desires me to inform you that he will preside at the Mass on the 21st inst. celebrated for peace and unity in Ireland, and that you are quite free to mention that fact in your personal approach to the Parish Priests of the areas in which you are interested.
I am, etc.
M.P. O'Connell, Secretary.

27. J. Cashin, Financial Sec. for and on behalf of the executive National Association, Old Fianna, 51, Parnell Square, Dublin to JCM, 23 Nov. 1948 –

A Dhuine Uasail,
Last year, the Executive of the above Association decided to give a Christmas party to the children of those members whose position in life did not allow for the provision of Christmas luxuries. The party was a major success, and close on two-hundred and fifty little children went home very happy. Thanks is entirely due to your magnificent contribution.
This year, the Executive of the Association have decided to make the party one which will cater for the children of members of all units who, otherwise, would not taste the joys of Christmas as seen through the eyes of a little child.
In order to make the party a success, the Committee, with a certain amount of reluctance, must again encroach on your generosity and appeal to you to help us, once again.
The Committee takes this opportunity of wishing you and yours health and happiness this year and all future years.
Mise, etc.

28. J. Cashin, Financial Sec. for and on behalf of the executive
National Association, Old Fianna, 51, Parnell Square, Dublin
to JCM, 22 Dec. 1948 –

A Chara,

I am directed by my Committee to convey our sincere
appreciation of your generous response to our appeal for funds for
Children's Christmas Party.

The party was held on Sunday 19th December at Stella Maris
Boy's Club, and way successful beyond all expectations. A
wonderful feast was prepared and each child received a small gift
as a souvenir of the occasion. We feel sure that our benefactors
would have been repaid by the sight of so many little ones
looking so happy.

My Committee, once again, express their gratitude for your
magnificent gesture and wish you and yours health and prosperity
in the coming year,

Mise, etc.

29. James Brennan, Hon. Sec. 1st Battalion Old I.R.A. Dublin
Brigade, 41, Parnell Square to JCM, 11 Dec. 1948 -

[The letter included suggested wording for a plaque to Dick
McKee, Peader Clancy and Conor Clune which was to be placed
in the Church of the Holy Trinity in Dublin Castle and asking for
JCM's approval of the wording.] JCM commented that he 'did not
oppose the erecting of the plaque, but would suggest that you
insert the words "the happy repose of" before "souls of"'.

30. Gerald Monaghan, Hon. Gen. Sec., National Association Old
Fianna, 21 Connaught St., Phibsboro, to JCM, December
1949 –

Your Grace,

Last year through the generosity of our many friends in Dublin, we were able to hold our annual Christmas Party for the children of our members whose position in life did not provide for Christmas luxuries. The party was a major success and two-hundred little children went home happy.

This year it is hoped to entertain a greater number of the little ones and to make this possible we are, once again, going to encroach on Your Grace's well-known generosity by asking Your Grace to help us in this worthy cause.

Contributions will be very gratefully received by the Executive at the above address.

I remain, etc.

[Handwritten note on letter by JCM '£5 granted'].

31. James Brennan, Hon. Sec. 1st Battalion Old I.R.A. Dublin Brigade, 5, Granby Row, Dublin to JCM, 21 Aug. 1951 –

Your Grace,

I have been instructed to inform you that it is the intention of the Council of the 1st Battalion, Old I.R.A. to present to each school in the Area from Cabra to the River and from Phoenix park to Blessington Street (which was the Old 1st Batt. Area) with a small framed copy of the Proclamation of 1916, with small pictures of the signatories.

The Department of Education, we believe, will offer no objection, provided the Manager of each school accepts same.

Hoping Your Grace will offer no objection.

Assuring Your Grace of our continued Loyalty and devotion to Yourself and Mother Church.

Obediently Yours,

James Brennan.

32. Telephone message –

Mr Brennan inquired if there is any answer to his letter to JCM's secretary, Fr. Mangan. The Protestant Archbishop has replied and agreed.

33. Draft written by JCM of his concerns about presenting copies of Proclamation to schools, 14 Sept. 1951 –

Re: present of 1916 Proclamation from old I.R.A.

1. HG is grateful for your letter and for expression of loyalty
2. Considers the proposal inadvisable, for it is equivalent to putting pressure on managers from an outside Body.
    Many managers may not wish to put up <u>Proclamation</u> of 1916, because it may give rise to controversy which has no meaning to the children of school going age. We all ought to live peacefully under the present <u>Constitution,</u> which is what now matters.
3. If Proclamation is put up, may not logically refuse to put up any other historical document, say [*inserted:* Treaty of 1922 (diff. Sides)], 1947 Declaration of The Republic, at request of some other Body.

[Handwritten note on draft from Fr. O'Connell – he has seen Brennan and 'He received the reply very submissively'].

34. Maire Comerford,[19] *Hon. Sec. Anti-Partition Association, 196 Pearse Street, Dublin to JCM, 30 March 1953 –*

Your Grace,
I am directed to ask for your consent for wreaths to be left in memory of men from the Four Provinces of Ireland who lost their lives in the struggle for Independence, at Dublin Castle on Easter Sunday, probably at the Church.

This is part of our programme in the All-Ireland Anti-Partition Parade and Robert Emmet Commemoration on that day.
We are looking for the names of specific persons whose heads were exposed on the Castle walls but they are more difficult to verify than was anticipated.
I am,
Yours very respectfully,
Maire Comerford.

[Handwritten comment on letter by JCM –'Matters concern AB. only if wreaths left in Church. AB. will not object to wreaths in memory of Catholics only being left in Church. +JC, 31.3.53'].

35. Maire Comerford, Hon. Sec. Anti-Partition Association, 196 Pearse Street, Dublin to JCM, 15 Aug. 1953 –

Your Grace,
We desire to inform you that Rev. Edward Lodge Curran, Chairman of the Anti-Partition Committee of the A.O.H. of America will be visiting Ireland from Sept 19th to Oct. 24th.
With your Grace's permission he will speak at a public meeting in O'Connell St on Sept. 26th, the day of the Football Final.
He writes to tell us he will be available to speak here and for the Anti-Partition League, 17 Howard St., Belfast subject to the consent of the Cardinal, of your Grace, and of the Bishops in whose dioceses it is proposed to hold meetings. He informs us he will call on your Grace as soon as possible after his arrival in Ireland.
We would be very grateful for your Grace's permission to announce Father Lodge Curran's meeting ....,
Maire Comerford.

36. Handwritten draft reply by JCM to Maire Comerford, 17 Aug. 1953 –

Dear Miss Comerford,

I am asked by HGaB. to acknowledge the courtesy of your letter of 15th inst., in which you state that the Rev. Edward Lodge Curran will, with the AB's permission, speak at a public meeting in O'Connell Street on Sept. 26th on the subject of Anti-partition.

HGaB. desires me to inform you that he regrets that he cannot regard it as advisable to give permission to Rev. Edward Lodge Curran to address any meetings in the diocese of Dublin. Accordingly, you will be good enough to inform Rev. Edward Lodge Curran of the AB's decision and refrain from making any announcement in this diocese of his projected visit.

37. Letter from P. Carroll, on letter headed 'An Garda Siochana', Commissioner, Garda Siochana, Phoenix Park to An Rúnaí, An Roinn Dlí agus Cirt, [23 Sept. 1955]

Confidential

'"An t-Óglach"

I am directed by the Commissioner to forward for the information of the Minister, attached typed copy of "An t-Óglach" for September 1955.

This publication is issued only to active members of the I.R.A., but we were able to obtain a loan of a copy from a friendly source for the purpose of copying it.'

38. Copy of An t-Óglach: official organ of the I.R.A., September 1955, price 3d.

[Issue is devoted to various aspects of guerrilla warfare – town fighting, tanks, mobility on the battle-field, training camps, duties of a volunteer and the conduct of members of the Irish Republican Army.]

39. Copy of typescript list of 'The active strength of the Irish Republican Army in the month of August, 1955'.

List organised by division, e.g. Carlow/Kildare with numbers for each division and remarks; total number is 618, 'as against 432 in 1954, 387 in 1953, and 337 in 1952'.

40. Copy of typescript copy of 'General directive for guerrilla warfare' [1955]

[This document details lines of organisation, column armament, numbers of training officers and active service units in Six Counties, lines of operations, and an assessment of morale of units.]

41. Handwritten draft of letter from JCM to the clergy, [20 Jan. 1956]–

The Clergy will have read the statement issued on behalf of the Hierarchy by the Standing Committee, in their meeting of the 17th. inst.
I would urgently request the Clergy of this Diocese, while firmly adhering to the ruling of the Bishops, to use great gentleness in their endeavour to persuade young men not to join the new I.R.A. and kindred groups or, if they have joined, to dissociate themselves from such groups.

42. The clergy will have read the statement issued on behalf of the Hierarch [sic] by the Standing Committee, in their meeting of the 17th January 1956.

I would urgently request the Clergy of this Diocese, while firmly adhering to the ruling of the Bishops, to use great gentleness in their endeavour to persuade young men not to join the new I.R.A. and kindred groups or, if they have joined, to dissociate themselves from such groups.
John C. McQuaid,
Archbishop of Dublin, etc.
Read at January Conferences 1956.

43. Handwritten letter from JCM to clergy and Provincials, 21 Jan. 1956 –

Very Reverend and dear Father,
I beg to enclose a statement which I have requested the Vicars General to read at the Conferences of the coming week.
May I ask you to ensure that this statement will, without any publication, be made known to all the priests under your control in this Diocese.
With your kind assistance I hope thus to secure the firm obedience to the ruling of the Bishops which will avoid the scandal and confusion of divided opinion and attitude.
I remain,
Very Reverend and dear Father,
Your faithful servant in Christ,
+John C. McQuaid, Archbishop

44. Printed statement from the Archbishops and Bishops of Ireland

We, the Archbishops and Bishops of Ireland, feel it our duty to warn all Catholics against erroneous ideas and claims which are being advanced in regard to the raising of military forces and the waging of war.

Catholic moral teaching lays down precise conditions in order that war be at all lawful. War is the cause of very great evils, physical, moral and social. It is not lawful, unless it be declared and waged by the supreme authority of the State. No private citizens or group or organization of citizens has the right to bear arms or to use them against another state, its soldiers or citizens. Just as no private citizen has the right to inflict capital punishment, so he has not the right to wage war. Sacred Scripture gives the right to bear the sword and to use it against evil-doers to the supreme authority and to it alone. If individuals could arrogate to themselves the right to use military force there would be disorder and chaos leading inevitably to tyranny and oppression.

The second condition for a lawful war is that there be a just cause. It must be certain that all peaceful means have been tried and found unavailing, that the matter at issue far outweighs the havoc that war brings and that it is reasonably certain that war will not make things worse. No private individual has authority to judge these issues, or to involve the people from whom he has received no mandate, in the serious losses inevitable in hostilities. But of all wars, a civil war between the people of one nation causes greatest injury and is most to be avoided.

Acting then in virtue of the authority conferred on us by our sacred office, we declare that it is a mortal sin for a Catholic to become or remain a member of an organization or society, which arrogates to itself the right to bear arms and use them against its own or another state; that it is also sinful for a Catholic to co-operate with, express approval of, or otherwise assist, any such organization or society, and that, if the co-operation or assistance be notable, the sin committed is mortal.

With paternal insistence we warn young men to be on their guard against any such organization or society and not to be induced by false notions of patriotism to become members of it.

We appeal also to the general body of our people to avoid violence, cherish peace, and, as a Christian nation, give an example to the world of order, forbearance, concord and goodwill.

45. Handwritten draft statement by JCM [1956]

Headed – 'For the Conferences Concerning the new I.R.A. and kindred groups'
I would urgently request all the clergy, with due discretion, to use every endeavour to persuade young men not to join the new I.R.A. and kindred groups or, if they have joined, to disassociate themselves from such groups, for the reason that the purpose and activities of these groups are gravely immoral.
I do not wish any reference to be made (in the pulpit [inserted 'in public']) at the moment, to this request or to the groups and their activities.
If I request all the clergy, diocesan and religious, to act in this manner, it is that I wish to avoid, either now or at any future date, the scandal and confusion of a situation in which some priests in their pastoral work will be seen to favour, and some to reprobate, the aims and activities of unlawful movements.

46. Draft letter by JCM, [January 1956] –

For the Major Superiors, <u>Confidential</u> [sic],
Very Reverend and dear Father,
I would ask you to be good enough to request, by word of mouth, through the local Superior, all your priests who hold faculties in this Diocese, with discretion to use every endeavour, etc., etc.

47. *Letters from Dominicans, Jesuits, Capuchins, Holy Ghost Fathers, Redemptorists, CMJA, Passionists, all confirming that they will communicate the statement of the bishops to their priests in the Dublin diocese.*

48. *Copy of a typed report on letter from [N. Costigan], Commissioner, Headed 'An Garda Siochana', Commissioner, Garda Siochana, Phoenix Park to Secretary, Department of Justice, 30 Jan. 1957*

Report of a Conference on 25/1/56 [?57] on I.R.A. Problem...held to discuss the I.R.A. problem, The Conference was attended by the Chief Superintendents in charge of all Garda divisions. The purpose of the conference was to get reports on the situation from all divisions, to give each divisional officer an opportunity of getting an overall picture of the situation, to discuss future actions and to give instructions. Topics discussed included IRA strength in each division, IRA men from here engaged in Six Counties, arrests of IRA men, Sinn Féin, public opinion, instructions to divisional officers.

49. *Typescript report [no date]*

I.R.A. in University College [Dublin].
Number in College: 50 all told. Of these 20 are active.
During the Christmas holidays steps were taken to contact the 20, with the result that the majority of them have promised to give up all connection with the I.R.A. Incidentally, the I.R.A. in University College have been disowned by the I.R.A. in the city and country.
Saor Uladh: 4 members in College – not yet identified.

50. 'A Catholic' to JCM, 19 Nov. 1961 –

Dear Sir,

When you were so good as to end the Eire police strike, I wonder would I be asking too much of you, to now intervene and try and stop the recent shedding of innocent blood across the border. As I am a man that has travelled a lot of the world it makes me ashamed that I am an Irish man.

I [hope] you have the power to stop this and it would bring about the unity of Ireland far sooner than shooting and murdering from behind stone walls.

Not forgetting to congratulate you on your high office.

Yours respectfully,

A Catholic.

51. Thomas Fehily, Dublin Institute of Catholic Sociology, 62-63 Eccles St., Dublin to JCM, 12 Nov. 1961 –

My Lord Archbishop,

As your Grace requested I have pleasure in forwarding the names of those who are presently prominent in the I.R.A. The information is accurate and has been carefully checked with the latest lists available both to the Army Intelligence and the Guards. I await any further instructions from your Grace in this matter.

I beg to remain, my lord Archbishop,

Your most obedient servant,

Thomas Fehily.

52. Handwritten note by JCM, 14 March 1969 –

When the Special Branch was searching Howth, the German agitator, guest of Cruise O'Brien, with Kohn-Bendit were kept at Mrs Maura "Woods", 81, Ailesbury Road.

53. Cutting from Evening Press [21 Sept. 1971] –

Confusion over "Pope's message"-reported that Pope urged JCM 'to persevere in his effort to limit the scope of conflict calling on the most ardent supporters of the Irish Republican Army to show moral and Christian feelings'.

Notes

1 J. McGarrity to JCM, 31 Jan. 1961 (AB 8/B/XXIV/1/40/3-4); (AB 8/B/XXIV/1/44) July 1966.
2 DDA AB/8/A/1/10.
3 Tomás Óg Mac Curtain (1915–1994) a leading republican and member of the IRA Executive. He was sentenced to death by the de Valera government for mortally wounding a member of the Garda Síochána, John Roche, in Cork city on 3 January 1940. The sentence was commuted to penal servitude for life and he was released after seven years.
4 McQuaid papers, Subversives (DDA, AB8/B/XXIV/1/1/1)
5 McQuaid papers, Subversives (DDA, AB8/B/XXIV /1/5/1)
6 Thomas Joseph Williams, more commonly known as Tom Williams, (12 May 1923–2 September 1942) was in C Company, 2nd Battalion of the Belfast Brigade. He was hanged in Crumlin Road Gaol on 2 Sept 1942 for his involvement in the murder of RUC police officer Patrick Murphy. Six IRA members were convicted and sentenced to death for murder. Five, Henry Cordner (19); William James Perry (21); Sean Terence Oliver (21); Patrick Simpson (18); and Joe Cahill (21) (who went on to become a senior figure in the IRA) had their sentences commuted. Williams, who acknowledged that he was the leader of the IRA unit involved, and took full responsibility for the actions of his men, was not.
7 Winifred Una Gordon, the widow of an RIC inspector, who married Austin Stack (1879–1929) republican and Sinn Féin TD for Kerry and Limerick West until 1927.
8 McQuaid papers, Subversives (DDA, AB8/B/XXIV /1/5/2)
9 Seán MacBride, (1904–88), lawyer and politician, was the only child of the marriage of Major John MacBride and Maud Gonne. He was one of the founders in 1931 of a new party called Saor Éire, which was effectively the political wing of those on the anti-Treaty side who were opposed to de Valera's espousal of constitutional politics.
10 Count George Noble Count Plunkett (1851–1948), scholar and revolutionary.
11 Mary MacSwiney, Mary (1872–1942), republican, sister of Terence MacSwiney (1879–1920).
12 William Frederick Paul Stockley (1859–1943), scholar and republican. He was professor of English at UCC (1909–31).
13 Brian O'Higgins (1882–1963), republican, author, and manufacturer of greetings

cards. From 1932 to 1962 he published the *Wolfe Tone Annual*.

14 John Joseph O'Kelly ('Sceilg')(1872–1957), writer, journalist, republican, Irish-language activist, member of the first and second Dáils and member of Sinn Fein.

15 Roger Joseph McHugh (1908–87), writer and academic. A republican, he was close to leading figures in Sinn Féin and served on several support committees for IRA volunteers imprisoned in Ireland and Britain during the 1940s. He was professor of English in UCD (1965–7) and UCD's first professor of Anglo-Irish literature and drama (1967–78).

16 Charles Kerins (1918–44), IRA chief of staff from 1942. He was convicted in October 1944 for the murder in 1942 of Garda detective-sergeant Denis O'Brien and was hanged in Mountjoy prison on 1 December 1944. The Kerins Reprieve Committee was organised in October 1944 under the auspices of the Kerry county council and was supported by members and TDs of the Labour party, the National Labour Party, Clann na Talmhan, and some independent TDs.

17 Martin O'Sullivan (1891–1956), trade unionist and politician, Labour Lord Mayor of Dublin 1943 and 1944.

18 George Plant (1904–42), republican. He was executed by military firing squad on the morning of 5 March 1942 in Portlaoise for the murder of Michael Devereux, quartermaster of the IRA Wexford battalion

19 Maire (Mary Eva) Comerford (1893–1982), republican and journalist. She joined Sinn Féin in 1916 and Cumann na mBan the following year. She was employed as secretary to the historian Alice Stopford Green and, from 1935 to 1964, wrote for the *Irish Press*.

Chapter five

'That would be an ecumenical matter'

Ecumenism and J.C. McQuaid[1]

In December 1961 Pope John XXIII summoned the Second Vatican Council. It opened in October 1962 and the final session took place in December 1965 under Pope Paul VI. It was seen as a means of spiritual renewal for the Catholic Church and an opportunity for Christians separated from Rome to seek opportunities for reunion. In the opinion of Deirdre McMahon, McQuaid did not see the need for a Council, laid particular emphasis on the jurisdiction of bishops and insisted that bishops must be free to administer their dioceses without interference.[2] He was particularly stringent towards members of the clergy writing or speaking about ecumenisim without his approval. One cleric who fell into disfavour with the Archbishop was the Jesuit Ronald Burke-Savage.[3]

1. JCM [John Charles McQuaid] from Irish College Rome to C. O'Conor, S.J. , 8 Nov. 1962

Very Reverend and dear Father,
I am profoundly disturbed by the published report of Father Michael Brennan's lecture on Adam and Anthropology which I have seen to-day in the *Independent* of 2nd November.
Even if the hypothesis put forward by the Father were true, I

would never have agreed to their being published in a daily newspaper, read by the ordinary Faithful who have been committed to my care.

The matter was never referred to me. I must request that the text which may be proposed to release after any of these lectures be first submitted to the Vicar-General, Right Rev. Mgr. Boylan. I am, Your sincerely in Christ, etc.'.

2. P. Boylan to JCM, 13 Nov. 1962

My dear Lord Archbishop,
I have received Your Grace's letter of 8th November and the copy of Your Grace's letter to the Jesuit Provincial.

I, of course, heard of the Milltown Course of Lectures from newspaper advertisements and reports only. I took it for granted – indeed I was aware – that the Dublin newspapers are received at the Irish College, and there was nothing I could report to Your Grace about the Lectures that would not have been available in the Dublin papers.

The Jesuit Fathers are becoming very active in the ecumenical movement, and they, with many others, are inclined to be active in theological "vulgarisation". This is common on the Continent and Catholic writers there frequently deal popularly with themes like that discussed in Fr. Brennan's Lecture. I suppose we could not hope to escape here from the general effects of such an attitude. The Jesuits will probably take somewhat unkindly to any control exercised by me – even though it is entirely in Your Grace's name! I will do what I can, but I am not an expert in higher dogmatic theology.

We have trouble at the moment in this Parish. Poor Father Hawkes got a breakdown yesterday which looked very ominous. He lost consciousness for some hours, but this morning he is fully conscious again. The Doctor, however, takes a very serious view of his condition. Mgr. O'Regan is very helpful in all matters that have reference to dispensations and analogous questions.

I have heard that Zerwick is still in some secondary teaching position in the Biblical Institute.

I should like to hear some of the discussions on the Sources of Revelation. I find that Fr. Simpson, S.J., is to lecture publically at Milltown on 'Holy writ or Holy Church'. I hope the newspaper summary of his discourse will not be awkward!

Your Grace will please understand that the Jesuit Fathers never discuss any of their plans with me – and there is no special reason why they should do so. They have I presume all the rights of an official Theological Faculty.

I remain,
My dear Lord Archbishop,
Very respectfully yours.

3. Charles O'Conor, S.J., Donnybrook to JCM, 12 Nov. 1962 –

My dear Lord Archbishop,
Your Grace's letter of Nov. 8th reached me by this morning's post.
I am very sorry for the appearance of the notice you mention in the Irish Independent.

I have already instructed Milltown Park that no press-releases of lectures are to be issued in future without submission to Right Rev. Mgr. Boylan as Your Grace directs.

This is obviously a very wise precaution and I thank Your Grace for having given me a direction in the matter.

May I express the hope that for all its great interest, Your Grace has not found the work of the Council too wearing, though I am sure the break in December will be appreciated by all.

I remain,
With all respect and esteem,
Your Grace's most obedient servant in Christ,
Charles O'Conor, S.J.

4. Ronald Burke-Savage to JCM, from 35, Lower Leeson Street,
   13 December 1962

My Lord Archbishop,

I was glad indeed to have the opportunity of saluting Your Grace
at the airport on Sunday and of seeing for myself that the Council
hadn't taken too great a toll out of you. You are very welcome
home. Despite the long sessions and wearisome repetitions the
Council must have been a fascinating experience.

Your Grace will, I think, be pleased to know that I have David
Hore[Hone?] ready for reception into the Church. I should be
grateful if you would have the documents made out giving me
leave to receive him and also a second convert, a Miss Janice
Williams, a post-graduate student from Cardiff studying in U.C.D.
I should like to receive David just before Christmas and Miss
Williams in January.

In the New Year when you have had time to catch up on things
and have had a chance to rest, I shall be grateful if Your Grace will
see me sometime at your convenience. I want to report on what
we have tried to do for Protestants and to ask your advice and
approval before making the next move. I want also to ask Your
Grace about [tonsure?] and minor orders for Arthur Cox who is
very settled in his way of life in Milltown.

I hope Mgr. Boylan[4] makes a complete recovery. Mentally he
seems wonderfully lively ... Did you find Fr. Dan O'Carroll in
good spirits.

With every best wish, and asking Your Grace's blessing,
I am,
Yours obediently in Christ,
Ronald Burke-Savage, S.J.'.

*5. Michael O'Connell to JCM, from Our Lady of Refuge, 54,
Lower Rathmines Road, Dublin 6, 21 Jan. 1963 –*

Your Grace,
A fortnight ago a parishioner, Mr. Liam Herlihy of the
Praedicanda Curia of the Legion of Mary, asked me to give a talk
to Non-Catholics in St. Joseph's Hall in this parish.
I consented, on condition that controversial matters would be
excluded & that it would be clearly understood that my remarks
could only concern published facts.
I now realise that I should have first sought Your Grace's
permission. I beg Your Grace's pardon and I beg to ask Your
Grace's leave to speak.
I expect that there will be very few present. If "sharpshooters" are
sent in, I hope to be able to deflect any attacks on the Church and
confine remarks to known facts about the general organisation,
procedure and freedom of discussion.
It would, I feel, be a preparation for the talk in St. Columba's
School on Ash Wednesday night.
I would be grateful if Your Grace would not go to the trouble of
writing a further letter but would ask Rev. Dr. McMahon to
communicate Your Grace's wishes to me.
Very obediently and respectfully,
Michael O'Connell.

[Handwritten note on letter by JCM 'Certainly you will do good.
St. Columba's will be more interesting'].

*6. Patrick Lavelle, P.P. Barndarrig, Kilbride, Wicklow, to JCM, [24
Jan. 1963]*

My dear Lord Archbishop,
A local Church of Ireland minister – Rev. Mr. Baird – is
organising a discussion between clergymen of different
denominations to see if he can help the Church Unity Campaign,

in a local way. He proposes to hold the meeting in a Protestant schoolhouse, at Redcross, on 30 January.

To my surprise, he has invited me also to be present. I told him I could not, of myself, undertake to do so, but that I would bring the matter to the notice of Your Grace.

May I respectfully ask Your Grace for a ruling in this matter, so that I can give the Rev. Mr. Baird a final answer?

I remain,

Your Grace's obedient servant,

Patrick Lavelle'.

[Handwritten note on letter by JCM 'It would be very hard to explain to your own people. I am sorry that you used my name for now my authority will be quoted. You can still retrieve the position without reference to the last court of appeal, the Archbishop. You ought to have said simply that you would think about it and then to have refused. +J.C. 26-1-63.'].

7. *Patrick Lavelle, P.P. , Parochial House, Barndarrig, Kilbride, Wicklow, to JCM, [29 Jan. 1963]*

My dear Lord Archbishop,

In reply to Your Grace's letter of January 26th, I have made known to the party in question, as coming from myself alone, the fact that I shall not be in attendance at the meeting which he proposes to hold.

I find it difficult to express how deeply I regret that Your Grace should have been caused any inconvenience in this matter.

I remain, my dear Lord Archbishop,

Your Grace's obedient servant,

Patrick J. Lavelle, P.P.

8. C.F. Humphrey, Unitarian Church, 112, Stephen's Green to JCM, 7 Feb. 1964 –

Your Grace,
The Reverend Kenneth Wright, B.A. will be ordained and installed as Minister of this Church on Thursday, the 20th February, 1964. The Service will be conducted by the Reverend William McMillan, M.A., Moderator of the Synod of Munster, at 7 p.m. I have been requested by the Managing Committee to extend a cordial invitation to your Grace, or a representative, to be with us on this special occasion in the life of this Church.
I shall be pleased to hear from you, and beg to remain,
Your Grace's obedient servant,
C.F. Humphrey.

9. JCM to C.F. Humphrey, 15 Feb. 1964 –

Dear Mr Humphrey,
I thank you for the courtesy of your kind invitation to be present at the ceremony of ordination and installation in the Unitarian Church, St. Stephen's Green.
May I ask you to thank your Managing Committee and to request them to understand that it is not a ceremony at which I may assist.
I remain,
Yours sincerely,
+John Charles McQuaid,
Archbishop of Dublin, etc.

10. John Deasy, Loreto Abbey, Dalkey to JCM, 17 Feb. 1964

Dear Reverend Father,
The Reverend N. Styles, who is Church of Ireland Curate in Dun Laoghaire and teaches with me in the Technical School there asked me if I would give a talk to the Young People's Coffee

Club. He would like the talk to be an informal and non-controversial one on the II Vatican Council. I would be glad to supply any further information or details on Request.

However, I would not like to accept such an invitation without seeking the approval of His Grace. I would be grateful therefore if you could bring this letter to his notice.

With kind regards and thanks,

I remain, etc.

[Handwritten comments on letter by JCM 'What is his competence' and 'I would think not'].

11. Memo to JCM, 19 Feb. 1964 [from J. Ardle McMahon] –

Your Grace,

Father John Deasy asks Your Grace's permission to accept an invitation from a Church of Ireland Clergyman to talk to his Young People's Coffee Club on the Council, informally and non-controversially.

Rev. N. Styles is a C. of I. Curate in Dun Laoghaire and teaches in the Tech. there, as does Fr. Deasy.

[Handwritten comment by JCM after 'non-controversially' – 'It is the questions after that one has to fear']

12. Memo to JCM, 25 Feb. 1964

Your Grace,

I learn, on enquiry, that Fr. Deasy has no special competence to speak on the Council. He is, I learn, very competent, and prudent in his work in the Vocational Schools. To learn more of what Fr. Deasy has in mind I wrote to him to enquire what he proposed, and received his reply of the 23rd inst. Would Your Grace consider asking Fr. Deasy to submit his text to Mgr. O'Connell?'.

[Handwritten comment by JCM – 'Yes, most certainly'.]

13. John Deasy to J.A. McMahon, 23 Feb. 1964

I wish to thank you for your reply dated 21st inst.
The way I intended to treat the Second Vatican Council was to
give an illustrated talk. Don Bosco Filmstrips have issued a strip
on the Council and are about to issue another on the Second
Session and I intended taking parts of these and presenting them
as slides to illustrate a talk which would deal only with why the
Council was convened, how it was organised, what has been
achieved and what is planned for the future. I feel the slides would
help to avoid the controversies of the Council itself and would
appeal more to a group of Protestants. I hope these details will be
of help to you.
Yours, etc.

[Handwritten comment by JCM against phrase 'what is planned
for the future' – 'Even I cannot say what is planned'].

14. P.F. Cremin from St Patrick's College Maynooth to JCM, 20 Jan. 1965 –

[In January 1965 McQuaid made what was described as 'a unique
gesture for the Church Unity Octive'[5] by permitting the Professor
of Theology and Moral Law at St Patrick's College Maynooth, P.F.
Cremin,[6] to speak on the work of the Vatican Council at Trinity
College Dublin (TCD). Dr Cremin was duly grateful.]

My Lord Archbishop,
Thank you for your kind letter... Yesterday's sessions went well
also, thank God. The attendance at the talk was nearly double that
of the first day. Evidently word had got around. Quite a number
of the Staff were present, as at the Question-time also, including
one of the Professors of Divinity. The Question-time, which goes
on for over an hour, went even better than on the first day,
inasmuch as there was no evidence of a certain polemical spirit

introduced the first day by the Presbyterian Dean of Residence in the questions he asked and kept following up, in regard to, e.g. – What is the doctrine of the Church? – he seemed to think all our doctrine should be available to him in a single compendium! – and what about the doctrine contained in Encyclicals since 1870, and what about the Assumption, etc? I refused to react "unecumenically", and insisted in being sweetly reasonable when he came up to me after to make some points privately. So perhaps overnight he came to appreciate that he had been on the wrong wavelength for an occasion such as this, for his questions and contributions yesterday were presented in keeping with the spirit of goodwill which I had been careful to establish for my part in the beginning.

The most remarkable thing yesterday, and the ultimate measure of the change in emphasis over the years, was that in Sammon's seat of learning there was no mention even of infallibility by anyone even in the questions asked, not even by the Professor of Divinity although he asked quite a few, even though I had to speak briefly on infallibility in dealing with the Constitution on the Church in my talk.

It has been an experience, especially with those present drawn from so many different denominations, or from none. And I am grateful that I have not had any difficulty really so far in dealing with the issues raised, and they have ranged widely; but of course I am not thereby justified – at least not in their systems [sic] of justification! I have struck a few blows in private also, of which I will tell you again.

So getting back to some thoughts for tomorrow, with great respect and gratitude.

I remain, my Lord Archbishop,
Obediently yours,
P.F. Cremin.

15. *William O'Brien, Oblate Fathers, Inchicore, Dublin 8 to JCM, 22 Jan. 1965 –*

My Lord Archbishop,
Many thanks for your letter today permitting Fr. Bourke to address the Protestant Community in Malahide on the use of the Crucifix in the Catholic Church.
Fr Bourke will send his manuscript in good time before the meeting to Monsignor O'Connell. In the light of what you say it is most probable that there will be a number of questions from the floor. I think Fr. will have both the knowledge and experience to deal with them in an amiable and friendly manner and thus help in some way dispel ignorance of some of the Fundamental Truths of our Faith.
With respectful and sincere good wishes, I have the honour to be, my lord Archbishop, Your Grace's devoted and obedient servant, William O'Brien, OMI, Provincial'.

16. *Prionsias Mac Aogáin [Frank Aiken], T.D. Minister for External Affairs to JCM, 10 March 1965 –*

My lord Archbishop,
I am anticipating that I may be receiving today an invitation from the Swedish Ambassador to attend a Memorial Service in the Lutheran Church, Adelaide Road, on Saturday next. The service is to mark the occasion of the death of Queen Louise of Sweden.
I should be grateful if Your Grace would let me know if you would see any objection to my accepting such an invitation if it reaches me.
I remain, my Lord Archbishop,
With great respect and esteem, etc.

17. *Memo from J.A. McMahon, 10 March 1965*

<u>Department of External Affairs</u>
Mr G. Woods, Chef du Protocol, said that the Swedish Ambassador had arranged a Lutheran service for the late Queen Louise. There would be some State representation; President and Taoiseach could find Protestants to represent them. There might be difficulty in finding Protestants who would represent the Department; Mr. Aiken might be required to attend; so might Mr. Gallagher, former envoy to Sweden, and possibly one or two others.
The Archbishop said that each Catholic who wished to attend should apply to him personally for permission, and I conveyed the message to Mr. Woods.

18. *JCM to Frank Aiken, Minister for External Affairs, 10 March 1965*

Dear Minister,
In view of your position as Minister for External Affairs, I should not object to your attending passively at a Lutheran Service on the occasion of the death of Queen Louise of Sweden, if an invitation be issued by his Excellency the Ambassador of Sweden.
With kind wishes,
I remain, dear Minister, Yours sincerely,
+John C. McQuaid.
[J.C. McQuaid gave similar permissions for 'passive attendance' to the ambassadors of Argentina and Spain].

19. *J.M. Rogers, Sec. United Council of Christian Churches and Religious Communions in Ireland, to JCM, 13 March 1965 –*

Your Grace,
At the half-yearly meeting of the United Council, held on Thursday 11th March, in Dublin, the following resolution was

adopted: 'The United Council of Christian Churches and
Religious Communions in Ireland has noted with interest the
lately published Decree of the Vatican Council "On Ecumenism"
and is grateful to God for every indication of a growing desire for
renewal within all our Churches. The Council accordingly
welcomes all efforts towards a clearer understanding between
Protestants and Roman Catholics'.
The resolution was ordered to be communicated in the first
instance to His Eminence Cardinal Conway and to Your Grace;
and later to the press.
Yours etc.

20. Draft letter from JCM to J.M. Rogers, 16 March 1965 –

Dear Reverend Mr. Rogers,
I thank you for the courtesy of your gracious message, I cannot
but rejoice at the resolution which sees in our Decree on
Ecumenism an effort of genuine charity.
I remain, etc.

21. JCM to J. W. Armstrong, dean of St Patrick's Cathedral, 23 Oct. 1965 –

Very Reverend and dear Dean Armstrong,
I thank you for your letter inviting me to send a priest
representative to a public meeting that the Dublin Council of
Churches proposes to hold in the Unity Octive next January.
The question of such meetings is a matter for the Hierarchy to
consider. No such consideration has yet taken place in the
Council sessions. We have been very hard worked.
May I then ask you to be good enough to withhold the invitation
on this occasion.
With kind wishes, etc.

22. JCM, from Pontifico Collegio Irlandese, Rome,[7] to Ronald Burke-Savage, 17 Nov. 1965 –

My dear Father,

I am grateful for your letter.

I am not worried about what you will write: it will be well meant, I am sure, and I shall endure it, like so many aspects of this coming Jubilee.[8]

You would be mistaken if you thought I am suffering much by reason of what people say. In fact, scarcely anything is now a surprise to me. If one has been a whipping-post for years, another few strokes do not hurt so much. Besides, if God did not permit all these comments, interpretations and calumnies, they could not be uttered at all. Some good is meant by Him. And, in the end, he gets His way.

Your project of a Mansion House Ecumenical week is premature. I fear that you are forgetting. We as a Hierarchy must await the Directorium Generale and, then, must ourselves elaborate a Directorium for our own circumstances. Neither Directorium has been even adumbrated. I may not then anticipate the decisions of my fellow Bishops, even by a "dramatic Christian (I would say Catholic) gesture".

If you had a week of lectures by Catholics of sure doctrine and balanced judgement who would explain the Decretum de Oecumenismo, your Centre[9] would do a worthwhile work in the Unity Octave. Be certain that relatively few educated people understand Oecumenism. Ordinary people are merely ignorant or confused … I am glad you are feeling better and prepared to improve <u>Studies</u>.

With grateful regards,

I remain,

Yours very sincerely,

+ John C. McQuaid.

23. Ronald Burke-Savage, to JCM, [n.d. Dec. 1965]

[Draft programme of talks and speakers for Church Unity Octive: 18 -25 January 1966, the lectures to be held in the Mansion House Dublin every night at 8.00 p.m. The proposed programme was a main speaker each night, to be followed by two responders.] 'The lectures will attempt to explain in simple terms the meaning and significance of the Decree on Ecumenism with special reference to the historical situation existing in Dublin'. Each evening proceedings were to conclude with 'the public recital of the prayers prescribed to be said during the Church Unity Octive by His Grace the Archbishop of Dublin'.

24. R. Burke-Savage from Clongowes Wood College, to JCM, 11 Dec. 1965

My dear Lord Archbishop,
I have had second thoughts as Your Grace suggested and enclose a revised panel of speakers for your comment and approval.
Where I have put down a Fr Provincial I have in mind that he nominates the member of his order whom he thinks most suitable – or else fills the bill himself. I have tried to make the list representative of the Church in Dublin.
As we end with the Bishop of Ferns I thought we could well lead off with one also – so I put down Dr Corboy[10] provided your Grace approves and that he is willing to remain in Ireland until 18th. I haven't approached him: he is not due in Dublin until Thursday next.
I came down here last night to make my retreat and shall be here until Sunday 19th. Please give me a remembrance in your Mass. I hope you get at least a quiet week-end.
With gratitude and affection, and asking Your Grace's blessing,
I am,
Yours obediently in Christ, etc.

25. JCM to R. Burke-Savage, 14 Dec. 1965 –

Confidential
My dear Father,
I thoroughly dislike your proposed amalgam of clergy and politicians.
God alone could predict what such a week would produce in the way of ecumenical understanding among our own people.
You should be content with a Benediction in each parish Church, with the prayers for Unity, and with one lecture by Mgr. A. Ryan on Tues. 18th, with the Nuncio presiding. I shall attend.
With kind wishes,
I remain, etc.

26. R. Burke-Savage to JCM, 16 Dec. 1965 –

My dear Lord Archbishop,
On this the sixth day of my retreat I take Your Grace's thunder-bolt in my stride. Poor Fr Ned Coyne used to say to me long ago that it was good at least to try occasional excursions into the third degree of humility!
Your judgment I respect. Perhaps you are wise to rein me in. I suppose it is better to organize one really [telling] night than a long drawn out octave.
I am sorry if I scared you by nightmarish vision of politicians and 'get with-it' clerics putting their feet in it all over the place.
Actually I had intended to brief them all. I wrote to Rome the day I left Leeson Street to augment my supplies of material.
There is no real harm done. The only people I sounded were the Nuncio, Fr Carroll of Clonliffe and Dr Corboy who is to get my message today when he returns home. Also the man in charge of the Mansion House bookings, Fr Maurice, O.F.M. Cap. who I asked to postpone an event he was holding and similarly an official of the I.N.T.O. who had the hall booked for the last night.

All this can be easily put right and I shall do exactly as you tell me so you can't say I'm too turbulent a priest even if you think my imagination has run away with me.

May I send out the invitations under the address of the Centre in Merrion Square but in your name – or would you prefer it otherwise. I hope you are not too tired. Please keep me in your Masses.

With gratitude and affection even when you shoot me down, and asking Your Grace's blessing.

I am,

Yours obediently in Christ.

27. Arthur H. Ryan, St Brigid's, Derryvoglie Avenue, Belfast 9, to JCM, 28 Dec. 1965

My Lord Bishop,

Your charity will have devined that nothing but illness could have prevented my acknowledging your most gracious letter before now ... Consequently I hasten to assure you that I will do the best that is in me to respond to the confidence and the compliment of your invitation to give the single lecture of your Unity Octave on January 18th next under the presidency of the Apostolic Nuncio and in your presence.

As soon as I have a script prepared, I shall send you a copy.

May I add my word of congratulation on the twenty–fifth anniversary of your consecration and on the beautiful tribute of Pope Paul.

Apologising again for a most embarrassing delay and begging a blessing.

I remain,

Your Grace's devoted servant,

A.H. Ryan.

28. R. Burke-Savage to JCM, 14 Jan. 1966

My dear Lord Archbishop,
Your Grace has always treated me with such exquisite courtesy
and kindly forbearance that I feel very unhappy that I failed to
clear the press release[11] with you. I have accepted your rebuke as
completely deserved. In extenuation, though not excuse, I did
think that I had mentioned that I thought the Our Father was a
simple ending.
I think I may recall the anecdote you told me about R.M. Smylie
[sic][12]: Then the Archbishop added astringently –: 'You may put
your steel through me but you will not put it through my back'.
'That I could never do' said Smylie. And from that moment the
two were friends. I set this down in the hope that your well-timed
and, from my point of view deserved, astringency this morning
will lead to a deeper friendship on our part rather than the reverse.
Were I not snowed under with proofs of my next issue, I should
have gone over to consult you about the press release. Please God,
I have done no serious harm. When Fr Tommy Byrne made me
superior here in 1951 he gave me only one piece of advice: 'Don't
be afraid of making mistakes!'. I have made my share of them and
can say mea maxima culpa!
I know that you are at your best in dealing with people who have
put a foot astray – so I count on your full forgiveness. I should be
greatly upset if you banished me into the 'suburbs of your great
pleasure'.
With my humble apologies and my gratitude and affection, and
asking Your Grace's blessing,
I am,
Yours obediently in Christ,
Ronald Burke-Savage, S.J.

Mgr Ryan's script was due last Monday but seems to have been
delayed by typist. I shall send you a copy as soon as it arrives,
RBS, S.J.

29. JCM to Fr B. Barry S.J., Provincial of the Jesuits, 14 Jan. 1966 –

My dear Fr Barry,
You will have seen today's <u>Irish Times</u> front-page notice supplied by Father Burke-Savage and written up by Michael Viney.
I telephoned at once, for it was sent without the least authorisation. From what I said, I thought that such an error could never again be repeated. This Evening's Press has an incredible additional explanation.
Yesterday evening I explained to the Apostolic Nuncio that it was a question only of a lecture. He accepted my word.
This morning I saw His Excellency to apologise for the <u>Irish Times</u> report.
It would be hard to convey to you the gross sense of embarrassment caused me in face of my clergy and people, in face of the Hierarchy and Apostolic Nuncio.
I remain,
Yours very sincerely,
+John C. McQuaid, Archbishop of Dublin, etc.

30. JCM to R. Burke-Savage, 14 Jan. 1966 –

Dear Father Burke-Savage,
I thank you for your letter handed in.
In view of the incredible statement attributed to you in this Evening Press, you will understand that no one except Mr O.G. Dowling[13] is authorised by me to issue any statement concerning the Tuesday meeting, either before Tuesday, or on Tuesday or after Tuesday.
I am,
Yours faithfully in Xt. [Christ],
+John C. McQuaid,
Archbishop of Dublin, etc.

31. Evening Press, 14 Jan. 1966

'Dublin's two archbishops, Most Rev. T.C. [*sic*] McQuaid and
Most. Rev. G. D. [sic] Simms, will pray together in public at the
Mansion House on Tuesday – "because it is time to soften up the
climate here," the Rev. Roland Burke-Savage, S.J. said today.
Father Burke-Savage, who is Director of the Centre for Religious
Studies and Information, organised the "get together" added: "We
have been a bit slow to move in the spirit of ecumenism here, and
with 1966 marking the Golden Jubilee of 1916 I decided this was
a good time to start moving".

Apart from invitations to members of other Christian Churches,
an invitation to participate has gone to Ireland's rabbi, Dr. Isaac
Cohen. The two Archbishops will join in a recitation of a Catholic
shorter version of The Lord's Prayer which will conclude an
address on the Decree of Ecumenism by Monsignor Arthur H.
Ryan, formerly reader in Scholastic Philosophy at Queen's
University Belfast.

In the chair will be the Apostolic Nuncio, Most. Rev. Dr Joseph
M. Sensi.

The president, Mr de Valera, and the Taoiseach Mr. Lemass, will
also be there with members of the judiciary, the diplomatic corps,
representatives of public bodies, industry and trade unions.

Approximately 700 tickets have been printed and about 400 of
these will be sold to members of the public through various
Dublin bookshops.

But these will not go anywhere near meeting the demand for
tickets. The telephones have been ringing busily at the Institute of
Catholic Sociology and the Centre for Religious Studies and
Information with requests for tickets.

A spokesman said: "It will not be possible to meet this heavy
demand. Tickets sufficient only for seating capacity in the
Mansion House were printed".

32. R. Burke-Savage to JCM, 14 Jan. 1966 [Note added in JCM's handwriting, 'Recd 17.1.66 Monday'] –

My dear Archbishop,

I accept humbly the severe formal reprimand which I received in this afternoon's post. I hope that I shall never give you occasion to write another formal letter.

For long years I have received constant encouragement from Your Grace whose friendship I so greatly value. It grieves me greatly to think that unwittingly I have caused you pain and embarrassment. I shall explain to the Nuncio that it is I, not Your Grace, who offers a sincere apology.

On the phone this morning you generously accepted my apology. When I was a boy Fr Charlie Mulcahy used to say he could forgive a mistake once but that he found it hard to do so twice. Please God, I shan't put Your Grace to that test by repeating my mistake.

I received a copy of Mgr's address to-night; in his covering letter he mentioned he was sending a copy directly to Your Grace. I had expected to receive his paper last Monday but his typist had held him up. I had hoped to discuss with you the brief speeches to follow it: I have in mind Mrs Josephine McNeill as the first speaker and I propose to speak briefly – five minutes – myself. I shall be grateful if you would ask Dr McMahon to let me know to-morrow whether Mrs McNeill is acceptable – and if not, I shall be glad if you nominate a speaker. I shall let you have the typescript of what I propose to say by Monday morning's post. The problems remain on which I should like your guidance: seating arrangements and dress. Protocol demands that I put Mr Lemass on the President's right. I had thought of putting Your Grace next to Mr Lemass with Dr Simms beside you. When I first proposed my list I had put you in that chair but you replied that you would prefer to sit in the front row. I suggest that I should put Mrs Lemass on the President's left – Mrs de Valera will not be present. I shall welcome whatever directions you care to give me in this matter of seating.

The second problem is dress: the Nuncio, I presume, will wear his soutane and feriola. Would you prefer to come in [illegible] suit or with feriola? And what about the Monsignor?

As I have caused you to suffer and have suffered myself in this matter I feel we shall have God's blessing on the meeting. The attendance will be most representative – and the demand for unreserved seats far outruns what we have to offer,

With renewed apologies, with deep gratitude and affection, and asking Your Grace's blessing,

I am, etc.

33. Osmond Dowling to J.A. McMahon, 14 Jan. 1966 –

Dear Dr McMahon,

I think it well, if only for the sake of emphasis, to put in writing the point I made to you on the telephone this afternoon.

If I am invited to the function in the Mansion House on Tuesday next, I will be happy to accept, without necessarily becoming involved or interfering with the press relations on that occasion. However, if I am personally or through you instructed by His Grace, or requested by Father Burke-Savage to assist in dealing with the press on Tuesday night, I will certainly do so provided that I am given in advance all the information which I require, and so do not again get placed in the position of being asked questions about something of which I have not been informed.

Yours sincerely

Osmond Dowling.

34. J.A. McMahon to R. Burke-Savage, 17 Jan. 1966 –

Dear Father Burke-Savage,

His Grace asks me to thank you for the draft of your speech. The

Archbishop does not think it necessary that you call on the Chief Rabbi.

His Grace also thought that it might be unnecessary for you to issue the acknowledgements indicating numbered seats. Numbered seats might seem to make too much of it. I return your card.

The order of thanking, His Grace also indicated: there was no need to mention all the religious heads.

Thanking you for your kind co-operation,

Yours, etc.

[Handwritten note by JA McMahon on letter ('note: His Grace subsequently agreed that the several cards could go out, and I informed R.B.S. accordingly, 17/1/66')].

35. Draft of R. Burke-Savage's speech for the meeting on 18 Jan. 1966 [corrected, shortened and commented on by JCM as 'jargon'].

36. Memo by J.A. McM., [n.d.] -

Mgr. Arthur Ryan's lecture under the auspices of the Catholic Information Centre, Mansion House, Tuesday, 18th January, 1966. The Irish Times issue of the 14th January, 1966, carried a report of this lecture.

The Archbishop called on the Nuncio and said that this report was not released by the diocesan press office.

At the Archbishop's request I explained to Mr. Dowling that His Grace had no knowledge of the recital of the Our Father by the Archbishop and Dr. Simms. He could tell the editors; the report was substantially true.

His Grace also asked me to get in touch with Fr. Burke-Savage who had released the story to the Irish Times. I told Fr. Burke-Savage that His Grace wished all future press releases regarding this function to be channelled through the diocesan press office. Fr. Burke-Savage also agreed to come and see me, and to ensure that the Taoiseach would be on the right of the President. I also asked Fr. B.S. to submit to the Nuncio and the Archbishop the text of his own address.

37. Memo J.A. McMahon to JCM, [17 Jan. 1966] –

Some notes on the Mansion House lecture of 18/1/66

1. The Archbishop will suggest 2 changes in Mgr Ryan's Ms. The text is accurate for the cognoscenti in these 2 instances, but might be misinterpreted by others.
2. Hence the text will not be available for publication until after the Archbishop sees Mgr. Ryan on Tuesday afternoon.
3. Which brings up the question of the diocesan press officer. His Grace mentioned yesterday evening that he would like Mr. Dowling to take charge of the reporters and photographers at the lecture.
4. Mr. Dowling had written to me that if he were to be asked – and I think the request ought to come from you – he would want all the information concerning the arrangements for the lecture.
5. Regarding seating arrangements: The Archbishop rather states that the Taoiseach go on the President's right, Mrs Lemass on his left. If the Tainiste/Minister for External Affairs should be present – you mentioned he would almost certainly not be present – he would come next. The Archbishop will be on the right of the Nuncio on the platform. Dr. Simms will not be on the platform.
6. The Archbishop would like to see your draft of your address beforehand, as promised on Monday.
7. His Grace asks that there be only one Speaker – yourself.

Your Grace, I made the above points to Father Burke-Savage, who called at 10 a.m. He gave me the attached copy of his address, to

which is only to be added the expression of thanks to Your Grace,
the Nuncio, Mgr. Ryan, and the distinguished guests. The Nuncio
has approved what he has written.

The Rabbi has been reported as coming, but he has not yet been
invited. Should Father Burke-Savage call on him to-day, he asked
[Handwritten comment 'No']

He also asked if he might say that there were Wine and Savouries
after the speeches on the attached acknowledgement card.
[Handwritten comment 'No'].

38. [JCM] to R. Burke-Savage, 19 Jan. 1966

Dear Father Burke-Savage,

I am grateful for the proofs and send a few notes – which are in
my opinion worthwhile.

Last night's lecture was widely appreciated – to an extent that
surprised me greatly, in view of its technical character.

I thank you for the pains you took to achieve the result which
gave so many persons an accurate account of Ecumenism.

With kind wishes,

I remain, etc.

39. [JCM] to Fr B. Barry, S.J., 19 Jan. 1966

My dear Father Barry,

I am grateful for your letter, God uses such situations for his own
purposes.

I shall see you soon, if I may. I have to be absent for a few days.
With kind wishes, etc.

40. JCM to Mgr A.H. Ryan, 19 Jan. 1966 –

My dear Monsignor Ryan,

For your lecture last night I am very grateful. On all sides, I have heard it praised by lay-folk – which particularly pleases me – and by priests.

You succeeded, on a nation-wide viewing, in giving an accurate account of Ecumenism. So, vicariously, I have fulfilled my motto: *Testimonium perhibere veritati.* You can guess how happy I am.

With every good wish,

I remain, etc.

41. JCM to the Apostolic Nuncio, Joseph M. Sensi, 19 Jan. 1966 –

Excellency,

Before I leave for a few days' rest at Rockwell, again I thank Your Excellency for having presided at the lecture last night. It was a gesture that merited wide appreciation.

Apart from the poor organisation due to Father Burke-Savage's trying to do everything himself, the meeting was a distinct success. So far, I have heard, especially from lay-folk, an excellent reaction.

In to-day's papers I have inserted explicit reference to Chapter 2, par. 8 of the Decree on Ecumenism.

With my grateful esteem,

I remain, Excellency,

Yours very devotedly in Xto.

42. 'An ordinary Catholic' to JCM, [22 Jan. 1966] –

With good intentions, I beg to express what very many are saying about Lecture in the Mansion House.

Why was Dr Simms and his people so treated and if it was necessary for Lecturer and Father Burke-Savage to eulogise you, the Pope and the Government why was the lecture on the Church and confined to Catholics. Apart from this the Lecture did not contain anything to help Unity – it will very much hinder Unity. Why were the seating arrangements so bad and why the

awful delay in commencing. Why did not the Chairman rather
than Father Savage say a few words. A gathering of those who
couldn't care less about Unity including Mink Coat woman.
More contacts between clergy and laity very necessary which
would have avoided such a disastrous meeting – particularly
between local clergy and people.
With respect,
An ordinary Catholic.

[Handwritten comment from JCM – 'Keep: one day he will sign
his name, +J.C. 22.1.66'].

43. Sunday Independent, 23 Jan. 1966 –

Ecumenism at the Mansion House, from a special correspondent.
It was so unfortunate that what promised to be in many ways an
historic night at the Mansion House fell far below what we
expected.
First there was the trouble about the seating. No system of
numbering or control had been arranged. What a ghastly situation
it was when President de Valera found himself with nowhere to
sit.
Mr James Dillon quickly arose and offered his seat. In offering it
to the President Mr Dillon addressed him in Irish. To my surprise,
the President replied in English. Everything and everybody
seemed to have got mixed up.
We were surprised, too, that Most Rev. Dr. Simms was not on the
platform. We had expected that, from the advance publicity, which
told us that the two Archbishops would join together in The
Lord's Prayer and we were invited to join with them.
Instead we found Dr. Simms merely a member of the audience.
Questions have been asked about the empty chair on the
platform. Was it intended for Dr. Simms. I am told that
Archbishop Simms said to friends there was never any proposal

that he would be on the platform.

It was hard to fit all this in with the spirit of Ecumenism. We listened to a very fine paper by monsignor Arthur Ryan, but were sorry that the very subject on which he spoke – Ecumenism – did not seem to be helped that night.

44. Handwritten draft of statement by JCM to Conferences of Diocesan clergy, [7 Feb. 1966] –

To be read at the Conferences (Strictly for the Diocesan Clergy) To dispel the confusion about the Mansion House meeting, I should like the priests to understand that:

1. The Archbishop was responsible only for the invitations to Mgr. Ryan to lecture and the Apostolic Nuncio to preside. The title chosen by me was the Decree on Ecumenism: in no sense, Ecumenism in Dublin. I agreed to Most Rev. Dr. Simms and Mrs Simms being invited. The question of Most Rev. Dr. Simms being on the platform never arose.

2. No other aspect of the meeting was arranged by the Archbishop or Archbishop's house. The first intimation of a common prayer was discovered in the Irish Times. The notice, once given, I agreed to the Our Father, because to omit it would have caused limitless criticism, hurtful to the Church. The invitations, titles on invitations, seating, stewarding, reception: not one of these was in a remote way the responsibility of the Archbishop or Archbishop's House.

+John C. McQuaid,

Archbishop of Dublin.

45. Brendan Barry, S.J., Provincial, to JCM, 20 April 1966 –

My Lord Archbishop,

In reply to Your Grace's letter of 14th April, I am now able to say that I am nominating Father Matthew Meade to the Missioners

Committee. Father Meade lives at 37, Lower Leeson Street, Dublin 2.

I should like to ask Your Grace for a directive in another matter. Father Michael Hurley has been invited by the "Dun Laoghaire and District Council of Churches" to address a meeting of the Council in early December on the occasion of its 25th anniversary. The meeting will probably take place in the Knox Hall, Monkstown. –The Council is, I understand, an exclusively Protestant body.

I should be most grateful if Your Grace would let me know whether Father Hurley may accept this invitation.

With respectful good wishes,

I remain, etc.

[Handwritten note by JCM on letter – 'I shall not oppose the lecture, but I would ask you to see that he does not make it difficult for the Hierarchy, in view of the fact that the Hierarchy has still to receive the directory from the Holy See and then to adopt it to the circumstances of our country. +J.C. 24.1.66'].

46. R. Burke-Savage, from Farm Street Church, London, to JCM, 29 April 1966 –

My dear Lord Archbishop,

I send Your Grace with my compliments a copy of the current number of Studies.

By putting in an extra hard stint of work I have been able to get the Summer number already prepared and after a few days here I am going to a small place near Lausanne for eighteen days holiday before going on a busman's holiday in Rome, Palermo and the near East. I leave Naples for Beirut by sea on 5 June and after a few days there go on to Damascus, Jordan and finally Israel. Father Barry has been urging me since last September to take a long break to freshen up my ideas after twenty years in Leeson St. I expect to be back in Dublin on 25th July.

I greatly wish that I had had an opportunity of meeting Your Grace before the Mansion House meeting or after it. You very graciously accepted my apology but I never had the chance to explain the misunderstanding. From the severity of Father Barry's reprimand I realize how annoyed you were with me. You are at your best when people make mistakes and so I am hoping that by the time I return your magnanimity will have overcome your displeasure. You have helped and encouraged me so consistently for fifteen years that I should be deeply hurt if I failed to gain your complete forgiveness by the time I return.

Whatever your ultimate decision I shall continue to serve in my limited capacity Your Grace and the diocese in which I was born and bred and in which I have worked all through my priestly life. Without fear or favour and with a loyalty to Your Grace that I have shown consistently throughout the years I think I deserve not to be thrown over.

Asking Your Grace's blessing, and with real gratitude and a deep affection that I shall take to the grave.

I am,

Yours obediently in Christ,

Ronald Burke-Savage, S.J.

P.S. Please excuse the biro. I have left my good pen at home. RBS.

[Handwritten draft reply by JCM on letter – 'There is nothing to forgive. I have long since forgotten. Have a proper holiday. +J.C. 4.5.66'].

47. Dan [O'Carroll], from Specola Vaticana Rome to JCM, 29 April 1966 –

Dear John,

…I am very sorry indeed to hear of the disastrous meeting in the Mansion House. I have not seen any account of it, but I have had a letter from Fr. John Ryan a few days ago, telling me what a fiasco it was, and how much embarrassment and trouble it has caused you. He and the Superior, Fr. Ingram, and the Provincial are very worried about our friend.

On Anzac day, April 25th, there was an ecumenical service in S. Silvestro, I will tell you about it when we meet.

Looking forward to seeing you soon.

With every good wish,

Ever yours in Xt.,

Dan.

48. S.G. Poyntz, St. Stephen's Church, Dublin to JCM, 23 July 1966 –

Your Grace,

In connection with the Week of Prayer for Christian Unity 1967 I would like to organize a Meeting in my Parochial Hall for members of my parish on say the 18th or the 25th January and invite four clergymen from different denominations to speak on Unity from their point of view.

I propose to invite a Presbyterian, a Methodist and a member of the Church of Ireland. I wrote to ask your permission to invite an R.C. priest from your Diocese. If you agree to this, in principle, a number of names come to mind – Father Michael Hurley S.J., Father Austin Flannery O.P. and Father P. O'Donnell, O. Carm. – all known to me personally and would be most acceptable in my Hall. But perhaps you might wish to add other names.

I have discussed the proposed meeting with my Archbishop and he has given his approval. I would be grateful to you personally if you can allow us to have the privilege of the presence of one of your clergy.

Yours respectfully, etc.

49. JCM to S.G. Poyntz, 27 July 1966 –

Dear Reverend Doctor Poyntz,

I thank you for your kind inquiry.

I should not object to your inviting one of the priests named to speak at your Unity symposium in the coming January.

May I suggest that the Major Superior or Provincial should be approached.

With kind wishes,

I remain, etc.

50. W.P. Pike, Dublin Junior Clergy Fellowship to JCM, 29 Aug. 1966 –

Your Grace,

The Committee of the above Church of Ireland society wish to ask Rev. Kevin McNamara,[14] Professor of Dogmatic Theology at St. Patrick's College, Maynooth to speak to their opening meeting of this session on September 23rd. We contacted Professor McNamara by telephone and he explained that we ought to write to you first to ask you if it met with your approval.

Our society is only open to our twenty members, the average number of Junior Clergy attending being eight to ten. We meet once a month on a Friday morning.

As it is the opening meeting, our Archbishop, Most Rev. Dr. G.O. Simms will probably be present for a short while.

Yours respectfully, etc.'.

[Handwritten draft reply by JCM on letter –'Thank you for courtesy. A pleasure to sanction Father McNamara addressing your Society. +J.C. 30.8.66'].

51. Handwritten draft by JCM to R. Burke-Savage, 6 Oct. 1966

Dear Father Burke-Savage,
I have put to my Council your two proposals to invite Father
Rideau S.J. to lecture on Père Teilhard de Chardin, S.J. and to
organise another Mansion House meeting during the Octave of
Unity in 1967.
It is the unanimous opinion of my Council that neither proposal
is advisable.
With kind wishes,
I remain,
Yours sincerely,
+John C. McQuaid, Archbishop of Dublin, etc.

*52. Maurice Carey, Parish Church of St Bartholomew, Ballsbridge,
to JCM, 18 Nov. 1966 –*

Your Grace,
In connection with the Octave of Prayer for Christian Unity I
should be pleased if it can be arranged to have one of your clergy
to speak in our parish on Wednesday 18th January 1967. At the
present time we have no parish hall and I am planning a service in
the church, according to the order of service used in the Basilica
of St Paul Without-the- Walls on the occasion of the visit of the
Archbishop of Canterbury to Rome, to be followed by the
address.
I have known Fr. Michael Hurley for some years since he
accepted an invitation, when I was Dean of Residences, to speak
to students at the Queen's University of Belfast, and I would be
glad to invite him again on this occasion.
I am, Your Grace,
Yours sincerely,
Maurice Carey

P.S. The Rev. Alan Crawford, who was my curate until recently, much appreciated Your Grace's kindness in helping him to secure a seat at the closing of the Council, and in receiving him afterwards at the Irish College.

53. Handwritten draft reply by JCM to M. Carey, 23 Nov. 1966
—

'Dear Reverend Mr Carey,
I am asked by HGaB. to thank you for the courtesy of your letter suggesting that you invite Rev. Michael Hurley, S.J. to speak in your parish Church on Wednesday 18th January 1967 at a service of the order of that used in St. Paul's outside the Wall.
HG. regrets that he cannot consider such an invitation as advisable.
I am,
Your sincerely, etc.

54. P. Boylan, to JCM, 4 Jan. 1967

My dear Lord Archbishop,
I am sorry to hear that the Nuncio is worrying about presiding at the Lecture in the Stadium.[15] With Father Carey in charge of the arrangements I feel sure that the confusion of the mansion house will not be repeated. If, as it might appear, he fears that my poor Lecture will be a source of trouble, I should like to assure him that what I shall try to say will be simple and quite innocuous. My own fear about the Lecture is that it will be both unimpressive and rather boring.
I have not yet succeeded in getting it all on paper. It is a serious trouble to me to have to fear that my attempt will be quite unworthy of a great occasion.
With thanks for Your Grace's kind message,
I remain very respectfully yours,
P. Boylan

[Handwritten note by JCM – 'Don't worry. 5.1.66'].

55. P. Boylan to JCM, 11 Jan. 1967 –

My dear Lord Archbishop,
I regret that I have only this poor document to submit to Your
Grace's inspection. It will show the general method and manner
of treatment, and to me at least, it indicates how poorly I have
done the work of conveying to a Catholic audience the thoughts
of the Decree. From the beginning I was convinced that I should
not attempt anything more than a mere summary of the Decree. I
have found the Decree rather illogically arranged, and slightly
incoherent and repetitious. This I say pace Consilii. If Your Grace
will be so kind as to let me have the MS back I intend to iron it
out somewhat, but I dread the verdict it will receive in the
Stadium.
I remain, my dear Lord Archbishop,
Very respectfully yours,
P. Boylan.

[Handwritten note by JCM – 'I am very glad to say that you are
very much mistaken. +J.C. 11.1.66'].

56. J.A. MacMahon to JCM, 11 Jan. 1967 –

My Lord Archbishop,
I wish to apologise for typing this letter, but I have lost my
fountain pen. I hope Your Grace enjoys good weather at
Rockwell.
On reading the text of Your Grace's letter [for Church Unity
Octave 1967], which is being printed, I thought Your Grace might
like to have my view of the reaction of publicists, on its publication.
I think these publicists may try to show that important aspects of
ecumenical teaching have not been mentioned. I enclose some
excerpts which I have drawn from the Decree on Ecumenism
which illustrate the point.
I am sorry to bother Your Grace with these observations.

Your Grace's obedient servant,
James Ardle MacMahon

[Handwritten reply by JCM on letter: 'My dear Doctor, Thank
you. I have been "true and fair". I am giving a direction to the
Clergy, not a disquisition on ecumenism. And no matter what I
write I shall be wrong. You all forget that the Octave is not one of
Ecumenism, but of <u>conversion</u>, i.e. of unity. +J.C. McQ.'].

57. Handwritten draft of JCM's letter for the Church Unity Octave, 12 Jan. 1967

The Church Unity Octave

Very Reverend and dear Father,
Between the 18th and 25th January, the Church Unity Octave
will be celebrated throughout the world.
Urged by the charity of Christ, we shall all humbly ask that God,
by the intercession of Our Blessed Lady, may be pleased to grant
to all Christians separated from the Holy See in doctrine and
discipline the light to see the claims of his one true Church and
the strength to accept those claims.
This is the Will of the Divine Founder of the Church: "that there
be one fold and one Shepherd," (John x, 16)
For that intention we hereby prescribe that in this Diocese from
Wednesday 18th till 25th January inclusively, on each evening at
an hour to be determined by the Parish Priest or Rector of a
public Church the Rosary shall be recited during Benediction of
the Blessed Sacrament.
I remain,
Very Reverend and dear Father,
Your faithful servant in Christ,
+John Charles,
Archbishop of Dublin,
Primate of Ireland.

58. Seósamh Ó Ceannaigh from Glasnevin to JCM, 14 Jan. 1967 –

'An tAtair a chara,
As I was at early Mass yesterday I did not see your letter until later in the Press.
In general most of our Laity do not take any of your announcements seriously. The Church established by Christ is of course the true Church but we deviate so much from what is true that trueness lessens its meaning. To us such things as the Trinity Ban or the G.A.A. Ban are contrary to Truth. We would not follow Bishops who advocate or order such things.
Thanks to God and our good Pope John we now know that many of the regulations of the Church which excluded Charity and love were altogether wrong.
We Laity will just have to do our little best to bring about Christian Unity. We feel that our Bishops or Priests do not want unity. They are just sitting back (not altogether) but throwing an odd spanner into the works now and then.
The Clerical members of the Church down through the ages have been wrong in their interpretation of truth. At the Reformation the higher Clergy in Rome like ours sat back and did nothing when perhaps a little discussion, Charity and love would have saved the day.
When we live truth, let us then go to our separated Christians.
Go raibh an Tiarna libh
Seósamh Ó Ceannaigh.

59. [Letter for Church Unity Octave 1968]

11 Jan. 1968
'Very reverend and dear Father,
The Church Unity Octave will be celebrated between the 18th and 25th January. It is an Octave of prayer.

This Octave is frequently made the occasion for conferences and discussions between persons drawn from different Christian denominations. Where such discussions have been initiated by those who are adequately trained and properly authorised, the results of the genuine ecumenism advocated by the Second Vatican Council have been achieved in the clearer and more charitable understanding of the difficulties that beset full Christian unity.

It is to be regretted that the Faithful may be confused by these discussions as if there were not only one true Church of Christ, the Catholic Church. They may also be induced to forget that the Octave is chiefly an occasion for humble prayer that God, in His mercy, by the intercession of Our Blessed Lady, may hasten the day when all Christians now unfortunately separated from the Holy See in Faith and discipline may accept the one true Church of Christ.

How difficult and how distant such a unity must seem, in human calculation! Each and every individual must personally accept the claims of the one true Church, of which the supreme Head is the Pope, successor of St. Peter, in which the rulers are the Bishops, under the Pope, and, in communion with him, the lawful successors of the Apostles. In that Church alone are found all the means of holiness given to us by Our Divine Lord, Jesus Christ Himself.

And yet it is the explicit will of God made Man, Founder of the Church, that there should be one Fold of Faith and discipline and holiness, one Shepherd.

To afford the Faithful an opportunity of interceding for the accomplishment by us on earth of this will of Jesus Christ, we hereby prescribe that the Holy Sacrifice of the Mass be offered each evening during the Octave, in every parish Church and public Church of the Diocese, at an hour to be determined as most suitable by the Parish Priest or Rector.

I remain, Very Reverend and dear Father,

Your faithful servant in Christ,

+John Charles,
Archbishop of Dublin,
Primate of Ireland.

60. [Padraig Mac Cathmaine] Harmondstown Park, Dublin 5 to JCM, [15] Jan. 1968 –

My Lord Archbishop and Shepherd as one of your flock I beg to enclose a cutting from today's daily *Independent*.
I must say these boys are very quick, as your letter was the topic of a large number coming out of Holy Mass. It is unfortunate that our slow development of Ecumenism should have received this shock.
Pope John of happy memory gave us the lead as regards our divided Brethren and called them our Brothers and Sisters in Christ Jesus which the world received joyously. [He prayed with them].
Is it too late at this 11th Hour to call all Christians in Dublin to an Evening of Prayer at the Mansion House with Choirs from our own and other Churches!!
An event like this would help to take the real meaning of your over zealous letter and would cheer the Hearts of all of us.
Yours most obediently, etc.

[Handwritten comment by JCM on letter – '16.1.68. Just acknowledge courtesy of letter. (He is becoming a nuisance – as he is retired and likes writing)'].

61. Cornelius Lucey,[16] Bishop's House, Cork to JCM, 16 Jan. 1968 –

Your Grace,
I feel must write and tell you how glad I was to read your Letter of last Sunday for the Church Unity Octave. It is absolutely right and absolutely at the right time. Already the feeling is abroad here

that any one religion is as good as another and that Church Unity is to demonstrate that in practice, Ecumenism, of course, is fast becoming an exercise in criticising the Catholic Church and all belonging to it while extolling all the other Churches and non-Churches.

The letter in today's IRISH TIMES, I presume from a Catholic, is a clear proof that we should let the people know that we do claim to be the one true Church and do [sic] we do claim, not as monopoly of holiness and belief exactly, but a far larger measure (to say the least) of holiness and belief than other churches.

With all prayerful good wishes I remain,

Yours Very Sincerely,

+Cornelius Lucey.

62. Handwritten draft of letter by JCM to Lucey, 18 Jan. 1968

My dear Lord Bishop,

The letter that Your Lordship has sent me concerning my letter on Church Unity is one of the most consoling that I have ever received. I am indeed grateful for this very kind support.

The confusion here among upper-class Catholics is very disturbing. It has become, I am assured, with many, a necessary fashion to criticise the Church and to line-up with non-Catholics. The students are infected at least in part, such as the [Lomos?] group and its adherents.

A very significant fact – that I may not publish – is that in 1967 we had only 61 converts, whereas hitherto we had up to 120 each year. Your Lordship will be glad to hear that the priests and good ordinary Faithful have expressed great satisfaction at the clear statement of the position.

With my very grateful regards,

I remain, my dear Lord Bishop,

Yours very sincerely,

+John C. McQuaid.

63. Amy Morris, on behalf of Regina Publications, Dublin 1 to JCM, 24 Jan. 1968 –

Your Grace,
The members and associates of Regina Publications are deeply grateful for the clear statement of principles on occumenical [*sic*] dialogue as set out in your letter read in our Churches on Sunday 14th January.
We pledge ourselves to give your statement the utmost support in the limited circles of our own families, work and recreation and assure you of continued remembrance in our Masses and prayers.
Yours respectfully in Christ,
Amy Morris (Miss) for Regina Publications.

[Handwritten draft response by JCM on letter: –'I am grateful for the support of prayer in my office of preaching the truth of the Catholic Faith. +J.C. 27.1.68'].

64. Rev. Patrick Dunne, St Mary's, Haddington Rd to JCM, 29 Jan. 1968 –

My Lord Archbishop,
I came back on Saturday night to be told of the insolent letters in the papers, etc. Your Grace said only what many people were anxious for someone to say and need have no regrets.
With kind wishes
I remain,
Respectfully and sincerely yours.

[Handwritten draft reply by JCM on letter – 'Your consoling letter is an encouragement. The criticism can, by its injustice, be explained only by the demon who is hurt by the truth'].

65. Anon. to JCM, 31 Jan. 1968 –

Your Grace,
Please accept my congratulations on your fine Pastoral Letter,
explaining clearly once again the true doctrine on Church Unity.
It is significant that the liberal 'Irish Times' failed to publish either
the full text thereof or Father McSweeney's popular sermon ...
We Catholics, however, are worried about the constant
inopportune statements of "expert priests", whether they be
Professors or editors or article writers. I regret to have to mention
the confusion caused to so many of us by Jesuit Professor
Simpson's statement on Divorce at "The T.D.'s Hotel"; Father
O'Connor's unfortunate generalisations about Church and State
leaders and very strange remarks re. Divorce; Father Sweetman's
allowing himself to be used as a dupe for unpatriotic agitators &
his speaking down to a notoriously sensual pack of
undergraduates; the article in "Brief" which highlights the errors
of the mixed-up Church of Holland.
We know how much this must pain you as Guardian of Faith and
morals and we look forward to more courageous statements of our
Faith.
MAY GOD SPARE YOU LONG,
'Member of your flock'.

66. JCM to Rev. D. Herlihy[17], 9 April 1968 –

Confidential
My dear Lord Bishop,
I have learned that there is a proposal to coopt Rev. Michael
Hurley, S.J. on the Advisory Commission on Ecumenism.
My Diocese contains the largest group of non-Catholic Christians
and pagans in Ireland.
I regret that my experience of the Reverend Michael Hurley, S.J.,
has been such that, if he is coopted I shall feel obliged to

withdraw my representative, Mgr. O'Connell.

I remain,

My dear Lord Bishop,

Yours, etc.

67. Rev. Michael O'Connell, Our Lady of Refuge parish, Rathmines, 27 April 1968 –

Dear Father MacMahon,

I enclose for His Grace a summary of our last Ecumenical Advisory Commission Meeting.

My suggestion about additional laity (no names mentioned) was to try and circumvent the proposal to add Fr. Hurley. There are in fact many good laity who would actually restrain the Maynooth clergy on this Commission.

The Abbot's[18] proposal is typical of his outlook.

I brought in Milne's History[19] and read it out to the members.

I went to this Meeting resolved to keep quiet – but I was forced to speak in view of the silence of Bishop Herlihy and Mgr. Ryan. Leaving the Hotel Bishop Herlihy said that he doubted whether the Hierarchy would agree to Fr. Hurley's inclusion.

Very sincerely yours.

68. J.A. MacMahon to M. O'Connell, 29 April 1968 –

Dear Monsignor O'Connell,

Many thanks for your letter of the 27th inst. enclosing the report of the last Ecumenical Advisory Commission. I shall at once convey your report to His Grace.

I see that you had very much stood in the gap of danger!

With respectful good wishes

Yours sincerely, etc.

Notes

1 The correspondence on ecumenism are mainly in the McQuaid ecumenism files (Dublin Diocesan Archives, (DDA), AB/8/B/XLVI) but there is additional material in the McQuaid censorship files(DDA, AB/8/B/XXV).

2 Deirdre McMahon, 'John Charles McQuaid, archbishop of Dublin, 1940-72' in James Kelly and Daire Keogh (eds), *History of the Catholic diocese of Dublin* (Dublin, 2000), pp 349–80, at p. 373.

3 Roland ('Ronnie') Marcus Anthony Burke-Savage (1912–98), Jesuit priest and editor of the *Irish Monthly* (1947–50), and of *Studies* from 1950–68. He served as superior of the Leeson St. community from 1951 to 1959 and he was director of the Central Catholic Library from 1959 to 1968.

4 Patrick Joseph Boylan (1879–1974), priest, and biblical scholar. He was professor of eastern languages at UCD from 1912 to 1956, chairman of the censorship of publications board in 1930 to 1942 and vicar-general of the Dublin diocese from 1939.

5 *Irish Times*, 19 Jan. 1965

6 P. F. Cremin (1910–2001), DD, professor of moral theology and canon law at St Patrick's College, Maynooth

7 The Archbishop was attending a session of the Second Vatican Council.

8 December 1965 was the Silver Jubilee of J.C. McQuaid's consecration as Archbishop of Dublin. Ronald Burke-Savage was the author of an article in *Studies* to celebrate the occasion; Ronald Burke-Savage, 'The Church in Dublin, 1940–1965: a study of the achievement and of the personality of the Most Rev. John Charles McQuaid, Archbp. of Dublin on the occasion of the Silver Jubilee of his episcopate' in *Studies: an Irish Quarterly Review*, liv (1965), pp 296–346.

9 Centre for Religious Studies and Information, 74, Merrion Square.

10 Dr James Corboy, S.J., Bishop of Monze.

11 Reports in the *Irish Times*, 14 Jan. 1966 and *Evening Press*, 14 Jan. 1966 that McQuaid and G.O. Simms, the Church of Ireland Archbishop of Dublin, would pray together at Mansion House meeting on 18 Jan. 1966.

12 Robert Maire Smyllie (1893–1954), journalist and editor of the *Irish Times*.

13 Osmond G. Dowling, director of the Diocesan Press Office from 1965.

14 Kevin McNamara (1926–87) was appointed to the chair of dogmatic theology at Maynooth in 1954. From 1968 to 1973, he served as a consultant to the Vatican Secretariat on Christian Unity. He was appointed Roman Catholic Bishop of Kerry in August 1976 in succession to Bishop Eamon Casey and was installed as Roman Catholic Archbishop of Dublin in 1985.

15 In 1967 the lecture for the Unity Octave took place on Sunday 15 Jan. 1967. It was organized through Archbishop's House and by the Dublin Institute of Adult Education in the National Stadium. Patrick Boylan, parish priest of Dun Laoghaire, was the invited speaker and Patrick Masterson of UCD invited to give the response.

16 Cornelius Lucey (1902–82), ordained Roman Catholic Bishop of Cork in 1951, and in 1958 bishop of Ross, he retired in 1980.

17 Donal Herlihy, Roman Catholic Bishop of Ferns

18 Rev. Augustine O'Sullivan, Abbot of Glenstal. He had suggested that visiting

Anglican clergy might be allowed to celebrate their liturgy in 'a remote part of a religious house'; McQuaid papers Dublin Diocesan Archives (DDA) AB/8/B/XLVI/207).

19 Kenneth Milne, *The Church of Ireland: a history* (Dublin, 1966).

Chapter six

Censorship and
J.C. McQuaid

The files on Censorship, Arts & Culture are held in the Diocesan Archives in Drumcondra[1] and have not been fully calendared to date but contain correspondence on a wide range of censorship issues; the theatre, film, the Index and the press. In many cases the original concerns were raised by concerned members of the public. Frequently His Grace referred the matter back to the correspondent for individual action. In 1954 Archbishop McQuaid established a Committee which was to 'keep an eye on Communist and other anti-Catholic activities'[2] which had a very wide remit, investigating the activities of the People's College, the Irish Housewives Association,[3] the IRA, Teddy boys as well as Saor Uladh, Sinn Féin and the Irish Workers League.

For cinema, with representatives on the Censorship Board, he could directly influence decisions of the Board and could also impose, either directly or indirectly, his views on the desired standards of films released in Ireland. The Irish theatre was more challenging and there were some very public confrontations. The most notable of these was the debate over the *Rose Tattoo* in 1957[4] but the following year the Archbishop's objections to two productions planned for the Dublin Tostal[5] theatre festival resulted in the festival being cancelled.

The Vigilance Committee

1. Memo to JCM [John Charles McQuaid], [22 March 1954]

In May 1954 His Grace met Dr O'Halloran, Fr. Kavenagh, Fr. Crean and Fr Michael Clarke and put the following suggestions to them.

Your Grace will remember deciding to appoint a Committee composed of V. Rev. M. O'Halloran, Rev. C.P. Crean and Father Kavanagh, who would have the function of keeping an eye on Communist activities and other anti-Catholic activities, such as Liberalism.

The following are some suggestions as to what should be the objects of such a Committee: I believe that one needs to be pretty explicit in assigning objects to such a Committee, as Secular priests are rather literal in their reading of assignments from authority.

1. To keep an eye on subversive movements, e.g. the Irish Workers' League; to keep a file on these movements and their members; to devise means of counteracting the activities of these movements, e.g. some years ago the Irish Workers' League, through a Students' Council, which was a subsidiary organisation, decided to try to influence Technical School and University students – means were then adopted to counteract these efforts of theirs.

2. To [provide for infiltration of] legitimate organisations, that are being used by communists or liberals or that are likely to be used by them for their own ends, e.g. The Irish Housewives Association, the Unemployed Association, The Civil Liberties Association.

3. As it is a fact that Communists and Liberals are much quicker than Catholics in setting up associations to provide for the needs of the people, another aim of this Committee should be to anticipate our opponents by being watchful to see the

existence of such needs and through suitable Catholic laymen and women, whether professional or Trade Unionists, inspiring the founding of such societies or groups, whose aims could be cultural or educational or recreational.

4. To try again, through suitable Catholic laymen and women, to influence from the Catholic view-point the Radio, the press. For instance, we hear on the Radio talks on foreign affairs by people like Sheehy-Skeffington[6] and Nevin and Green– it should be possible to have their influence counteracted by seeing that competent Catholic laymen should be heard also on the Radio both in giving talks on foreign affairs and in discussions, when men like Sheehy-Skeffington etc. are talking.

5. To try and give a more instructed Catholic outlook (through the University, Guilds, Inst. of Social Science) to such groups, as Trade Unions, Doctors, lawyers, etc. For instance, if the I.M.A. had shown some initiative in promoting a voluntary insurance scheme before the State got going on the matter, a lot of unpleasantness could have been avoided and the beginnings of socialisation could have been nipped in the bud. Similarly lawyers as a group are a very influential organisation and at times they have much to say in the government of the country – it should be possible to imbue them with Catholic principles.

6. There are many individual Catholics and Catholic organisations that are anxious to combat communism or liberalism. A number of them come to Archbishop's House for advice and it is better that they should not be directly advised from Archbishop's House. Such people could be advised by this Committee and their zeal properly channelled.

I think that this Committee should report progress to Your Grace (at least) twice a year and see Your Grace in a body (at least) once a year, so that its policy could be directed in accordance with Your Grace's wishes.

[Comment by JCM – 'I will always have to be free. I am in full agreement. +J.C. 22.3.54'].

2. Rev. M. O'Halloran to JCM, 24 Jan. 1955 –

My lord Archbishop,
I wish to make my report to Your Grace on the Committee's activities during the past six months.

Our difficulty has been that we have been so busy with our parochial problems that we have got out of touch somewhat with the problems mentioned in our terms of reference. Father Kavanagh was our link with these. Hence I suggest that Father Fehily be added to our committee. He is in constant contact with trade union executives, and many of the problems that arise are referred to him in the first instance. It would be essential to have him with us.

We had three formal meetings

1. Father Crean has kept in constant touch with the Bakers Union, the I.T. and G.W. Union and the Local Government Officials Union. We have discussed the matter of the People's College. It is the official body for adult education sponsored by T.U.C. Father Crean has a file on it since 1949 which is kept up to date.
2. We discussed the position in trade union circles of Michael O'Riordan.[7] I spoke to Fr Killian O.F.M. He and Fr. Crean have the problem in hand.
3. We discussed the case of Miss Blake Loreto Convent North Great George's St. after consultation with Fr. Denis Daly, Fr Crean advised Rev. Mother on her course of action.
4. Fr. Clarke has been watching the activities of the Irish Housewives Association and had talks with two ladies. Membership has been greatly reduced and he thinks the movement under control. He has a small file on the question.

He also has in hand the problem of Communist literature sent to Students in U.C.D. by the International Students Union. The method employed has been approved by the President.[8]

5. Recently complaints have been made to Father Crean about new trends in dancing in some of the Dublin Dance Halls – they are intimately immoral. We have discussed the matter and now wish to draw Your Grace's attention to the problem. We think that where such abuses exist the attention of the police should be attracted.

Such, Your Grace, is my report. We are working under difficulties, but we have not overlooked our commission.
I am, etc.

3. Memo [to JCM] [1955] –

Objects of the 'Vigilance' Committee.
Intelligence work.
The objects of the Committee as described in the original memorandum fall under six headings. Only the first heading deals with specifically intelligence work, namely, the keeping of an eye on subversive movements. The other five headings envisage the:
Infiltration of neutral organisations,
Setting up of cultural and educational associations,
Influencing of radio and press by talks, etc.,
Instructing of Catholic professional bodies,
Advising on problems as they arise.
Intelligence work, certainly, is related to all of these objects. Knowledge must precede enlightened action. Yet it must appear doubtful that the same committee could deal adequately with objects which are so diverse in nature as to require a great deal of activity in addition to specifically intelligence work ... Good intelligence work demands a good technique, involving intelligence methods, the building up of contacts and information,

the classification of information and so on. Specifically intelligence work, then, would best be done by a committee devoted solely to intelligence work. This conclusion is reinforced in the case of the present Committee by the fact that the members, as far as one can see, are not skilled in intelligence technique. It is unlikely that this technique can be acquired unless and until the members devote themselves solely to intelligence work.

On the other hand the importance of the other five headings which have been mentioned can hardly be over-stressed. In fact they are so important that they require the special attention of special groups. In point of fact, in setting up the Guild of St. Francis de Sales, in reforming the C.A.I.R., and in many other ways, His Grace the Archbishop has dealt with these problems by using specific groups and associations.

Censorship board.

The first Censorship Board was set up in 1930, six months after the passing of the Act and was composed of five men, chosen by the Minister. They were Canon Patrick Boylan (Chairman), Professor W.E. Thrift[9] of TCD, W.J. O'Reilly LLD, W.B. Ward, representative of the Dublin branch of the INTO and Patrick J. Keawell MA. The membership of the Board varied very little over the next decade, with individual board members being replaced from time to time. Under a new censorship Act in 1946 the first board appointed was chaired by Senator William Magennis.[10]

4. Rev. Joseph Deery,[11] the Presbytery, Leinster Rd., to JCM, 26 Jan. 1948 -

My dear Lord Archbishop,
Lay members of the Censorship board have been restive under criticism for some time past. I have done what I could to persuade them to continue, uncomplainingly, at their task. However,

yesterday's editorial in the "Sunday Independent" has roused them again. Two of them have already said that they regard it as a consequence of O'Faoláin's[12] recent letter in the "Irish Times", and that it will be impossible for them, or for any Catholic laymen, to continue unless they get some expression of ecclesiastical approval or support. "Nobody will do it" is the opinion of one of these men. In his letter Mr O'Faoláin had said that no approval had ever been given to the Board, and suggested that a great number of priests actually disapproved of it. The following-up of this letter by an official attack in the paper which, in the view of many people, is Ireland's leading Catholic newspaper, has knocked my two colleagues out of their stride. They have urged, demanded in fact, that I should put their views before your Grace. Their hope is that it may be possible to obtain backing for their work from higher Ecclesiastical authority. They would not, of course, want approval for each act of prohibition, but would welcome an official statement on the necessity for censorship, especially for the protection of youth, and on the general principles underlying Censorship. Your Grace will understand that I am merely a mouthpiece in this matter. For my own part I am quite happy to continue without demur, the work your Grace entrusted to me, for as long as Your Grace wills. I remain, etc.

5. Dermot O'Flynn[13] of Loyola, Church Drive, Milltown to JCM, 7 March 1958 –

My Lord Archbishop,
In view of an official reply that may be in transit to the Secretary of the Hierarchy I beg to submit the following facts and some observations.
In a recent Dail reply the Minister of Justice[14] stated that the new Board was now working efficiently and reducing its arrears. The true position is that some 500 books were outstanding when this

new group took over in Nov. '57 – now almost 800 are awaiting attention.

I am informed on reliable authority that in the prejudiced report prepared by the Secy. Dept of Justice[15] – for the recent meeting of the Government a number of distortions appear.

1. It is stated that after the arrival of the letter from the Hierarchy on 4th Feb. the Dept. consulted with the Gardai and requested them to examine a report on the type of paper-back book offered for sale in the shop. The Garda report showed that little or no evil books are on sale.

What is <u>not</u> stated is that the Secy of the Department waited until Feb 28 to call the Garda Chiefs. During this period of 24 days the newsagents and street stalls had reacted to the Statement of the Hierarchy, and, in the light of a [new] public opinion had returned books to the wholesalers, or had placed them under the counter.

2. The Chairman of the present Board is reported as being confident that they will clear excess at their current rate of 90 books per month. They are not anywhere near this target. For February 1958 – the incoming books exceeded those disposed by 63.

Rev. Burke Savage, S.J. visited the Dept. last week and was with Mr. Coyne for a long private session. It is felt in the Dept that he was collecting data to justify the present regime at his next lecture on Friday 14th out at Dun Laoghaire.

The following items give a clear indication of the liberal standards of the new Board.

(a) Copy of the Red Room by Francoise Mallet-Jones (enclosed) was decided "No action" on 8/5/57 by a 2/3 vote. The 2 new members Comyn[16] and Figgis[17] outvoting Pigott,[18] O'Reilly[19] and O'Flynn. This amoral book is detailed , e.g. P89/90 or P. 58/59.

(b) Copy of Clementine – recently decided by the present Board as "No Action" (This cannot be used as evidence – just yet – and

I must return the copy <u>at once</u>). This book was stopped by a Revenue Officer. Such a rejection by the Board affects their standards. It discourages them in the conscientious exercise of their duty. They tend to take less care in future as the result of an official snub. I shall endeavour to procure another copy as evidence.

c) <u>The Dead, the Dying and The Damned</u> – The marked pages alone condemn this book. Yet the present Board has recently decided "No Action" on the paperback and adult editions.

(d) <u>The Green Crow</u> by O'Casey was submitted as a test case copy covering letter and official reply herewith.

The last 4 stories in this book are from *Windfalls* banned 4/12/34. It was ruled by the Chairman that as it did not contain <u>all</u> of *Windfalls* it was not automatically banned, and this was open for reconsideration. This slender legal ruling was used as a loophole for a "No Action" decision. "We do not wish to make ourselves appear foolish (as did a previous Board) by banning the works of the great O'Casey". Unfortunately all this cannot be used without disclosing the source of our information.

I enclose Dec. '57 copy of *Continental Film Review* (now stopped). This was omitted from a previous group of evidence.

Copies of *Psychologist* demonstrate another very subtle type of poison.

The Western novel enclosed (released this week) shows how the virus can attack an innocent boy eager to read a straight-forward adventure story.

I am sorry if I have gone on too long Your Grace – but the problem is far deeper that [than] the paper-back menace we have fought till now. It is not easy to get adults to agree on adult book censorship. We [With] Mr Coyne's liberal men in command we can look forward to reduced standards and many pitched battles from the County Libraries.

I remain, etc'.

6. Éamon de Valera, Oifig an Taoiseach to JCM, 8 March 1958 –

My dear Lord Bishop,
I have given careful consideration to the observations of the
Standing Committee of the Hierarchy on the subject of evil
publications, conveyed in the letter addressed to me on the 30th
January by Your Lordship and His Lordship the Bishop of
Raphoe,[20] as Secretaries of the Hierarchy.
As regards the extent to which the number of those publications
has increased, although the evidence is not conclusive, I do not
doubt that some increase has taken place as a result of difficulties
that existed for a time concerning the membership and
functioning of the Censorship of Publications Board. Of these
difficulties I think their Lordships are aware.
The observations and suggestions made by the Bishops fall under
two main heads, namely, the extent to which the powers of the
Gárda Siochána are exercised and the composition and procedure
of the Censorship Board.
As to the Gárda Siochána, it is necessary to explain that they have
no powers to deal with the importation and sale of crime and sex
fiction, as such, but only with the publications that are obscene
and that, even in this field, action by the Gárda is necessarily
restricted, in practice, to publications that are manifestly in this
class. The Gárda have no special power to enter a bookseller's shop
and examine his stock; they can do this only to the extent that it
can be done by any member of the public. A warrant for the
search of the premises can be obtained, but only where a Justice is
satisfied, on the oath of an officer not below the rank of Chief
Superintendant, that there is reasonable ground for suspecting the
presence of either indecent pictures or publications prohibited
under the Censorship of Publications Acts. For these reasons, the
Gárda cannot readily take effective action, even when they think
that obscene publications are for sale, unless they are informed of
the places where they are for sale, by persons who have themselves

made an adequate examination of the publications.

An extension of the existing powers of the Gárda Siochána in regard to objectionable publications would require legislation by the Oireachtas, and it is obvious that there would be very serious difficulty in framing such legislation in a form that would be at once effective and likely to secure majority acceptance.

With regard to the Censorship Board, since it was reconstituted in October 1957, it has, I am informed, been working harmoniously and well. The Chairman[21] considers that it will be able to handle the problem, notwithstanding the arrears that resulted from the difficulties concerning its membership and functioning to which I have already referred.[22] Incidentally, I would like Their Lordships to be assured that, to the best of my belief, each member of the Board desired to perform his duties as a member in a conscientious manner and is endeavouring to do so.

Their Lordships will appreciate that the functions of such bodies as Bord na Mona, the Electricity Supply Board and Bord Failte Eireann are of a character fundamentally different from those of the Censorship of Publications Board. The special statutory provisions regarding the procedure of that Board and the establishment and functions of the Appeal Board[23] were decided upon as safeguards against any abuse by the civil authorities of powers given to them to regulate the choice of matter for private reading.

If it should become clear, at any stage, that the Censorship Board, as at present constituted, could not handle the volume of work with which it has to deal, we would have to consider how best the Board could be assisted in the performance of their task. I am afraid that a considerably larger number of members, working in groups, would find it very difficult to maintain uniform standards of judgment and that, in consequence of this, there might be a serious growth in adverse criticism of the censorship arrangements.

I think that it is generally known that the Censorship Board are now obliged to examine any particular book in respect of which a complaint is made by a member of the public, as well as any book referred to them by an Officer of Customs and Excise; it would greatly assist the efforts to deal with this whole problem if complaints by individuals and societies were made in a specific rather than a general form. This has been pointed out by a number of Catholic organisations which have made representations in recent months, and we hope there will be a satisfactory response.

I am addressing a letter in the same terms to His Lordship the Bishop of Raphoe.

I remain, etc.

Newspapers

7. *Norah O'Connor, 9 Berkeley Road, Dublin 7 to JCM, 1 June 1962 [and also signed by two friends, Mairin Nolan and Joan Shine] –*

It has come to our notice the enclosed paper [*News of the World*] is on sale in the shops in Dublin and throughout the country. We are of the opinion that the articles, and one article in particular, as well as a photograph in the issue of 28th May are offensive and could, in our opinion, be constituted as dangerous to the morals of young people. Is there any action which can be taken about this matter.

Yours respectfully, etc.

[The issues of the paper were sent from Drumcondra to Peter Berry at the Dept of Justice whose ultimate reply on 6 July 1962 to J.A. McMahon was that he had 'read (distasteful task) the issues of the 'News of the World' since 10 June. I regret to say that while the paper published offensive, vulgar matter I have come to the conclusion that the Censorship Board would not regard the publications as meriting the issue of a prohibition order'].

8. Richard Graham to Anon, 5 June 1966

Dear Revd. Father,
With the compliments and Good wishes of the 3rd Order of St
Francis Church Street Merchants Quay (Dublin), we are
reluctantly compelled to draw your attention to this seemingly
ugly and suggestive Propaganda in an Irish journal which boasts of
printing and circulating Sermons and Extracts of various R.C.
orders as a regular feature, and always under the caption "De
chum Glóire Dé and Onóra na hEireann".
Br. R. Graham (T.O.S.F.)
P.S. Would this be a case for our good Archbishop to study?

[Handwritten draft response by JCM 'Just say it will have AB's
careful attention'].

[N.B. The advertisement in question was for an advert for Veet
underarm depilatory and included an illustration of a woman in
underwear].

9. Memo to JCM, 5 June 1966 –

Your Grace,
A Mr Graham, a Third Order member from Merchant's Quay,
called here last evening to ask that the attached advertisement
from the Evening Press be brought to Your Grace's attention.
Mr Graham protested, he said, about this advertisement last
December in a personal call to Mr. Moore, Advertisement
Manager at Burgh Quay, and again by letter to Mr. E. De Valera in
May of this year. He states he received no acknowledgement from
either.
Mr Graham asked whether Your Grace could endeavour to have
such advertisements discontinued.

10. *John D. Horgan, Whitehall Dublin to JCM, 13 Jan. 1960*

My Lord Archbishop,

I beg to enclose herewith a letter from professor Cunningham, together with the letter from the Irish League of Decency, and the circulars concerning the C.D. Indicator, which your Grace had sent me.

Professor Cunningham confirms what I wrote in my last letter to Your Grace and adds that the Indicator is not entirely accurate and may be misleading. It seems to me, however, that this is a medical rather than a moral matter.

I have not seen the Advertisement in the <u>Readers' Digest</u>, and I do not know why the League refers to its 'pagan philosophy'.

I beg to remain, my Lord Archbishop,

Your Grace's most obedient servant.

[Handwritten draft reply on letter by JCM: 'Thank you. I thought the machine of no special value. Tables are found in standard textbooks. I am grateful for your letter explaining further your views on our present position in face of unwholesome publications'].

11. *Thomas J. Coyne*[24] *of Ballsbridge Dublin to JCM, 5 April 1960 –*

Dear Archbishop,

I was relieved to receive an acknowledgement of my letter of the 28th March for I was afraid that I might have lost Your Grace's favour, not so much for what I had said but rather for what I had left unsaid.

I had no sooner dispatched the letter (with more haste than prudence) than I began to think that I had either said too much or too little. For one thing, I thought that my omission to say <u>expressis verbis</u> that I thought the magazine you had sent me was the most unwholesome trash (which is, of course, the case) might lead you to suppose that I thought otherwise.

For another, I felt I had not shown a sufficient awareness of Your
Grace's concern to safeguard the morals of your subjects and of
the good grounds there are for supposing that publications of the
kind in question have a demoralising effect not merely on the
weak-minded but on the weak-willed as well and are a greater
menace because they are retailed at a price which is low enough
to give them a relatively wide circulation.

Thirdly, I thought it was wrong (if not impertinent) of me to say
that I did not understand why Your Grace and the other Bishops
did not exercise your powers to specify particular publications by
name as being publications which ought not to be read without
indicating that I could think of a number of good reasons,
prudential and otherwise, for their not doing this, as, for example,
the practical impossibility of specifying all such publications and
the risk that those left unspecified might be wrongfully presumed
to have ecclesiastical approval.

Finally, it occurred to me that I might have said (what has been
uppermost in my mind for a number of years) that one of the
reasons why I regard State censorship as an evil, albeit a necessary
one, is because of the possibility amounting, in my view, to a
possibility that, if the State is encouraged or even allowed to
become an arbiter of morals, it may be tempted to usurp the
functions of the Church and that one day a Government may be
found, even in this country, which is only too ready to invade the
province of the Church and to tell the people that ecclesiastical
pronouncements on this or that subject are not fit reading for
them, as has happened elsewhere.

More than ever am I convinced that the battle for the
fundamental decencies of life is a battle that must be fought
chiefly by the Church with such assistance from the State as may
be expected from an unreliable and potentially dangerous ally.
What is needed, in my opinion, to check the false emphasis on sex
that is a feature of our times and of which obscene publications
are a by-product is the creation of a public opinion which will

react against the prevailing moral flabbiness and the false philosophies that are so much in vogue. This, as I see it, is a task for the priest, not for the policeman.

To illustrate what I mean I enclose a cutting from last Sunday's Observer (which as you know, is one of the so-called "quality" newspapers) containing an advertisement that is certainly not obscene in the eyes of the law but which shows quite plainly how small girls and their parents are being systematically indoctrinated with the idea that sex appeal (to use the jargon) consists in a provocative display of secondary sexual characteristics. This is the sort of thing that cannot possibly be suppressed by the State without the State appearing to make itself ridiculous which the civil authority is always unwilling to do. But since the wisdom of God is the foolishness of man it seems to me that the Church need have no such inhibitions and that the public will in the long run listen to the Church if it is consistent and persistent in denouncing what is false in present day philosophies and that in this way, and only in this way, can there be brought about a reversal of the present trend.

Not that I think the laity can be left out of the reckoning or that they have only a passive role to play though I deplore the harmful excess of zeal of some of them. Nor am I to be taken as suggesting that the wearing of brassieres (or their advertisement), to take that example, is a thing that should be denounced by the Church. What, in my view, is required is something much more radical than symptomatic treatment: it is a root and branch denunciation of the philosophy underlying the aberrations which have resulted in the apotheosis of the teen-ager and which is best exemplified in this country by the fate of a school teacher (or even a parent) who is known to have smacked a naughty child. Yours sincerely,

Thomas [J. Coyne].

[Enclosed is a cutting from the Observer, 3 April 1960, of an

advertisement for 'new bras and girdles specially designed for 11-
16 year-olds'].

12. JCM to T J Coyne, 13 April 1960 –

Dear Mr Coyne,
I am grateful for your letter explaining further your views on our
present position in face of unwholesome publications.
I agree with all that you have written –and you have written well.
The plan of approaching proprietors and advertisers has been
worked by me already, when I got educated ladies to call the
management. The result in every case was effective, because it was
understood why the ladies felt it necessary to call.
Unquestionably we have a great task facing us in the incessant
effort to educate a sane public opinion. One can only keep
working for the time allotted by God.
If you assure me that you are concerned to safeguard public
morality, it is not, I trust, because you believe that I am among
your detractors. I am conscious of your work and I am grateful for
what you have achieved.
With kind wishes
I remain, etc.

13. J.A. MacMahon to Basil Clancy, editor of Hibernia, 8 June 1962 –

Dear Sir,
I have been directed by His Grace the Archbishop to inquire on
what principle your paper has given facilities to a Protestant
theologian to expose his errors in doctrine while reviewing a
Catholic work.
It has not escaped His Grace's attention that, in your issue of June,
an unsigned article (and I am to point out that so many of your
articles are unsigned) treats this incident as an advance, a good

example of the new climate of opinion and of the need for a
meeting of minds.
I am, etc.

14. Basil Clancy to JA MacMahon, 12 June 1962 –

Very reverend and dear Father,
I wish to acknowledge with thanks your letter of 8th June and to
say that my reasons for asking a Protestant to review a Catholic
work on Church Unity were that I thought this would be a
suitable gesture at the present time and that such a review, by a
responsible Protestant theologian, would be in the interests of the
ecumenical movement.
On a few previous occasions in 1958–59 I had published some
contributions by non-Catholics on the same general theme and in
all good faith I thought it would be appropriate to do so on this
occasion. I sincerely regret that the review has caused anxiety and
I am willing to arrange for a reply to it if considered desirable.
The main sections of 'Hibernia' are produced by panels of
Catholic contributors who work largely on a voluntary basis. As
the comment of such groups does not easily lend itself to
publication under an individual name, such comment as is finally
published is accepted as an editorial responsibility.
I would be grateful if you could convey to His Grace my sincere
thanks for his kindness in writing to indicate the dangers in such
matters.
I remain. etc.

15. J. C. Bushe of Independent Newspapers to Sec. at Archbishop's House, 8 July 1963 –

Dear Reverend Father,
The enclosed is a copy of an advertisement we have received for
publication in the "Irish Independent", Special Notices column.

We have a feeling that, some considerable time ago His Grace The Archbishop advised that he did not approve of such charitable appeal notices from Convents, etc., appearing over a box number address. We shall therefore, be obliged for His Graces' [*sic*] guidance on the matter.

Your reply at earliest convenience will oblige, Yours truly, etc.

[The advertisement intended for the small ads (1¹/₂″ special notices) was for a piano for a community of teaching sisters in Limerick −. The original draft advert read −

'Think it over − You have a good piano which is rarely used now, as your family have grown up and have homes of their own or you have not the time to play it. A Catholic community of teaching sisters could make this piano work for God. What about selling it to them at a reduced price for mission work. They have about £5. God will not be outdone in generosity'. The final draft was amended by JCM to read −' Think it over − You have a good piano which is rarely used now, as your family have grown up and have homes of their own or you have not the time to play it. A Catholic community of teaching sisters could use it for mission purposes and would consider its purchase'].

16. Archbishop's House [Leon O Cuinnleain] to J.C. Bushe, 12 July 1963 −

Dear Mr Bushe,

Thank you for your letter of the 8th concerning the enclosed advertisement for a bargain in a piano in the name of a missionary cause.

I welcome the opportunity to state that the Maynooth Synod of 1956 (S. 311), rules that any appeal for a pious or church purpose in a public paper must have the permission of the place of publication. This permission should be printed with the appeal itself.

With appreciation for your care in referring this matter to us,
Yours, etc.

[On 18 July 1963 the Bishop of Limerick, Henry Murphy, gave
permission 'subject to the permission of the Bishop of the place of
publication'].

17. Leon O C. to J.C. Bushe, 30 July 1963–

Thank you for your letter of 20th inst. concerning Mr Sexton's
proposed advertisement. His Grace agrees to the advertisement, but
asked if it could be altered as I have it in the enclosed page.
Again, with many thanks for your care.
I remain, etc.

18. JCM to Vivion de Valera, 11 Jan. 1968 –

Personal
My dear Viv,
May I ask you to study p. 10 of yesterday's *Evening Press*.
One reads: "The important thing about Mary is that her Son turned
out so well". I am shocked by such a statement.
In effect, this is blasphemy. It is suggested that God made Man
could have "turned out" other than well.
With kind wishes,
I remain,
Yours very sincerely.

19. JCM to Angela McNamara, 28 Sept. 1968 –

Dear Mrs. McNamara,
I am grateful for your note.
If I may, I shall retain the enclosures for a few days.
You will remember that I did refer at Lent to the growing
sensuality of these magajines [*sic*], but it is for you women to act

with courage, openly.

I cannot see how you can be prevented from making representations to your Editor, by the mere fact that you are yourself a contributor.

With kind wishes,

I remain, etc.

20. [Anon] to JCM, 7 Oct. 1969 –

Your Grace,

I wish to draw your attention to this "Irish" Magazine. I realise the moral harm such advertising has on a Christian country. Can any thing [sic] be done to stop this barrage of sex on our young people. Every magazine published in our country is imported or geared to sex. The result being there is no Christian modesty or Christian restraint or discipline among our young couples – even in public.

Has Your Grace ever been to a dance hall in Dublin during any celebrations or festivities – such as an all Ireland Final?

I certainly would not like any daughter of mine to attend such a function.

Catholic Dublin Girl

(23 years old – engaged).

21. JCM to Louis McRedmond, Dundrum, 2 March 1970 –

Dear Mr McRedmond,

Kindly pardon my delay in answering but my work obliged me to be absent for some time.

I thank you – and your Editor – for the suggestion that a series of articles on me and my episcopate should appear in the *Irish Times*. Your Editor is correct in thinking that you would be a competent person, for, at least you would wish to be just and you are, by your education, fitted to undertake such a task.

But I fear that your Editor, for all the good intentions that I am willing to allow him in this instance, would give you a quite impossible task.

Unless you had access to my private archives you could not describe my episcopate. They will remain closed for long after my death. And they will contain many surprises for those who have already attempted to assess my years as Archbishop of Dublin.

You could, of course, state what you have already come to believe is my character. But, you will readily understand that, as you graciously suggest you would first show me your text, I could not sanction the praise you might think it necessary to apportion. The blame that you would find in me, I would at once allow to pass without comment. Both you – and your Editor cannot fail to know that I have not yet answered when I was blamed or even reviled. I do not intend to change. All that side of one's life can be very safely left in the hands of God.

You will, I hope, now understand that it is not merely an encroachment on my time, as you kindly suggest, that would make your task impossible.

And, with respect, I do not see at all that the articles "would be valuable in helping many people to appreciate an important chapter in the history of the Irish Church". You are kind to write in such a strain, but I must wait for the judgment of God on that chapter, a merciful judgment, I hope, for myself and for all with whom I have had to deal or who have dealt with me.

With kind wishes,

I remain,

Yours sincerely,

+John C. McQuaid.

22. Memo from Fr. D. Williams to J.A. MacMahon, 7 April 1970

Subject: Censorship

I had a phone call from Monsignor O'Connell asking His Grace's

direction concerning the May issue of REALITY.[25]
Monsignor told me that in the March issue Father Wadding wrote
an article in which he queried the Sunday Mass obligation as
binding under mortal sin. Subsequently, in the April issue, Father
Seery wrote a letter (under Dr. Curtin's guidance) in which he
outlined the traditional moral theology on this question. The May
issue has now reached Father Stephen Green and in it Father
Wadding has submitted a letter in which he criticises the Sunday
Mass Law but does not deny it. He admits that Father Seery's
view is not the traditional view but questions the motivation for
attending the Sunday Mass. He also quotes from Father Haring in
support of his rather "fuzzy" letter. Both the Monsignor and
Father Greene consider that it is the lesser of two evils to allow
this letter to be published in REALITY. If it is not published,
Father Haring may take his case elsewhere and John Horgan who
is on the Editorial Board of REALITY would certainly take up
the matter in the *Irish Times*.

The Archbishop asked me to phone the Monsignor and say that
he agrees that the letter should be let through but to ask him to
try and find some way of pointing out that the motivation is not
in question and is truly a red herring. It is the actual law of
Sunday Mass that is the issue in this correspondence.

[Note by JCM on memo 'Acknowledge with thanks 16/4/70'].

23. JCM to Rev. Joseph Dunne of the Communications Centre, 3 Sept. 1970 -

I note your paper Intercom is publishing sermons on doctrinal
matters of Faith and Morals.
I shall require that the text of such publications be submitted to
the Ordinary of this Diocese, in advance of circulation.
I am, etc.

24. Rev. Joseph Dunne to JCM, 10 Sept. 1970 –

My Lord Archbishop,

Thank you for your kind letter directing that the sermons in "Intercom" should be submitted for publication.

As I am sure Your Grace is well aware, it is difficult to get priests to submit sermon material at all, never mind well in advance of publication. When the sermons are tied to a particular Sunday, there is also a critical deadline for printing and distribution. In view of these factors I think it important for us to have a censor who would not have many other censorship commitments, and who could review and return material quickly. I will be happy to hear whom Your Grace will suggest.

Once again, may I express personally our gratitude for Your Grace's support in the recent collection. The final returns are not in, and are unlikely to be before the end of the bank strike. However, a fairly accurate forecast would be in the region of £125,000. It is a lot of money – the only pity is that so much of it has to go on paying off debts.

With every good wish,

I remain, etc.

Cinema

25. John Costelloe, Hon. Sec. National Council of the Federation of the Catholic Young Men's Society of Ireland to JCM, 25 March 1948 –

Your Grace,

The Central Committee have been in communication with the Film Censor's Office regarding the forthcoming production of a Film entitled "Duel in the Sun"[26] which has been advertised for showing in one of Dublin's leading Cinemas.

Your Grace is no doubt aware that this Film was condemned very strongly by some of the American Bishops on the ground of its indecent tendency with the result that the Central Committee wrote to the Irish Film Censor enquiring the circumstances which made it possible for the film to be passed by his office and shown in Dublin.

I enclose for Your Grace's information a copy of a letter which I received from the Censor.

The Central Committee is disposed to accept the invitation contained in the letter, but having regard to the condemnation of the American Bishops we believe that Your Grace might desire to have the film viewed by a priest who would report his opinion therein to Your Grace. If this belief is correct perhaps Your Grace would forward the name and address of a Priest to the Film Censor's Office, Harcourt terrace, Dublin.

I have the honour to remain,

Your Grace's Most Obedient and Humble Servant,

John Costelloe.

[Letter is annotated on 27 March 1948 by JCM, 'HG desires me to thank you and to assure you that he has already been active in the matter. The AB considers, in the circumstances, that it would be better for your Assoc. to invite a priest, on your own responsibility, to view the film. The AB. will take the measures that he himself considers best'.]

26. Joseph Deery to JCM, 16 July 1955 –

My dear Lord Archbishop

I have the honour to submit to Your Grace some contents on the films exhibited for the Grand Prix of the O.C.I.C. [International Catholic Cinema Conference].

I saw all the films and discussed them with individual members of the Jury. Their award was governed by their interpretation of the terms of reference. These may need some modification, for it seems incongruous that a film which needs cutting by a State Censor should be given a Catholic award, especially when there is an entirely unobjectionable alternative, which is technically well done.

Such a film was available in "Marcelino, Pan y Vino". The Jesuit on the Jury disliked it because of its [illegible], whose sole purpose he held to be the trivial one of saving the Franciscan community from eviction; another considered it "niais". I wondered would they have thought differently if it had been centred round their order. However, the majority evidently ruled it out as being "unsuitable for a non-Catholic audience," though since then it has got 2nd prize in Berlin.

Only two other films were able to avoid a [sic] embrace in the telling of their story.

One was "Le Defroqué", which left Mr. Tom Sheehy limp, but which the Canadian priests said was shown in Quebec, in its entirety, without shocking or scandalising the faithful. The other was a Danish film, "Ordet" with the best photography of all. It was profoundly religious, but absolutely Protestant. The scene in it was an accouchement, resulting in the death of both baby and mother. The Chairman of the Jury considered it very discreet; to me it was horrible: the agonised cries of the mother struck the same note that is constantly being stressed in modern fiction.

Of the other films, "Marty" and "[On] The Waterfront" had cuts which caused the Jury no qualms, though they would probably be shown uncut elsewhere. An English film, "The divided heart" dealt with the struggle for possession of a boy between his adopted mother and his real mother (believed dead) . . . the sympathy appeared to be weighted in favour of the adoptive mother. The Abbé Pierre story "Les chiffoniers d'Emmaus" was hardly up to the technical standard of the others, but gave a magnificent film, marred by one embrace. Can no other means be devised of signifying love?

I hope Your Grace's address to the Congress will bring about a

change in O.C.I.C. standards. In my opinion, it is needed.
I remain, etc.

[Handwritten comment by JCM, – 'Quite clearly the standards are not fully Catholic in my way of thinking. Have you seen Fr. Burke's Tablet article in which I am bracketed with the State Censor as, in effect, a fool. +J.C. 18.7.55'].

27. L. Donoghue to Sec. Archbishop's House, [March]1956

Dear Reverend Father,
It is our intention to bring in to the Schools a Film Show of the various All Ireland Hurling and Football Finals covering the period 1947 to 1955.
We have been requested by a Parish priest to contact you to obtain the necessary permission from His Grace for the showing of these films in the various schools in the diocese.
These films being of the National games and their outlook being on sound moral grounds, we feel that it would be helpful in the formation of the character of our future citizens.
If we can be of any further assistance please ring 336744.
Yours , etc.

28. JCM to L. Donoghue, 22 March 1956 –

Dear Sir,
I have been directed to reply that His Grace the Archbishop does not consider the request advisable, inasmuch as the Schools are disturbed by every such intervention and there are other means of showing films to the children.
Yours, etc.

29. Leo Quinlan to JCM, 21 May 1962 –

Your Grace,
The film censor, Mr O'Hara, wishes to inform Your Grace that he
has had the film of Graham Green's "The Power and the Glory"[27]
submitted for censorship. He intends to reject it, but asks if Your
Grace would care to view it [Comment by JCM –'No desire']. Sir
Laurence Olivier is cast as the priest.
The picture was made in America for television and
simultaneously filmed for the Cinema in Europe [Comment by
JCM – 'Very glad to see it thrown out'].
Leo Quinlan
Addenda 23 May –
Mr O'Hara said he had rejected it and the Appeal Board was
seeing it on Friday. There were 2 non-Catholics on that who only
objected to the violence in the film but not to sexual immorality.

*30. Editor of Irish Catholic, "the voice of the Irish", to JCM, 11
Jan. 1963*

Your Grace,
I write at the request of our Film Critic respectfully to draw your
attention to the presentation in a Dublin cinema of a nudist film
and to point out that this raises a big problem for all reviewers.
The fact that this film, though rejected by the Film Censor, was
passed by the Appeal Board suggest that the members of the latter
see nothing objectionable in the presentation of nude figures on
the screen and their being paraded before adolescent and child
audiences.
In common with other reviewers, our Critic was forced to
exercise restraint in viewing this film lest by giving it too much
publicity more harm than good would be done. They expect to be
faced with a similar problem later since once it becomes known
that nudity is permitted on Dublin screens there are other films of

a more blatant type waiting to be allowed in.

I have taken the liberty of enclosing herewith copy of a letter received from a reader who seems to consider inadequate references previously consulted by him about the Catholic attitude to nudity, especially in the film as an art form.

Both our Film Critic and I would welcome from Your Grace a comment on the issue involved in the passing of a nudist film as suitable for presentation before adults. In particular we would welcome – should Your Grace think well of it – a comment (not necessarily your own) which could be quoted as an authoritative guide on the matter,

Yours, etc.

[Handwritten draft on letter by JCM – 'Ansd. 14.1.63. This film got through in my absence. I have taken effective action against it. Saw Mr O'Flynn, Chief Knight and will have Laymen all over Ireland alerted to reject it quietly'].

[This letter enclosed with the letter from the *Irish Catholic* –]

Dear Sir,

I am after reading your remarks in the "IRISH CATHOLIC" [*sic*] on the film "Adam and Eve". I have not seen this film. I have a problem and as you appear very confident about the rights and wrongs of nudity, perhaps you can help me. My problem is this, I have been more or less "brought up" to regard nudity as an evil, which I feel is not correct. I would like to know why the portraying of nude figures in stone or on canvas are regarded as "art" yet on film or "in the flesh" (excuse the expression as necessary) are regarded as evil. As a realist I prefer photography to painting or sculpture. I do feel there can be beautiful film incorporating nude figures. There are many questions in my mind on the entire subject and I would love to get the Catholic Church's teaching on the subject. Any reference I have ever come across was not much use. At school, my teacher had produced paintings of various biblical themes. One was of Adam and Eve after the fall, very well covered with many fig leaves! I have a friend who is a reasonably able painter and has quote a few painting of nude figures, which he keeps at home. He does not hide these from his children and considers that to do so would be wrong. He feels that children should not be forced to form an unhealthy curiosity in "the opposite sex" and that this is a help to them in that they too will be "open" about any nude pictures, etc., that comes into their hands at school, etc., and he can advise them on "good" pictures and "bad pictures". Is my friend acting wisely? I will be obliged if you can answer my questions or pass my letter to someone who can.

I am a Catholic and my age is 28.

Yours, etc.

31. Margaret Conron to JCM, 29 July 1967 –

My lord Archbishop,

I would like to draw your attention to a film at present showing in the Academy Cinema, Pearse St – "The Pawnbroker". There are some very objectionable and suggestive scenes of nude women in this picture which in my opinion are not fit for young people of 18 yrs of age.

Incidently, I myself am in my 30s so don't think I am what some people would call sq. [square].Hoping I'm not wasting your valuable time as I don't often get to pictures but I thought you should know about this.

Hoping you are very well.

Yours, etc.

32. Draft by JCM to [Anon], 1 Nov. 1967 –

My dear Father,

I believe you will soon be asked to see the Ulysses film on appeal.

It is psychotic in its blasphemy and dirtiness. I cannot see any pagan allowing such a flood of dirt to flow over a people.

The opening scene is a subtle parody of the Mass and the definition of the Real Presence: which might be missed without the script.

With kind wishes, etc.

33. Undated memo by JCM on censorship –

1. I consider that a more strict moral classification is not necessary for Catholics. State censorship.
2. I would suggest no sanctions.
3. Present system is working excellently on the whole. Nat. Film Inst. is setting up a panel of reviewers.
4. Five, out of seven large cinema managers are K. of C. [Knights of Columbanus] Cinema renters are very different: English, Jewish, Catholic. Rank's organisation is controlled by a Catholic.
5. On 22nd I am seeing Mr Ryan who will be back from consultation in England and Scotland.

34. Sheila O'Flanagan to JCM, 27 April 1970 –

Dear Father,

You, I am quite sure, are well aware that many parents are very worried about the rather erotic films being shown in Dublin recently. I mean films like "A woman in love" so harshly criticised by Gerald O'Reilly in the *Evening Herald*.

Ordinary parents can do very little on their own except wring their hands. In fact many who consider the unfortunate Late Late Show as the source of all evils; have no idea what kind of films their older children are being subjected to.

Maybe a quiet word in their ear at Sunday Mass might do no harm. Thunder and [?] from the altar went out with high buttoned boots, but is silence always golden? I don't think St. Paul would approve.

Sincerely, etc.

P.S. Please forgive any errors in spelling – not my strong point.

35. Memo from J.A. MacMahon to JCM, 19 April 1971

Re: M.A.S.H.[28]

Your Grace,

I went to see this film, and found they had in fact not fully cut the scenes parodying the Last Supper. I mentioned the fact to Father Richard O'Donoghe [sic], whom was very surprised. His understanding was that the scene was to have been fully cut, and that all the Appeal Board were agreed on this. He is taking up the matter with Judge Conroy and the other members of the Board. I do not believe that this film on its own will do damage in any decisive sense. The parody scene follows one in the film of Bunuel, La Viridiana, which was not shown in this country. These so called black humour films are in vogue, and that it is likely that there will be more such parodies of religion. The parody in M.A.S.H. is only part of a satire on the U.S. army in Korea.

J.A. MacMahon.

Theatre

36. Jack Lynch[29] to JCM, 29 Nov. 1957 –

My Lord Archbishop,

I received your letter of 19th instant and also the parcel of books. I regret that I did not have an opportunity of showing them to my colleagues at the Government meeting on Friday, the 22nd instant, but I did show them to the Minister for Justice. I left the books with him and asked him to see if he could take any action in respect of the importation of these publications.

With regard to the discussion on the contentious matter of Tóstal plays, you may be sure that I fully appreciated your position. I since mentioned the matter to Mr Boland and he has asked me to convey his re-assurance that he fully understood the situation and that he regretted, as I did, any embarrassment that might have been caused to you.

I shall have the books returned to you personally, later.

I have the honour to be, My Lord,

Your obedient servant'.

37. Draft of letter from JCM to the T. A. Boyle, Secretary of the Dublin Tóstal Council, 7 November 1957 –

Dear Sir,

In your letter of 21st Oct. you requested from H.G. the Ab. permission to have a Solemn mass to initiate the proceedings of the Dublin Tostal, 1958. HG. in answer asked you to approach the V.R . [Very Reverend] Admistrator of the pro-Cathedral to have the facilities formally given for a Low Mass.

HG.Ab. wishes to know whether it is correct that your Council has sanctioned the production in Dublin of a stage version of "Ulysses" and of a play by Mr Sean O'Casey during the Tostal period, 1958.

I am, etc.

38. Memo from JA MacMahon to JCM, 11 Nov. 1957 –

Your Grace,

The Lord Mayor's Secretary phoned at 3.45 p.m. to ask for Father Tuohy's address or phone number. Then the Secretary said that the Lord Mayor wished to speak to me.

The Lord Mayor said he was anxious to have Fr. Tuohy's address in order to communicate with him concerning the two plays proposed for the Tostal.

The position was that the Lord Mayor did not wish to have in the City any plays that would reflect discredit on it. He had prepared a letter for the Tostal Council to that effect. Likewise Mr Brennan felt strongly on the matter to the extent that he was prepared to resign from the Council if these two plays are sanctioned... The Lord Mayor said that he wanted to explain his position.

39. JCM to Fr. Patrick Tuohy , 13 Nov. 1957 –

My dear Father Tuohy,
I fear that the opinion expressed by you in regard to the choice of "Ulysses" by the Dublin Tostal is being regarded as the opinion of Archbishop's House, because Father Martin recommended the Lord Mayor to consult you, without my knowledge.
I would like you to take means to remove any such misunderstanding, for I shall feel obliged to take very definite action if either Ulysses or O'Casey's play be chosen by the Tostal. The "Rose Tattoo" ought to have been a lesson to the Tostal.
With kind wishes,
I remain, etc.

40. Fr P. Tuohy to JCM, 14 Nov. 1957 –

My Lord Archbishop,
I wish to thank Your Grace for your kind letter, which I received this morning.
I am extremely sorry that you have been disturbed by what I have been represented as saying in reply to the enquiry by the Lord Mayor on the proposal of the Dublin Tostal Council to produce plays by Joyce and O'Casey.
I should explain that my reply to the query by the Lord Mayor was simply a conditional and private opinion to the effect that if the scripts contained nothing objectionable, there should be no objection to their production.

Since Your Grace has been misrepresented as giving approval to the selection of these plays, I shall take immediate steps to clarify the position.

With renewed apologies,

I remain, etc.

41. *T.A. Boyle, Sec. to Dublin Tostal Council to J.A.MacMahon, 15 Nov. 1957*

Dear Rev. Secretary,

I am to acknowledge receipt of your letter of the 7th instant and to state that the first paragraph, confirming that His Grace the Archbishop of Dublin allowed me to approach the Very Rev. Administrator of the Pro-Cathedral to request a Low Mass on the occasion of the opening of An Tostal 1958, is noted.

Referring to the information sought in the second paragraph of this letter I am to inform you that my Council has sanctioned the production of a dramatisation of Joyce's "Ulysses" and of a play by Sean O'Casey during the Tostal period 1958.

Thanking you,

Yours, etc.

42. *Draft by JCM of letter to T.A. Boyle, 28 Dec. 1957*

Dear Sir,

I have been directed by His Grace the Archbishop to acknowledge the receipt of your letter stating that your Council has sanctioned the production in Dublin of a dramatisation of Joyce's Ulysses and of a play by Sean O'Casey, during the Tostal period, 1958.

His Grace the Archbishop directs me to inform you that permission for a religious ceremony, more particularly for the celebration of the Holy Sacrifice of the Mass, in connection with the Dublin Tostal 1958, is hereby withdrawn.

I am, etc.

43. Memo to JCM, 3 Jan. 1957 [sic]

Father O'Regan has asked me to inform Your Grace that he has had the following telephone conversation with Charles Brennan: Father O'Regan; that Mr Charles Brennan had telephoned him to say that the Dublin Tostal Council at a meeting on the previous day had decided to withdraw their sponsorship of the two plays referred to.

Mr Brennan expressed the hope that the matter would be so handled by the Lord Mayor and the Dublin Tostal Council that unwelcome publicity would be avoided.

The Lord Mayor, according to Mr Brennan, was to communicate with Your Grace.

44. Memo to JCB, 10.15 a.m., 6 Jan. 1958

10.15 – Mr Charles Brennan telephoned me to say that he had been asked to take over matters concerning the two plays under discussion. He had been asked to do so by the Lord Mayor, and as the press had been making enquiries, he would like to discuss them. I reported the matter to His Grace and enquired if I should see Mr Brennan, and was told to do so. I made an appointment to see Mr Brennan at 11.30 this morning. Mr Brennan came as arranged.

45. Memo from JA MacMahon to JCM, 14 Jan. 1958 –

Tostal plays 1958
Mrs Rapple's query by telephone, 14 Jan. 1958. Mrs Rapple explained that she was in charge of a group of actors who are producing two plays for the Festival. One was Synge's "The Tinker's wedding". Could I please give her a ruling on the play. I replied that was not a matter for the telephone.

Mrs Rapple said that a priest figured in the play who wanted money before he would wed the tinkers. She would not like to put on the play if it should cause controversy.

I asked Mrs Rapple to write her query and enclose the script.

[Comment by JCM – 'No. To ask for the script is to suggest that AB's House is going to act as censor']

Mrs Rapple to be informed that if she has any doubts of conscience she should consult her Parish Clergy.

46. Memo to JCM, 14 Jan 1958

Father O'Grady S.J. Provincial, rang to ask that it be conveyed to your Grace that he had directed the Rector of Gardiner St to refuse the application of the Theatre Festival Committee of the Tostal for permission to stage a play of Beckett's in the new St Francis Xavier Hall.

Draft reply by JCM on memo –'Ansd. I am very grateful. It is significant that you are the first to uphold me in my resistance to the Dublin Tostal's production of Joyce and O'Casey. 14.1.58'].

47. John Dunne, Dublin Council of Irish Unions to Archbishop's House, 15 Jan. 1958

Very Reverend and Dear Father,

At a meeting of the above Council held last night, the question of the An Tostal programme was discussed, arising from the publication of an item of news appearing in Irish and English newspapers of last Sunday's date.

We have written to the Secretary of Tostal, asking if it is the intention of that body, to stage plays of an objectionable nature, as part of Festival programme.

In view of the newspaper reports referred to above, I am to ask has there been a decision made by His Grace, Most Rev. Dr. McQuaid, with regards to the celebration of Solemn Votive Mass for the opening of An Tostal.

I remain, etc.

48. Draft by JCM to Mr John Dunne, 17 Jan. 1958

Dear Mr Dunne,

I am asked by HGaB. to acknowledge the receipt of your letter of the 15th inst., and to state, in answer to your query, the following facts.

The secretary of the Dublin Tostal Council requested permission for a Solemn Votive Mass to inaugurate the Tostal. HG. gave permission to approach the very Rev. Administrator of the Pro-Cathedral to have celebrated a Low Mass, as on a previous occasion.

Then, having learned from the Dublin Tostal Council that it had sanctioned the production in Dublin of a dramatisation of Joyce's Ulysses and of a play by Sean O'Casey, HGaB. withdrew permission for any religious ceremony, more especially, for the celebration of the Holy Sacrifice of the Mass, in connection with the Dublin Tostal of 1958.

I am, etc.

49. T.A. Boyle to Archbishop's House, 17 Jan. 1958 –

Dear Rev. Secretary,

I am directed by the Dublin Tostal Council to refer to your letter of 28th December 1957 advising that His Grace the Archbishop had decided not to allow the celebration of the Holy Sacrifice of the Mass in connection with the 1958 Dublin Tostal.

The Council has learned of His Grace's decision with much regret particularly as the Council, in considering and deciding on the presentation of the two plays mentioned in your letter, had made arrangements from the beginning to ensure that their content and stage presentation could not fairly be regarded as objectionable. I should like to assure you that these arrangements are being fully implemented.

Yours, etc.

50. Joseph Rogers [Bishop of Killaloe], to JCM, 20 Jan. 1958 –

<u>Private and confidential</u>

Your Grace,
Yesterday I had a visit from Mr. Brendan O'Regan, Director of
Bórd Fáilte. Your Grace will remember him as a student in
Blackrock College. Mr. O'Regan is very disturbed over the
proposal to produce at the coming Tostal a dramatised version of
"Ulysses" and Sean O'Casey's "Drums of Father Ned". The main
cause of his anxiety is the fact that Bórd Fáilte has, as usual, given
a grant in aid to the Dublin Tostal Council for dramatic and
ancillary productions. In view of the very correct and laudable
stand taken by Your Grace Mr. O'Regan is afraid that a
controversy will arise and that Bórd Fáilte will suffer as a result.
When I asked him why Bórd Fáilte has sanctioned a grant towards
the production of the above mentioned plays he stated that the
Bórd Fáilte proper is only a part-time body, with a full time
Executive in Dublin, and that it was the latter who really dealt
with the matter.
He was anxious to see Your Grace in person. I told him that for
the present, at any rate, it would be better if Bórd Fáilte kept
completely out of the affair lest the old charge of "Rome rule" be
raised once again: that at the moment the matter rested between
Your Grace and the Dublin Tostal Council.
After discussing the problem we agreed that he should submit the
following three questions to a panel of three viz. Gabriel Fallon,
Seamus Wilmot and Roger McHugh.

1. Are the proposed plays offensive to Catholics, or do they
   contravene Catholic doctrine or belittle Catholic morals?
2. Are these plays likely to cause public controversy or even
   disturbance?
3. What is their literary value? Are they "good theatre" in the real
   meaning of the term, and can they be regarded as truly
   representing Irish life and Irish cultural and social conditions!

If the panel answer is "no" to the last question and "yes" to the first two questions Mr O'Regan would then ask that the grant be withdrawn, as it is the stated policy of the Board that all [matters] likely to cause public controversy be avoided.

As I am not acquainted with any of the "experts" whom Mr. O'Regan proposes to consult I cannot say what answers they will give to the questions submitted. Neither can I say what Mr. O'Regan can do if opinions are divided. I warned Mr. O'Regan that he was not to mention to anybody that he had approached me, and I told him that I would acquaint Your Grace concerning the matter of our talk. As an excellent Catholic he is totally opposed to the proposed production of those plays – as Director of Bórd Fáilte he fears that public controversy may prove harmful to that body. He sincerely wishes that they could be quietly withdrawn, and fully agrees that they should never have been put forward.

I hope Your Grace can follow what I have written. It is not easy to make it quite clear in a short letter.

Very kind regards and good wishes,

Yours, etc.

51. JCM to Joseph Rogers, 21 Jan. 1958

Confidential

My dear Lord Bishop,

I am very grateful for Your Lordship's kind note.

Brendan O'Regan could not be expected to act in any but a decent way about the Tostal plays: he is a good lad and always was. No matter what questions may be put to a panel of dramatic experts, no matter what answers are given, the Holy Sacrifice may not be linked with Joyce or O'Casey.

The Tostal Council had weeks to consider the Question and has decided to retain the plays: it takes the consequences of its own decision.

Your Lordship will realise that I understand at once your letter and why it was written and am very glad to hear from you.
With kind regards,
I remain, etc.

52. Joseph Rogers to JCM, 22 Jan. 1958 –

Your Grace,
I thank you for your very kind letter received this morning.
Brendan O'Regan's idea in having his questions examined by a panel of dramatic experts is this. If they are of the opinion that the plays in question do not merit production by An Tostal, then Bórd Fáilte would withdraw the subsidy already allocated to this Dublin Council. Fortified with this opinion Bórd Fáilte could not be accused of having acted under any "ecclesiastical presence" in withdrawing the grant.
Your Grace's refusal to have the Holy Sacrifice of the Mass linked with Joyce and O'Casey is warmly commended everywhere in Catholic circles.
Cordial good wishes and kind regards,
Yours, etc.

53. T.A. Boyle, Secretary Dublin Tostal Council to Secretary Archbishop's House, 21 Jan. 1958 –

Dear Rev. Secretary,
At a meeting of the Dublin Tostal Council held this evening the Council considered it would be advisable, in view of recent newspaper reports regarding the International Theatre Festival, to issue a Press Release.
The Council feels that as His Grace the Archbishop is mentioned in the enclosed draft release perhaps His Grace at this stage might be prepared to approve this press release or may wish to offer his comments on same.

The favour of an early reply would be greatly appreciated.
Yours, etc.

[Enclosed draft release −]
Draft press release
It has come to the notice of the Dublin Tostal Council that there
may be a certain amount of misunderstanding amongst some
members of the general public regarding the proposed Festival of
Dublin, 1958.
In order to clarify the position the members of the Dublin Tostal
council wish at the outset to assure the Dublin public that their
only desire is to present an International Theatre Festival worthy
of the capital city and of the country as a whole.
At no time has His Grace the Archbishop objected to the
inclusion in the programme of any of the plays already
announced. The members of the Dublin Tostal Council, who are
all voluntary workers, have given much of their time to the
consideration and final selection of productions which would have
the immediate support of the Dublin public as well as that of
audiences from abroad.
When it is considered that the 1958 Festival will rely for
practically 80% of its support from the Dublin public, it can
readily be realised that productions which in any way might
interfere with that support would be automatically avoided. As a
matter of fact precautions were taken from the beginning to
ensure that the programme items selected would not only be
attractive to the foreign visitor but also would not be
objectionable in any way to the Dublin public.
Being aware of this situation, and mindful of the magnificent
support afforded by the Dublin public last year to the Festival
programme, the Dublin Tostal Council would like to correct any
feeling that anything of an offensive nature would be included in
the 1958 programme.
In terms of dramatic writing, the Irish contribution to-date is

from Goldsmith, Beckett, Shaw, O'Casey and Joyce, all names of repute in the literary and/or theatrical world, the latter four writers being Dubliners.

The "Ulysses" adaptation is a free adaptation from – not "of" – the book by Alan McClelland, and entitled "Bloomsday". The decision to include it in the programme was based on many factors, not least being that the book is world famous, and, in the contemporary sense, is regarded as a classic of English literature. Goldsmith, Shaw, Beckett, and O'Casey are all classified as international writers and their plays are performed regularly in Dublin and throughout the country with great success. The Council was advised by Bord Failte Eireann that in promotional work abroad the inclusion of works by these writers would be an asset.

The policy of the Dublin Tostal Council has been to ensure, through its Director and other available sources, and also in consultation with appropriate authorities, that (a) only works of Festival quality and (b) only works that could be fairly considered to contain nothing of an offensive character, would be included in the Theatre Festival programme. As already announced, negotiations as to production and casting are progressing for the presentation of "Bloomsday" by the Edwards/MacLiamoir Company and the new O'Casey play by the Dublin Globe Company.

The Dublin International Theatre Festival was launched successfully in 1957. If it is to continue as a permanent feature, it must have the whole-hearted co-operation of the Dublin public, so generously provided in 1957. The Dublin Tostal Council are working in the interests of the public to provide a Theatre Festival worthy of our national theatrical traditions.

54. J.A. MacMahon to T.A. Boyle, Secretary of Dublin Tostal Council, 22 Jan. 1958 -

Dear Sir,

I am directed by His Grace the Archbishop to thank the Dublin Tostal Council for its courtesy in forwarding a copy of a proposed press release in which mention is made of the Archbishop.

The Archbishop regrets that he must take the gravest exception to the use of his name in the manner proposed.

His Grace gave permission for the celebration of Mass at the Pro-Cathedral to initiate the Dublin Tostal 1958.

Having learned of the intention of the Dublin Tostal Council to produce a dramatised version of Joyce's Ulysses and a play by Sean O'Casey in the Dublin Festival, His Grace inquired from the Secretary if it were correct to believe that the Dublin Tostal Council had sanctioned the production of these plays.

The Secretary replied that "his Council had sanctioned the production in Dublin of a dramatisation of Joyce's Ulysses and of a play by Sean O'Casey during the Tostal period, 1958".

His Grace, then, acknowledging the receipt of the Secretary's letter "stating that his Council had sanctioned the production in Dublin of a dramatisation of Joyce's Ulysses and of a play by Sean O'Casey during the Tostal period, 1958" withdrew permission "for a religious ceremony, more particularly for the celebration of the Holy Sacrifice of the Mass in connection with the Dublin Tostal, 1958".

It was, and remains, quite obvious, from the correspondence alone, that permission for a religious ceremony, more particularly for the celebration of the Holy Sacrifice of the Mass has been withdrawn, because the Archbishop had, on inquiry, been informed by the Secretary of the Dublin Tostal Council that his Council had decided to include in its Festival programme a dramatised version of Joyce's Ulysses and a play by Sean O'Casey.

I am, etc.

55. Draft by JCM of covering letter to religious Conferences, 21 Jan. 1958 –

My lord Bishop, My dear Monsignor,
I should be grateful if the following notice were read to the coming Conference, in order to correct the inexact reports of the newspapers.
With kind wishes,
I remain, etc.-

To correct the very inaccurate statements that have appeared in the daily Press, HGaB wishes the following statement to be read out at all the conferences.
On 21st October 1957 the Secretary of the Dublin Tostal Council requested permission for a Solemn Votive Mass to inaugurate the Dublin Tostal 1858. On 22nd October 1957 His Grace the Archbishop directed a reply be sent that the Secretary had permission to approach the Very Reverend the Administrator, the Pro-Cathedral, to arrange for a Low Mass to inaugurate the Dublin Tostal.
Having learned that it was proposed to include a dramatised version of Joyce's Ulysses and a play by Sean O'Casey in the Dublin Tostal Festival, the AB. had a letter sent the Secretary of the Dublin Tostal Council on 7th Nov.1957 asking if it were correct to believe that the Council had decided to include these plays.
The Secretary replied on the 15th November that his Council had sanctioned the productions in Dublin of a dramatisation of Joyce's Ulysses and of a play by Sean O'Casey during the Tostal period 1958. Having waited for some weeks, in the hope that better council would prevail, at length on 28th December, HGaB. wrote the Secretary of the Dublin Tostal Council as follows:

Text of letter
Dear Sir, etc.
On 2nd January a majority vote decided that the plays would be
cancelled. On 10th January, the Council stated that no changes are
envisaged in the preliminary programme...

56. Memo from Liam Martin to JCB, 11.15 a.m., 3 Feb. 1958

Mr Charles Brennan of the Tostal Council rang to speak to me.
He said that he had telephoned to inform me that a meeting of
the Tostal Council would be held this evening to decide finally
concerning the two plays, the dramatisation of Joyce's Ulysses and
that of O'Casey "The drums of Father Ned".
He said that the Council was very widely split on the matter. And
he thought that he might have a casting vote, or a decisive voice
in the matter.
He could not be certain if the plays as expurgated, or, rather,
planned as expurgated, would, if put on, have a good effect on the
Theatre Festival, since the foreign tourists would come expecting
sensationalism, and find none, and thus would not come again.
The whole affair might prove the ruin of the Festival. Again, if
they were put on as expurgated, even if they were attended, they
might induce people to read Joyce and O'Casey, out of curiosity.
He thought too much publicity had been given to the matter, and
that this had contributed to the difficulty... He said that he was
grateful, and that he would not act passively in the matter, as he
well could.

57. Memo from Liam Martin to JCB, 11.40 a.m., 3 Feb. 1958 -

Mr Charles Brennan telephoned again to say that he had it
indirectly and on very good authority that the Lord Mayor would
resign from the Council if the two plays were adopted.
Mr Brennan added that this would considerably add to the
controversy about the matter, as it would cause the matter to be

debated at the Corporation, and, eventually perhaps in the papers, etc.

58. JCM to Sir Lauriston Arnott, 21 Feb. 1958 –

Dear Sir Lauriston Arnott,
I should be grateful if you would do me the favour of calling at Archbishop's House.
If Monday, 24th inst. at 11.a.m. be suitable, I should be glad to see you. If the day and hour be inconvenient, I should be happy to learn what time would suit you.
I remain, etc.

59. Memo by JCM, [24 Feb. 1958] –

I had asked Sir Lauriston Arnott to call, by letter of 21st Feb.
Sir Lauriston Arnott called 11 a.m., 24th Feb. 1958.
Very gentlemanly, I explained the true position. Expressed disgust at the things that have appeared in the last 15 years in the Irish Times and great regret for the Tostal leader and letters.
Formerly his family had a controlling interest.
Asked if I would see Newman, the Editor, I declined, saying that he was without excuse, for a journalist and a gentleman would first have ascertained the facts. I said similar causes for complaint had often arisen. Sir I said that he would do all he could to have the controversy stopped and to prevent any future cause for worry.

60. Joseph Walsh,[30] St Jarlath's Tuam to JCM, 12 Feb. 1958 –

My dear Lord Archbishop,
May I say this? This morning I read with deep interest the account of the meeting of the Dublin Council of Irish Unions.
Your Grace has done a big service to the whole country. I thank and congratulate you.
Very sincerely, etc.

61. Edward Clancy, Superior General, Christian Brothers, Marino, to JCM, 17 Feb. 1958 –

Your Grace,
Accept our very sincere congratulations on Your Grace's highly successful efforts to prevent the production of unsuitable plays in Dublin in connection with the coming Tostal festivities.
All here are very pleased with Your Grace's timely intervention in this matter thus preserving our moral standards worthy of our best traditions
With deep respect and much gratitude,
I remain, Your Grace's very devotedly in Christ,
Edward F. Clancy.
P.S. This needs no reply.

[Handwritten comment by JCM – 'Thank you for your encouragement, +J.C. 20.2.58'].

62. John J. Pigott to JCM, 27 Feb. 1958 –

My Lord Archbishop,
I enclose for Your Grace's information a letter I have just received from the Civil Liberty Association and would deem it a great favour if Your Grace would advise me as to whether I should accept or refuse this invitation.
I have the honour to remain, etc.

[Handwritten comment by JCM – 'I should think it a mistake to gratify the Association in its desire to debate the Tostal Theatre Festival. 28.2.58'].

63. Edgar M. Deale, Irish Association of Civil Liberty to JCM, 27 Feb. 1958 –

Your Grace,
We are arranging to have a public meeting in the Mansion House to discuss "Freedom in the Theatre" and have been given two dates by Dublin Corporation, the 15th March and the 11th April. We as an Association have no opinions in the matter, but we wish to provide a public forum for discussion.
We asked Fr. O'Donoghue of the Pro-Cathedral who is interested in the drama to be one of the speakers, but he has told us that he cannot do so without authority. We would be honoured if you would give the necessary permission, or if you would nominate another speaker. It is most important that at a public meeting of this type we present all sides of the question. With this in mind we have asked professor Pigott, late Chairman of the Censorship Board, Mr Allan McClelland of London and Mr. Brendan Smith[31] who is organiser of the Tostal Theatre Festival.
It would be greatly appreciated if we could have a reply from you at an early date as organisation of such a meeting as this takes some time.
Yours sincerely, etc.

64. Handwritten draft reply from JCM to E.M. Deale, 28 Feb. 1958 –

Dear Sir,
I am asked by HGaB. to acknowledge the receipt of your letter of the 27th inst.
HG. asks me to say that the AB. does not consider it advisable to give permission to any priest of his diocese to speak at the public meeting organised by the Irish Association of Civil Liberty to discuss "Freedom in the Theatre".
I am, etc.

65. A. Newman, editor of the Irish Times to JCM, 28 February 1958 –

Your Grace,

Sir Lewiston Arnott gives me to understand that my newspaper's reporting of the Theatre Festival has misinterpreted your conduct and has provoked your reasonable anger. May I assure you that any comment which this newspaper made was not directed against Your Grace, but against the tactlessness of the Tostal Council?

I would beg you to believe that such reference to Your Grace as occurred in the columns of the Irish Times was not deliberate, and that no disrespect was intended to Your Grace in person, or to your sacred office.

May I assure you of my deep and continued respect?

I am, etc.

66. JCM to A. Newman, 3 March 1958 –

Dear Mr Newman,

I am grateful for your gracious letter.

May I say that I never associated you with the unfair leader. I knew that you were the Editor, but Monsignor Deery had years ago assured me of your honourable attitude.

I have not sought – nor shall I seek – to know who is responsible. You would err, if you should think I was angry. In somewhat similar circumstances I met the late Editor, Mr. Smyllie. I should be glad to meet you, if you did not find it inconvenient.

With kind wishes,

I remain, etc.

67. Memo from J. A. MacMahon to JCM, 7 March 1958 –

Your Grace,

Doctor MacNevin phoned this morning to say the proposed

Meeting organized by the Civil Liberties Association on Freedom and the Theatre has been cancelled as a result of Your Grace's letter to Mr. Deale. Father O'Donoghue, C.C., Pro-Cathedral received a communication from Mr. Deale's Secretary to this effect.

Your Grace's obedient servant, etc.

68. Patrick J. Murphy, P.C. to JCM , 14 Feb. 1965

Dear Reverend Father,

Re: <u>Burtons to read poetry at Abbey</u>

The above quotation which headed a news item in the "Sunday Independent" of date, has surprised and shocked me. For quite some recent time past it has been considerably emphasised that the ordinary layman forms a very vital part of the Church. He is therefore encouraged to take an active part in Church affairs and to raise his voice when need arises.

In acceptance of this, may I, an ordinary layman, and the father of a large family, raise my voice in protest at the proposed recital. It is particularly objectionable that this proposed affair is in aid of a Catholic charity, namely the Medical Missionaries of Mary.

There is absolutely no doubt in my mind that while there may be a few individuals who would attend for purely artistic motives, the vast majority would be co-operating in the exploitation of the unsavoury record of the featured performers, particularly the female performer. I can assure you that I am expressing the views of quite a number of responsible individuals who believe that any Catholic charity that lends itself to such exploitation has sunk very low indeed.

Yours respectfully,

Patrick J. Murphy, P.C.

P.S. Although I am writing to you as a private individual I wish to assure you that I am a responsible Catholic. I am an active member of the Knights of Columbanus and hold a Diploma in Catholic Theology.

[Handwritten comment by JCM – 'The AB. was quite unaware of the project and would never have sanctioned it'].

69. Edward Golden, President and Dermot Doolan, Gen. Sec. Irish Actors' Equity Association, to JCM, 20 June 1966 –

My Lord Archbishop,

Representing Equity, the association of those professionally connected with the dramatic art in this country, we respectfully beg permission to draw your attention to certain aspects of the synodal restrictions on priests of this country from attending theatrical performances in commercial theatres. In doing so, we voice a very strong feeling shared by all our Catholic members – who constitute the majority in our association – but which is also common to their non-Catholic fellow members.

We are aware that priests are forbidden by Canon Law to attend 'scandalous theatrical performances', but we do firmly believe that in the Irish theatre as a whole such performances are very rare occurrences; and it is a prime object of our association to ensure that they do not occur at all. We know that when the synodal law was first introduced, the theatre in Great Britain and possibly in Ireland had reached nearly its nadir. We wonder, however, whether their Lordships, the Bishops, have adverted to the enormous changes which have taken place since then, and, in particular, during the present century, in the theatre, and to the status which the legitimate stage has now for several decades achieved in every civilised country in the world and not least of all, by any means, in our own. At the annual Retreats of the Catholic Stage Guild which very many of our members most gratefully attend, they are constantly assured that they belong to 'an honourable profession'. This, indeed, is our belief, and to safeguard that honourable status is the chief end of our organization. It therefore seems strange to us that priests are forbidden in Ireland to enjoy the benefits this honourable profession provides for society, when in many other Catholic countries they are allowed to do so.

In an age when the principal forms of popular entertainment are mechanical, largely imported, and for the most part geared to a low general level of intelligence, religious belief, and moral conduct, we should very greatly appreciate the active support and informed criticism of the most stable, learned and deeply concerned class of people in the country, namely, the clergy, in our endeavour to keep the theatre alive as an art-form and as a principal source of intellectual and intelligent entertainment. But support will mean little unless it can mean active support of our theatrical endeavours; and criticism will not be informed or helpful if priests cannot come to see the plays. We are well aware of the great part played by the clergy in encouraging and directing the amateur dramatic movement in this country at the present time; this awareness, however, only serves to make us realize more exactly and more keenly how greatly we should benefit, in the professional theatre, from their support. Further, it may be observed that in places where the theatre is truly alive and responsible, there is always a close link between the professional and the amateur stage, the latter often forming an excellent apprenticeship to the former, a valuable means of encouraging appreciation of dramatic art, and a potent factor in maintaining moral standards in the theatre. At the moment, as it seems to us, such a link might be more closely forged in Ireland and the benefits we have mentioned ensue, if the clergy were less restricted in regard to the professional theatre.

It is for all these reasons that we have decided to bring this matter to your grace's attention. We do so in the confident hope that it will meet with your Grace's sympathetic consideration.

We have the honour to be your Grace's most obedient servants, etc.

70. *Typed comment to JCM re letter from Golden and Doolan, 23 June 1966 –*

Your Grace,

I wish to thank Your Grace for showing me the letter from the Irish Actors' Equity Association.

I expect that Mr Golden and Doolan have turned to Your Grace following their visit here last year. They cannot have adverted to the fact that it is not within the power of any Irish bishop to dispense from the theatre law except in individual cases, and for a just reason. Only the Holy See could change the theatre through a new plenary council, or by special rescript.

Neither can they have adverted to the fact that statute 33 does not speak of scandalous theatrical performances, but only of theatrical performances. Theatre and horse and dog racing are described as pursuits that are unworthy of the clerical state.

Their request is interesting in the light of the statement that has often been publicly made that the Church is out of touch with artists in this country, particularly writers. Does statute 33 need to be reconsidered in the light of the Constitution on the Church in the modern world, as far as the theatre is concerned.

71. *Edward Golden, President and Dermot Doolan, Gen. Sec. Irish Actors' Equity Association, to JCM, 23 Feb. 1967 –*

My Lord Archbishop,

Further to our letter of 20th June, 1966, when we bought to your Grace's attention our request to have the restrictions on the clergy attending the commercial theatre waived, we would now very much appreciate a discussion with you concerning this matter and would be most grateful if a date could be arranged to suit you.

We have the honour to be your Grace's most obedient servants, etc.

[Handwritten draft response by JCM on letter – ' AB of D. thanks for courtesy of communication and wishes me to point out that the repeal of a Statute pertains to all the Hierarchy. 24.2.67'].

72. Anne Swaine [et al] from St Brendan's, Cross Ave., Blackrock [but on Gresham Hotel notepaper] to JCM, 3 Nov 1966

My lord Archbishop,
In common with many other members of the audience, we have been saddened and enraged to see Irish theatre, culture and moral standards debased by acceptance of a most corruptly suggestive, sexually "sick" play – Love and the bottle[?], in the Gate theatre, which runs until the end of this week. We feel that your Lordship would share our disgust at seeing our fellow country men and women laugh long and loud at a scene of open homosexuality, and several scenes showing a most unhealthy attitude towards sex. In common with a number of the audience we left the theatre before the end of the first act. We can do no more. We appeal to your lordship
Respectfully,
Anne Swaine, Dervila O'Brien, Ann Boyle (Aer Lingus hostesses).

73. Draft reply by JCM, 12 Nov. 1966, to Miss Swaine–

Dear Miss Swaine,
I am asked by HGaB. to ack. the receipt of your letter, and to thank you. HG. considers that you and your companions and the audience who attend the theatre could usefully correct the Irish theatre, if you took measures to express publicly your disapproval, being careful to base your disapproval on facts that can be proved on examination.
I am
J.A. McMahon.

74. *Frances Fearon of 466, Howth Rd., Raheny, Dublin 5 to JCM, 1 Oct. 1967 –*

My Lord Bishop,
On Friday last my husband and I went to the Abbey Theatre with a view to being entertained. Instead of that we were shocked, insulted and outraged at the fare being meted out to the public in the name of entertainment. Is there no censorship of the plays being produced in this, our Irish national Theatre? I can't believe that you, who have the morals of your people so sincerely at heart, are aware of the flood of filth being poured into the Abbey audience night after night. "The loves of Cass Maguire"[32] is a masterpiece in obscenity scurrility and nauseating lewdness. The author, a Belfast-man, must be an absolute gutter-rat, and the actress who portrays the part, the once-wonderful St Joan, Siobhán McKenna, is equally depraved. Her very posture is an insult to womanhood, the vile jokes and obscene language, which leave nothing to the imagination, an insult to the gifts of speech and hearing.
I am the mother of six children and very seldom have an opportunity to go out for a night's entertainment. Perhaps I am narrow-minded, restricted as I am to contact with the world outside my home, and it may be that this is the standard of entertainment which is acceptable nowadays. If so, I shudder to think of the future of my children; for the future of the country. No wonder our morals are deteriorating when such iniquitous poison is being poured into our minds in the name of Art. The devil is never short of a name for the sugar-coating. I trust your Grace will give a sympathetic hearing to my plea to have this play, and any other of a similar diabolical nature, banned from our Theatres.
I am, my Lord Bishop, your obedient servant,
Frances Fearon.

75. Draft response from JCM, to Frances Fearon [no date] –

AB deplores bad plays and has specifically spoken about them. Please thank but say that it is the lay-people who attend the theatre who ought to use every means of lawful protest.

76. [Anon] of Main Street, Tipperary to JCM, 16 Feb. 1968 –

Dear Archbishop McQuaid,
Maybe you would do something to stop the terrible language in the play in the Abbey by Brendan Behan. I was shocked and left after half time. It was positively a disgrace being full of vile language and blasphemy and the taking of the Holy Name. Five times during the first act the name – Jaysus; and everyone laughed. Then the following unmentionable words:- "Shite", "Horshit", "Feck", "Fuck", "Bastard" and many of these words were spoken to the priest in the play. This surely does not pass for literature. Is this Ireland's National Theatre, and built by the Ratepayers [*sic*] money? What would outsiders to our country think? I am a father, but I would be ashamed if I had brought any of the children to see that performance.
I will pray for you,
X.

Television

77. JCM to Canon Cathal McCarthy,[33] Holy Cross College Clonliffe, 8 Nov. 1961 –

My dear Canon McCarthy,
I should like to confirm the findings of our interview this morning.
1. I agree that each Sunday there should be a Catholic religious service, in the afternoon or evening, as a fixed feature.

2. Benediction of the Most Blessed Sacrament is the most suitable service.
3. The Bl. Sacrament can be brought from Our Lady's Hostel, opposite Montrose, on each occasion, quietly, with due reverence.
4. The apartment used as a temporary Oratory will be equipped, for the purpose, only as an Oratory, on the occasion. I trust you to see to it that the altar and its appointments are strictly liturgical, in good taste, preferably austere.
5. I trust you equally to exact, even with severity, a rehearsal of each and every religious ceremony performed at the Studio.
6. Of necessity, the question of a Studio Oratory of a permanent nature will arise. I am prepared to accept such an Oratory. The means of providing such an Oratory, the site, style of building and uses to which such an Oratory may be put are matters for future consideration.

I remain, etc.

78. Cathal McCarthy to JCM, 10 Nov. 1961 –

My Lord Archbishop,
I am really most thankful for the trouble Your Grace has taken and for the beautiful books. It must be a unique phenomenon for a Television authority to have an archbishop as production artist.
I remain, etc.

79. Memo by JCM, 12 Jan. 1963 –

Re: proposed televising of Jubilee Mass of De la Salle Wicklow.
I phoned Canon McCarthy, who was equally amazed at the proposal of Bro. Arcadius.
I asked Canon to insist with Telefís Eireann that no religious broadcast or telecast on T.E. be permitted without the Canon's sanction.

This is an absolute rule, binding on all Orders, Congregations or Societies, for divine worship in the exclusive care of the Archbishop. +J.C.

80. JCM to C. McCarthy, 15 Jan. 1962 –

My Dear Canon McCarthy,
I think it would help Telefís Eireann if it were understood that the text of every Recollection to be given by a Catholic priest must first be submitted to, and passed by you.
With good wishes,
I remain, etc.

81. C. McCarthy to JCM, 15 Jan. 1962 –

My Lord Archbishop,
Your Grace's direction regarding the censorship of priest's scripts will certainly be welcomed by Telefís Eireann and it will remove all difficulty from me when I am asked for a ruling. I am very grateful.
I remain, etc.

82. JCM to E.J. Roth,[34] 3 Oct. 1962 –

Dear Mr. Roth,
I have pleasure in informing you that at the meeting of the Hierarchy the question of Catholic policy in television was again fully considered.
At the request of the Hierarchy His Grace of Cashel and I to-day called on the Taoiseach to discuss a policy which involves the people of the whole country in regard to the Faith.
The Taoiseach will duly communicate with you and the Authority.
With my gratitude for your cooperation.
I remain, etc.

83. Dermot J. O'Flynn, from the Supreme Knight's Office of the Knight's of St. Columbanus Ireland, to JCM, 7 March 1962 –

My Lord Archbishop,
Please find enclosed a Report, from a reliable source, on certain key personnel in Telefís Éireann.
The mental outlook of the Liberals has been reflected in the Plays so far produced – the publicity given last week to The Plough[35] and its "ideal of extreme socialism" and, the selection of boys and girls from non-Catholic schools to tell us of the wonderful opportunities for youth "in this country" or to demonstrate their hobbies in woodwork.
Some members of our Boys Clubs would certainly have reflected more credit than the hobbies of pupils from Mountjoy School. There is an urgent need for the selection and training of an elite to recover these vital lines of communication of ideas to the general public.
I remain, etc.

[The enclosed reports contain comments on the religious affiliations, social and education backgrounds and political inclinations of the Chairman (Eamonn Andrews), the Director-General (Edward Roth), the Controller of Progammes (Michael Barry) –'all Catholics' – and sixteen producers – 'only four are Catholic'.]

84. Draft of letter by JCM to Kevin McCourt[36], 12 Dec. 1963 –

Dear Director-General,
I am to ask you, at the direction of HGaB. of Dublin, to be good enough to state of by whose authority the stranger-priest, Rev. Gregory Baum, O.S.A. was invited to speak and did speak in my Diocese on matters of Faith and morals.
I am, etc.

85. *Kevin McCourt to JA MacMahon, 17 Dec. 1963* –

Dear Father MacMahon,
I thank you for your letter of the 12th December. For the information of His Grace the Archbishop, Father Gregory Baum, O.S.A. was interviewed in a television Newsview programme on Wednesday, December 11th, in connection with the proceedings of the Ecumenical Council in Rome.
Since Father Baum is a well known expert on the ecumenical movement and was attached to the Council, it was taken for granted that he was well qualified to comment on the proceedings there.
The responsibility for using Father Baum's services, of course, rests with Radio Eireann but we would assume that, if he required ecclesiastical clearance to participate in a programme of the kind involved, this would be a matter between him and the ecclesiastical authorities.
Yours sincerely, etc.

Handwritten comment by JCM –'No answer sent, 18.12.63'].

86. *JCM to Kevin McCourt, 12 Feb. 1966*

Confidential
My dear Kevin,
I have just seen the Late, Late Show. I am afraid that it was, in part, really unworthy... And I think that Gay Byrne need not, for a second week, return to the Bunnies. I wonder if you saw Weekend's article and pictures describing the strange American who conceived the plan. You would not, I think, let it into the house.
I remain, etc.

87. Kevin McCourt to JCM, 15 Feb. 1966 –

Your Grace,

The generosity and kindness of your letter about last Saturday's Late Late Show moved me to distress that you should have had cause at all to write on such a matter… Television possesses some magnetism for risk-taking and for being racy, especially in the field of light entertainment. But be assured, please, that I do not tolerate the tawdry, the depreciation of what I believe to be the inherent good taste and instincts of the Irish people.

I knew of that "bunny" man[37] and thus had his intended appearance cancelled immediately the intention came to my notice.

Not infrequently, to my frustration, I cannot be the policeman of all I want and still manage a large and complex organisation; but the mistakes, believe me are more from inexperience, enthusiasm, and sometimes bad judgement rather than malice or misery of outlook.

I am greatly strengthened in my concern to do justice to Ireland in this field by Your Grace's guidance and understanding.

I remain, etc.

88. Desmond [?] Dublin to JCM, 29 Jan. 1966 –

Your Grace,

I wish to protest in the name of Catholic laymen and women at this later attempt of foreigners to recruit innocent Catholic girls for such base and degrading work in Britain (The Bunnies). God only knows what dangerous ways they may happen upon.

I request that you as Shepherd of the flock make representations to the Government to put a stop to this dangerous thing.

Yours sincerely, etc.

89. Cathal McCarthy to JCM, 14 March 1966 –

My Lord Archbishop,
I have been asked by Telefís Eireann to put a request before Your
Grace. It is that the monthly Mass from Montrose for the sick and
house-bound might be celebrated facing the people. A
consideration, real though of course secondary, is that such an
arrangement would greatly facilitate camera work.
It is hoped to have a fortnightly Mass within the next few weeks,
and eventually one every Sunday.

90. JCM to Fr. McCarthy, 23 March 1966 –

Dear Canon McCarthy,
I thank you for your letter.
I am at a loss to understand why my authority is invoked for the
rubrical change of saying Mass at Telefís Eireann facing the
people.
Benediction of the Blessed Sacrament – which I had inaugurated,
was eliminated; a new form of religious service was introduced;
sermons and discourses and discussions pertaining to religion have
all been undertaken at Telefís Eireann.
The authority of the Archbishop has not been sought for these
activities.
I remain, etc.

91. C. McCarthy to JCM, 6 May 1968 –

My Lord Archbishop
Mr Thomas Hardiman, the new Director General has asked me to
ask if Your Grace would be willing to see him. He would like to
pay his respects.
As a Member of the Hierarchy's Communications Council Mr
Hardiman has shown himself perceptive of Catholic interests in

broadcasting. In my opinion such an attitude will be sorely needed in this field.
I remain, etc.

[Handwritten draft comment by JCM, –'Yes. Met him on 1st and will see him again. We shall need him, in view of the strange things priests are doing on T.V. +J.C. 8.5.68'].

92. [Anon] to JCM, 12 Dec. 1971 –

Your Grace,
I respectfully bring to your attention last night's "Late, Late Show" when Father Michael Cleary came out very strongly, he should <u>be banned</u> by you from taking part in these shows, he is too much of a <u>"firebrand"</u>, and in fact you should <u>ban all priests</u> in taking part in these controversial topics.
The Church is going through hard times and it is time you should take a firm hand with your priests.
An Irish Catholic Mother.

Notes

1 The correspondence on censorship is mainly in the McQuaid Censorship, Arts & Culture files (Dublin Diocesan Archives, (DDA), AB/8/B/XXV) but there is additional material in the McQuaid communications files (DDA, AB/8/B/XXVI).
2 McQuaid papers, (DDA AB8/B/XXIII/1)
3 Alan Hayes (ed.) *Hilda Tweedy and the Irish Housewives Association: Links in the Chain* (Dublin, 2012).
4 The small Pike theatre staged Tennessee Williams's 'The Rose Tattoo' in 1957 for the Dublin Drama Festival. After accusations that contraceptives were produced on stage, the director, Alan Simpson, was arrested and charged with producing an indecent and profane performance for gain. After proceedings that reached the Supreme Court, the charges were dismissed in 1958, leaving Simpson with large legal bills. The Pike Theatre closed in 1960,
5 An Tostal was an annual festival inaugurated in 1953 as a celebration of Irish life. Initiated by Bord Failte with the intention that it would extend the tourist season it continued until 1958 although it has continued to be celebrated, in Drumbshambo, Co. Leitrim.
6 Owen Lancelot Sheehy-Skeffington (1909–70), academic and senator, son of

Francis and Hanna Sheehy-Skeffington. He was an outspoken commentator on the role of the Catholic church, censorship and education and was a Senator for TCD from 1954–61 and 1965–70.

7 Micheál (Mick) O'Riordan (1917–2006), communist, founder of the Irish Workers' League (IWL) and later the Irish Workers' Party.

8 Michael Tierney (1894–1975), academic and president of UCD from 1947 to 1964.

9 William Edward Thrift (1870-1942), academic, professor of natural and experimental philosophy in TCD, (1901-29), vice-provost (1931-37) and T.D. for Dublin University 1922-37.

10 William Magennis (1867-1946), professor of metaphysics in UCD from 1909-41, he was a TD from 1922-27 and afterwards a member of the Senate. A member of the Knights of St Columbanus, he was a strong supporter of censorship.

11 Rev. Joseph Deery, appointed to the Censorship Board in 1945 and chairman from 1946 until 1956, when he was appointed Vicar General of the Archdiocese of Dublin.

12 Sean O'Faolain (1900–91), writer and editor.

13 Dermot J. O'Flynn, engineer and member of the Knights of St Columbanus. He resigned from the Board in protest in May 1957, along with Christopher O'Reilly and Pigott.

14 Oscar Traynor (1886-1963) revolutionary and politician; Fianna Fáil TD for Dublin North from 1932 to 1961 and Minister for Justice from 1957 to 1961.

15 Peter Berry (1909-1978), he joined the Dept of Justice in 1927 and was Deputy Sec. from 1957-61 and Secretary from 1961 to 1971.

16 A.F. Comyn, appointed to Board in 1956

17 R.R. Figgis, appointed to Board in 1956

18 John J. Pigott, lecturer in education in St Patrick's Training College

19 Christopher J. O'Reilly, member of the Board 1951 to 1967. He taught Irish in St Patrick's Training College, was a member of the Knights of St Columbanus.

20 William MacNeely, Roman Catholic Bishop of Raphoe.

21 Judge John Charles Conroy (1906–85), chairman of the Board from 28 October 1957

22 For more on this see Michael Adams, *Censorship: the Irish experience* (Dublin, 1968) pp 119-22.

23 The Censorship of Publications Appeal Board was first established in 1946.

24 Thomas Joseph Coyne (1901-1961). In 1923 he was one of the first administrative officers appointed to the new Irish civil service. In 1934 he became principal officer to the Dept of Justice (and served on the 1935-8 interdepartmental committee on censorship) and was Secretary to the Department from 1949 to 1961.

25 *Reality*, published by the Redemptorists.

26 A controversial film about prejudice and seduction, *Duel in the Sun*, was released in 1946 and starred Gregory Peck, Jennifer Jones and Joseph Cotton.

27 Based on the 1940 novel about a priest in Mexico on the run from the authorities who is an alcoholic and who fathered a child.

28 A 1970 satirical comedy directed by Robert Altman and starring Donald Sutherland, Elliott Gould and Tom Skerritt.

29 John Mary ('Jack') Lynch (1917–99), sportsman and Taoiseach. He was Fianna Fáil
    TD for Cork from 1948 to 1981 and Taoiseach (1966-79). In 1957 he was Minister
    for Education.
30 Joseph Walsh, Roman Catholic Archbishop of Tuam.
31 Brendan John Smith (1917–89), founder-director of the Dublin Theatre Festival.
32 'The loves of Cass Maguire' by Brian Friel was first presented in 1966 in New York.
    It opened in the Abbey Theatre on 24 Sept. 1967 for seven performances.
33 Head of the Committee on Television.
34 Edward Roth (1922–76), first Director General of RTÉ television, 1960-1962.
35 Sean O'Casey's 'The Plough and the Stars' is a play first performed in 1926 in the
    Abbey theatre in Dublin. Set in Dublin's tenements, the first two acts take place in
    1915 and the last during the Easter Rising of 1916. It caused riots when it was first
    performed in Dublin.
36 Kevin McCourt (1915–2000), Director-General of RTÉ from 1963 to 1968.
37 Victor Lownes of the Playboy Clubs had visited Dublin in Feb. 1966 with the
    intention of recruiting fifty Irish girls to staff London's first Playboy club.

Conclusion

The Lenten Regulations are uncatalogued in the archives, but every year they were displayed in Catholic Churches in the Diocese of Dublin. They give a sense of the rules associated with Lent in the 1940s and 1970s, the beginning and end of the archbishopric of John Charles McQuaid.

Lenten Regulations
For the Diocese of Dublin in 1949

The Season of Lent is set aside by the Church as a time of special prayer and penance... the Church prescribes the penance of fasting. If it is not possible to fast, other penance... works of charity ought with prudence to be undertaken by young and old alike. The... behaviour of a Catholic during Lent should be that of a person, who, at this season, keeps... in mind the Passion and Death of Our Divine Redeemer, Jesus Christ.

This year, owing to the restoration of more normal conditions, the general law... concerning Lenten fast and abstinence is to be observed in this Diocese.

The following Regulations are to be regarded as stating the law of the Church... able to fast, without danger to their health or without undue strain upon their sour...

The Faithful between the ages of twenty-one and sixty years are bound by the law of Fasting and the law... The Faithful, who are over seven and under twenty-one years of age, are bound only by the law of...Fast Days, the general law of the Church allows only one full meal to be taken each day...Fast Days, in addition to the one full meal, a light repast might be taken each morning and each evening...quantity and kind of food allowed at each of these repasts are regulated by the approved custom of...the Diocese of Dublin, custom sanctions the use at these repasts of milk, butter and cheese.

...this Diocese, during the Lenten Season of 1949, by a special concession of the Holy See, eggs...morning and evening

...days which are not days of Abstinence, meat is allowed.

...Divinity, for the spiritual nourishment of our souls.

VII. Parents have a most serious duty to secure a fully Catholic upbringing for their children, in all that concerns the instruction of their minds, the training of their wills to virtue, their bodily welfare and the preparation for their life as citizens. (Canon 113, Code of Canon Law.)

Only the Church is competent to declare what is a fully Catholic upbringing: for, to the Church alone which He established, Our Divine Lord, Jesus Christ, has given the mission to teach mankind to observe all things whatsoever He has commanded. (St. Matthew, xxviii, 20.)

Accordingly, in the education of Catholics, every branch of human training is subject to the guidance of the Church, and those Schools alone, which the Church approves, are capable of providing a fully Catholic education.

Therefore, the Church forbids parents and guardians to send a child to any non-Catholic School, whether primary or secondary or continuation or University.

Deliberately to disobey this law is a mortal sin, and they who persist in disobedience are unworthy to receive the Sacraments.

VIII. No Catholic may enter the Protestant University of Trinity College, without the previous permission of the Ordinary or the Diocese. (Canon 1374, Code of Canon Law, Statutes 385, 404 1, Plenary Synod of Maynooth, 1927.)

Any Catholic who disobeys this law is guilty of mortal sin and while he persists in disobedience, is unworthy to receive the Sacraments.

In this Diocese, it is reserved to the Archbishop to grant permission to attend Trinity College.

Permission is given only for grave and valid reasons and with the addition of definite measures, by which it is sought adequately to safeguard the Faith and practice of a Catholic Student.

IX. The National University of Ireland, with its three Constituent Colleges, is, by its Charter, a neutral educational establishment. For that reason, it must be regarded by Catholics as failing to give due acknowledgement to the One, True Faith.

In view, however, of the measures taken by the Ecclesiastical Authorities to protect Faith and Morals, University College, Dublin, in our Diocese, may be considered to be sufficiently safe for Catholic students. (Statutes 404; 2, 495; 1 and 2, Plenary Synod of Maynooth, 1927.)

X. The Church, to safeguard the Faith and Morals of her children, forbids everywhere and most entirely the marriage of a Catholic with a non-Catholic... (Canons 1060 and 1071, Code of Canon Law, Statute... Plenary Synod of Maynooth, 1927) unless

1. that the Catholic and non-Catholic parties promise to have all the children of the marriage baptized as Catholics and reared as Catholics, according to the prescriptions of the Church;

2. that the non-Catholic party promise not to interfere in any way with the Faith or practice of the Catholic party;

3. that it be morally certain that these guarantees will be loyally observed.

The Catholic party is obliged in conscience prudently to strive for the conversion of the non-Catholic party.

These guarantees are solemn pledges very gravely binding in conscience. Once given, they may not ever be disregarded or set aside.

A Dispensation given by the Church is not to be regarded as an approval; it is rather a permission, sorrowfully and grudgingly given.

Lenten Regulation
In the Diocese of Dublin, 1971.

1. In the tradition of the Church the weeks preceding the commemoration of the Sacred Passion and death of our Divine Redeemer
   have been devoted to penance and prayer.

2. Our Divine Lord, who is all holy, fasted for forty days and forty
   nights and frequently withdrew to pray alone, even to spend the
   night in prayer.

   He has taught us who are sinners, "Unless you do penance, you shall
   all equally perish," (Luke XIII 3-5) and again, "Take heed, watch
   and pray." (Mark xiii, 33) "He told them a parable to the affect that
   they ought always to pray and not lose heart. " (Luke xviii, 1).

3. In consideration for our present-day weakness, the Church has
   removed the obligation of fasting on each day of Lent.

   Only Ash Wednesday, 24th February and Good Friday, 9th April
   shall be days of fast and abstinence.

   On a fast day, the general law of the Church, for persons between
   the ages of twenty-one and fifty-nine years, allows only one full
   meal, with a light repast morning and evening.

   The law of abstinence, which binds the faithful from the age of
   fourteen years, forbids the use of flesh-meat, but not of a soup made
   from meat or meat-extract.

4. Although the Church has relaxed her disciplines of fasting, very
   many of our faithful will continue to fast and abstain, according to
   their means and opportunities.

   All, however, are obliged to do penance. All can practice humble
   prayer, can give alms, can devote time to charitable work of their
   choice, can refuse themselves many comforts, can, in particular, on
   occasion, give to God out of their day the brief period that is
   needed to assist at Holy Mass.

   All can, with the help of God's Grace, truly repent of their offences against God and can avoid the occasions of sin.

All can, with the aid of grace, each day, constantly and honestly, fulfill the duties of their calling in life, a task that demands unending self-denial such that Our Divine Lord spoke of it as "the daily carrying of our cross."

5. Occasions of sin are being multiplied by the means of communication. Our Divine Lord, who is truth himself, has given us an unfailing standard by which to judge, "by their fruits you shall know them." [Books] Newspapers, magazines, films, television features, especially stage-plays, of necessity, reveal the vulgarity of nobility of the authors and actors, directors and producers.

If men or women be unjust, their words and actions will be unjust. If they are uncharitable, they will belittle or subtly defame the object of their dislikes. If they are cruel, they will use their power to crush the lowly who cannot defend themselves. If they are sensual, they will search for anything that can stimulate themselves and others to unchaste imaginations and unlawful satisfaction. If, in addition, they are cowardly, they will have recourse to the slinking refuge of anonymous publication. And, what is worst of all, if they be themselves in error concerning the faith, they will spread confusion, under cover of so-called humanism, or even of co-called renewal of Catholic life.

What a fruitful cooperation with the grace of Our Divine Redeemer, the means of communication could achieve in the modern world, if only the masters, who give themselves the vocation to mould us, could instead keep constantly in mind the admonition of the Holy Spirit; – "Whatever is true, whatever is honourable, whatever is just, whatever is pure, whatever is lovely, whatever is gracious, if there is any excellence, if there is anything worthy of praise, think about these things." (Philippians iv, 8)

6. Our faithful people continue to be assailed by public pleas for civil divorce and contraception. Civil divorce is proposed as the right of minorities. Contraception is proposed as the right of married

persons to control birth.

The words "right" and "control" lend a false appearance of reason and morality.

But civil divorce is evil and contraception is evil. There cannot be, on the part of any person, a right to what is evil.

A right is the moral power of a human person to do or [to] possess or to exact. Being a moral power, it can be founded only in reason and in the objective moral law. Its purpose is to give to the human person the moral power or authority freely to choose what leads him securely to his final end, which is God.

Civil divorce and contraception are each a violation of the objective moral law, a very grave offence against God, author of that law. Our faithful people, as by an instinct of the faith, grasp at once this truth and will be guided by the Church which has been founded by Jesus Christ Himself to be the authentic interpreter of the objective moral law.

7. Seeing that Saturday is now, in great part, a day of leisure, it is inexcusable for the trading, especially the large trading interests, to open their establishments on Sundays.

8. Within the Paschal time, that is, in this Diocese, from Ash Wednesday, 24th February to Trinity Sunday, 6th June, the Faithful are commanded by the Church to receive the Blessed Eucharist, the Sacrament in which our Divine Lord gives us, in very truth, His body and blood, His soul and his [sic] divinity, for the spiritual nourishment of our souls. To receive Him worthily the best preparation is the humble, sincere confession of our sins in the Sacrament of Penance.

+ John Charles,
Archbishop of Dublin,
Primate of Ireland.

17th February, 1971.

Index

280 · His Grace is Displeased

Shine, Joan, 212
Simms, Dr. G.O., Church of Ireland
   Archbishop of Dublin, 174, 175, 177,
   178, 180, 181–2, 186
Simpson, Fr., S.J., 157, 196
Sinn Fein, 124, 201
Smith, Brendan, 249
Smylie, R.M., 172, 250
Social Encyclicals, 10
social policy, 9–10
Social Welfare Bureau, 5
socialism and communism, 18, 24, 108–9,
   115, 201, 202–3, 205, 260
sovereignty, 20, 21, 23
St. Columba's School, Dublin, 159
St. Joseph de Cluny, Chapelizod, 87
St. Kevin's Hospital, Dublin, 107
St. Kieran's College, Kilkenny, 30, 35
St. Kilian's German School, Dublin, 29,
   72–7
St. Patrick's College, Maynooth, 163, 186
St. Patrick's Diocesan School, 3
St. Ultan's Infants' Hospital, 81, 82, 83
Stack, Una C.A. de (Mrs Austin Stack),
   125–7, 135–6
Staunton, James, Bishop of Ferns, 30,
   88–90, 92–3, 97–8, 169
Stephenson, N., 77
Stockley, William Frederick Paul, 129
Styles, Rev. N., 161–2
subversive organisations, 119, 202, 205–6
Sunday Chronicle, 45–6
Sunday Independent, 42–3, 181–2, 207, 251
Swaine, Anne, 255
Sweetman, Fr., 196
Synge, J.M., *The Tinker's Wedding* (1908),
   236

Taylor, Elizabeth, 251
The Tablet, 227
Teddy boys, 201
Telefis Eireann, 258–60, 261, 263–4
television, 231, 257–64
theatre, Irish, 4, 201, 251–7
   complaints over bad language, 256, 257
   restrictions on attendance by priests,
     252–5
   see also Tostal theatre festival, Dublin

Thrift, William Edward, 206
Tierney, Michael, 103, 104–5
Togher, Captain Joseph, 119–24
Tostal theatre festival, Dublin, 201, 232–7,
   238–46, 248–51
   Irish Times and, 247, 250
   JCM's refusal of Solemn Mass to
     initiate, 233, 235, 237–8, 240, 241,
     244, 245
Trade Unions, 203, 204
Trevor-Smith, Dr., 82–3
Trinity College, Dublin, 5, 101, 163–4
Tuohy, Fr. Patrick, 233–4

Unemployed Association, 202
Unitarian Church, 161
United Council of Christian Churches,
   166–7
United States of America (USA), 118,
   145–6
Unity Octave, 167, 168–71, 185–6, 187–90
   JCM's letter (January 1967), 190–1
   JCM's letter (January 1968), 191–6
University College, Dublin, 3, 5–6, 29, 78,
   99, 104–5, 107, 151, 205
   JCM files unavailable, 4–5
University College, Galway, 87

Vigilance Committee, 202–6
Viney, Michael, 173
Viridiana (Luis Buñuel film, 1961), 232

Wadding, Fr., 223
Walsh, Mrs., 82–3
Walsh, Joseph, Archbishop of Tuam, 247
Walsh, Rev. Brother P.J., 78–9
Walsh, S., 68
War of Independence, Irish, 144–5
Ward, W.B., 206
Williams, Fr. D., 222–3
Williams, Miss Janice, 158
Williams, Thomas, 125–7
Wilmot, Seamus, 239
women, rights of, 13–15
Women in Love (British film, 1969), 231
Woods, G., 166
Wright, Rev. Kenneth, 161